RELIGION AND THE MEDIA

RELIGION AND THE MEDIA

AN INTRODUCTORY READER

Edited by

CHRIS ARTHUR

UNIVERSITY OF WALES PRESS · CARDIFF · 1993

British Library Cataloguing in Publication Data

A catalogue record for this book is available from the British Library.

ISBN 0 – 7083 – 1221 – 7

Published on behalf of the World Association for Christian Communication

Typeset by Action Typesetting Limited, Gloucester
Printed in England at The Bath Press

Working for a Fairer World

Contents

The Contributors

CHRIS ARTHUR was Gifford Research Fellow at the University of St Andrews from 1984 to 1986 and Research Fellow in the Faculty of Divinity at the University of Edinburgh from 1986 to 1989. He now lectures in religious studies at St David's University College, Lampeter (part of the University of Wales). His publications include *In the Hall of Mirrors* (1986) and *Biting the Bullet* (1990).

WILLIAM BIERNATZKI is an American Jesuit brother, now serving as Research Director of the Centre for the Study of Communication and Culture in London. He holds a doctorate in sociology and anthropology from Saint Louis University and is Professor of Anthropology at Sogang University, Seoul, Korea. Among his publications are *Roots of Acceptance: the Intercultural Communication of Religious Meanings* (1991).

JEANNE COVER is currently engaged in doctoral studies at the University of Toronto. From 1984 to 1989 she was Principal of Loretto College, Marryatville, South Australia.

D. P. DAVIES is John James Professor of Theology and Deputy Principal at St David's University College, Lampeter. He is a founder member of Cwmni'r Gannwyll, an independent production company geared to making religious programmes for S4C, Channel 4 and other channels. He has served on the Central Religious Advisory Committee (CRAC), which advises both the BBC and ITV about religious output. Cwmni'r Gannwyll's series on the religious traditions of Europe will be broadcast on S4C and on Channel 4 in 1993. The series will also be screened on various networks in Sweden, the Netherlands, Greece, Poland and Hungary.

JOHN ELDRIDGE is Professor of Sociology at the University of Glasgow and a founder member of the Glasgow University Media Group, whose publications include *Bad News* (1976), *More Bad News* (1980) and *War and Peace News* (1985).

WILLIAM F. FORE is an editor-at-large for *The Christian Century* magazine. Among his publications are *Television and Religion* (1987) and *Mythmakers: Gospel, Culture and Media* (1990). From 1964 to 1988 he headed the Communication Commission of the National Council of Churches in the USA. In 1971 he founded the National Coalition Against Censorship. From 1982 to 1990 he was President of the World Association for Christian Communication. He is currently a visiting lecturer in communication at Yale University Divinity School.

DUNCAN FORRESTER is Professor of Christian Ethics and Practical Theology and Principal of New College, the Faculty of Divinity of the University of Edinburgh. He is Director of the University's pioneering Media and Theological Education Project. Previous posts include eight years as an educational missionary in India. Among his books are *Beliefs, Values and Policies* (1990) and *Theology and Politics* (1988).

GREGOR GOETHALS is Professor of Art History at the Rhode Island School of Design and is also a freelance designer. She is author of *The TV Ritual: Worship at the Video Altar* (1981) and *The Electronic Golden Calf: Images, Religion and the Making of Meaning* (1990).

STEWART M. HOOVER received his Ph.D. from the Annenberg School of Communication, Univeristy of Pennsylvania. He is currently based at the Center for Mass Media Research, University of Boulder, Colorado. Among his publications are *The Electronic Giant* (1982) and *Mass Media Religion: the Social Sources of the Electronic Church* (1988).

PETER HORSFIELD is Dean of the Uniting Church Theological Hall and lecturer at the United Faculty of Theology in Melbourne. He is author of *Religious Television: the American Experience* (1984) and *Taming Television* (1986).

JIM MCDONNELL has been Director of the Catholic Communications Centre in London since June 1990. The centre is the communications development and training agency for the Catholic Church in England and Wales. He was previously at the Jesuit international research institute, the Centre for the Study of Communication and Culture. He has written extensively on all aspects of the media and, in particular, on the relationship between media and culture. He is co-editor, along with Fran Trampiets, of *Communicating Faith in a Technological Age* (1989).

COLIN MORRIS is a freelance broadcaster and consultant. He recently retired from the BBC, where he held a number of senior appointments including Head of Religious Broadcasting and Controller of BBC Nothern Ireland. Among his many publications are *God in a Box: Christian Strategy in the Television Age* (1984) and *Wrestling with an Angel: Reflections on Christian Communication* (1990).

S. A. SCHLEIFER is Distinguished Lecturer in Mass Communication and Director of the Adham Center for Television Journalism at the American University in Cairo. He is former NBC news bureau Chief in Cairo and a member of the Advisory Board of the World Media Association. His publications include frequent contributions to *The Islamic Quarterly* and *Arts in the Islamic World*.

ERIC SHEGOG was Religious Broadcasting Officer for the Independent Broadcasting Authority from 1984 to 1990. He is currently Director of Communication for the Church of England.

NEIL SIMPSON is a Church of Scotland Minister whose Ph.D., from the University of Edinburgh, was in the field of religion and the media. He is a frequent reviewer for *Media Development*.

PEG SLINGER, at the time of writing 'Television Commercials: Mirror and Symbol of Societal Values' (which first appeared in Vol. 78 of the journal *Religious Education* in 1983), was a Master of Divinity candidate at the University of St Michael's Faculty of Theology, Toronto.

DOROTHEE SÖLLE is one of the most influential and widely respected of contemporary theologians. She is a prolific writer and many of her books have been translated into English, including *Suffering* (1975), *Revolutionary Patience* (1977), *Death by Bread Alone; Texts and Reflections on Religious Experience* (1978),

Choosing Life (1981), *Of War and Love* (1981), *The Strength of the Weak: Towards a Christian Feminist Identity* (1984), *To Work and to Love; a Theology of Creation* (1984).

RACHEL VINEY is Religious Broadcasting Officer for the Independent Television Commission, a public body charged under the Broadcasting Act of 1990 with licensing and regulating all non-BBC television services in the United Kingdom. Prior to this post she worked in publishing and in radio, joining the Independent Broadcasting Authority in 1986. She was researcher for the award-winning BBC Radio 4 documentary about Martin Luther, *Fire in the City*.

DEREK WEBER has been Lecturer and Project Officer for the University of Edinburgh's Media and Theological Education Project since 1989. He is author of *Discerning Images* (1991).

Acknowledgements

The editor and publishers are grateful to the World Association for Christian Communication whose generous support and helpful advice did much to make publication of this volume possible.

For permission to reproduce material from works under copyright, grateful acknowledgement and thanks are extended to the following individuals and organizations:

Colin Morris and HarperCollins Publishers, for permission to reprint 'The Theology of the Nine O'Clock News', which first appeared in *Wrestling with an Angel*, London, 1990, Fount Books (an imprint of HarperCollins Religious, part of HarperCollins Publishers Ltd.). An early version of this chapter was presented as a Hibbert Lecture.

The Religious Education Association of the United States and Canada for permission to reprint Peg Slinger's 'Television Commercials: mirror and symbol of societal values' which first appeared in *Religious Education*, Vol 78, Number 1 (1983). Efforts to contact Peg Slinger have proved unsuccessful. The publishers would be interested to receive any information regarding her current address.

Jeanne Cover and the Religious Education Association of the United States and Canada, for permission to reprint Jeanne Cover's 'Theological reflections: social effects of television', which first appeared in *Religious Education*, Vol 78, Number 1 (1983). The Religious Education Association is based at 409 Prospect Street, New Haven, CT 06511-2177, USA.

Dorothee Sölle and the MIT Press, for permission to reprint 'Thou shalt have no other jeans before me', which first appeared in Jürgen Habermas (ed.), *Observations on 'The Spiritual Situation of the Age'*, translated by Andrew Buchwalter, Cambridge, MA: 1984, pp.157 – 68.

1 Introduction

CHRIS ARTHUR

In a book about religion and media it would be legitimate to look
at a vast and diverse range of topics. After all, every expression of
human religiousness is, inevitably, a *mediated* expression, which
comes to us through a variety of means of communication: words,
symbols, music, dance, architecture, and so on. An examination
of the cave paintings of our early ancestors; the way in which the
Ayatollah Khomeini relied on audio-cassettes to carry his sermons
and so maintain his authority and presence in Iran during his years
of exile; a study of the symbolism of Buddhist burial mounds or
Christian stained-glass windows; the role which TV has played
in modern American religiousness; the symbolism of the dancing
Shiva; a comparison of concepts of God in oral and literate cultures; the impact of printing on the expression and nature of
faith; the problems of communicating mystical experience in any
medium – these are just a few of the countless subjects that a
book about religion and media might choose to address. Much of
the activity of the world's great faiths is, after all, precisely concerned with the communication of values and ideas using a variety
of media. Indeed religions themselves could be seen as powerful
systems of mass media (and, conversely, it is now increasingly
being suggested that some forms of apparently secular mass media
in fact perform distinctly religious functions). It is clear, then, that
the field of interest suggested by 'religion and media' is daunt-
ingly extensive and any single-volume selection of material from
it would be bound to leave out a very great deal.

The presence of the definite article in the title of this book should
alert the observant reader to a narrowing down of focus. Yet even
looking at religion and '*the* media' (by which locution is generally meant television, radio and the press) still leaves us with an
enormous subject area. It is important, therefore, to make clear at

the outset that this particular volume does not attempt to cover the area as a whole or to present example material representative of every point of view. Its aims are much more modest. It seeks to do no more than provide an introduction to what, for many readers, will be a new area of interest. A concern about *modern* forms of mass media and their religious implications is the common denominator underlying the contributions which make up this book. This is not meant to suggest that other areas of relationship between religion and media do not exist or that this particular area is the most important. This is only one dimension of a massive subject and should not be allowed to obscure the existence or significance of others. The fact that in what follows 'the media' most often refers to TV is a reflection of the extent to which television is the dominant medium in contemporary society, rather than any indication that our contributors are blind to the interest and importance for religion of language, the press, radio, sculpture, computers and other important varieties of media, both ancient and modern. Likewise, the fact that 'religion' tends here to mean Christianity, is an indication of the background and interests of the contributors rather than of that theological blindness which does not recognize that there is more than one faith in the world. In fact the advances in communications technology which have done so much to mould the contours of modernity, have made a consciousness of pluralism, religious and otherwise, almost impossible to avoid. The purpose of the book is to give a series of pointers which will identify some of the ways in which modern mass media might be considered relevant to religion and religion relevant to such media. Often, when these two areas of human endeavour are mentioned together, people think solely in terms either of the religious *use* of the media, in order to propagate a particular message to as wide an audience as possible; or of a religious *critique* of the media of a particularly reactionary kind, usually focused on complaints about sex, violence and profanity. It will rapidly become apparent that the linkage between religion and the media is far richer than that suggested by such simplistic models.

As editor, I have been more concerned with gathering together a thought-provoking collection of individual chapters than with imposing some confining structure which demands strict conformity to an overarching blueprint. Whilst some such structure is essential in any book that seeks to present a cogent argument which progresses by logically acceptable steps from premises to conclusion, it has the potential to hinder the less ambitious aims of an introductory reader such as this. What follows is very much a case of being selected papers on religion and the media rather than a systematic study of this area. Such systematic study is, of course, needed, but it is not the task of the present volume to provide it. Whilst it would be nice to think that anyone with an interest in religion and/or the media might find something of interest in these pages (thus creating an audience far in excess of our print-run!), the book is primarily intended for students of theology and religious studies and for those in training for the ministry, areas where there is a dawning awareness of the relevance of media matters. Given the intended audience, many of the contributors are particularly concerned with the implications which the media have for programmes of education in these areas. There seems little point in summarizing the book chapter by chapter. The writing is clear, the chapters are short and the intended readership quite capable of performing such précising for themselves. However, it does seem appropriate to offer an orientating bird's eye view of some of the authors' main concerns and to suggest some questions which readers may find it useful to pose.

*   *   *

Gregor Goethals argues that, however drained it may be of explicitly religious subject matter, TV has assumed an iconic role in modern society. She offers a disturbing analysis of the potent myths which it disseminates and suggests that we have succumbed to the belief that if something important has happened it will invariably appear on TV. Non-appearance suggests that something is unimportant, or indeed non-existent (an ontological assumption which, its flawed logic notwithstanding, is likely to have serious theological repercussions for anyone in whose life it is operative). Such beliefs, Goethals argues, underlie one of the most powerful of all our media myths, the conviction that we live in an open information system. TV has become the common touchstone of what is real and what we should value. Beneath the giant canopy of images it creates, all religious traditions, says Goethals, are exposed to the same framing of reality

(a framing which, as she makes clear, is prey to political and commercial manipulation). Given the fact that for millions of people
TV rather than religion now provides the symbols which offer
answers to fundamental questions (such as 'Who am I?' and 'How
ought I to live?'), one is bound to wonder if media mythologies
will eventually eclipse more traditional religious outlooks. Asking
if religious groups may be able to reclaim the power of myth
through the electronic media, Goethals identifies various options
open both to iconoclasts and iconifiers.

Does television function in the quasi-religious iconic manner
which Goethals suggests? One of the abiding problems in studying
TV is the difficulty of assessing with any precision the extent to which
it influences us. Assessments of its significance are likely to depend on
two factors. First, the individual's own experience, both as a viewer
and as a member of a media-saturated society. Secondly, on a critical
consideration of interpretive accounts of that experience, such as
that offered by Goethals. Whatever verdicts we finally reach about
TV's role, whether we view it as potently mythopoetic or merely
entertaining, it is imperative that we honestly recognize the sheer
scale of its impact on society, both in terms of the time and resources
it claims and the size of the audience it addresses worldwide.

The iconic, culture-shaping role of TV in a modern society
for which Goethals argues, finds strong support from Peter
Horsfield, who voices particular concern that so profoundly
important a phenomenon as television is being largely ignored
by theologians. Although the whole cultural context in which
we live is, he suggests, media created, although the mass media
are forming a new symbolic environment within which societies
organize and express themselves, theology shows little sign of
taking media issues seriously. Horsfield makes clear that in our
new media-forged symbolic environment God is not only apparently absent but functionally no longer necessary. He argues that
modern mass media may be having a marked effect on religious
faith, not just in terms of their handling of explicitly religious
issues but, much more significantly, in terms of the influence which
they exert on perceptions of social reality within which religious
faith is understood and experienced. Stressing the risk of ending
up with an inadequate theological understanding of a large part
of the world in which ministry will actually be exercised, if TV
continues to be seen as unimportant, Horsfield urges theologians

to see media issues as being crucially important for theological education and ministerial formation. Just as hermeneutics has been
faced with the challenge of translating the biblical message from
a rural to an urban environment, so he believes that the emergence
in recent years of a new media environment which over-arches the
urban-technological one, takes the hermeneutical challenge a step
further. Part of that challenge demands working out the relationship between Christianity and consumerism, and establishing
how one translates religious meaning from print sources to people
whose understanding of truth is dominated by oral or audio-visual
communication. Horsfield also raises the important question of
the cultural impact of imported TV programmes and the extent
to which the concentration of media ownership in the hands of a
very few individuals and organizations worldwide may influence
the development and extension of religious thought.

Perhaps one of the most important issues raised by an examination of religion and the media concerns the extent to which
different media can influence religious thinking. That an understanding of truth dominated by oral or audio-visual communication
may be quite different from one dominated by print, as Horsfield
suggests, underlines the extent to which media are very much
more than neutral containers carrying whatever cargoes of meaning
we choose to put into them, without exerting any influence on
what they carry. The picture that emerges time and again in the
chapters which follow suggests a much more intimate relationship
between meaning and media than any simplistic cargo/container
analogy would imply. Whilst few would want to accept McLuhan's
creative exaggeration – 'the medium is the message' – without
qualification, it is clear that media changes open up new avenues
of thought and close down other intellectual routes. Media
facilitate and shape the whole commerce of our varied communication (and religious communication is no exception), rather than
acting merely as inert transportation devices for shifting nuggets
of media–independent information from A to B.

As William Kuhns put it in his study of *The Electronic Gospel*,
'The Entertainment milieu has transformed the ways in which we
believe and are capable of believing.'[1] Like Horsfield, Kuhns is
concerned that the intellectual shift occasioned by TV may have
a profound effect on how we think religiously. He suggests, for
example, that a belief in absolutes is eroded by the tentative and

elastic epistemology of modern media.[2] The very concept of faith, he believes, is threatened by a TV-informed mind-set accustomed to incessant visual impact.[3] This kind of recognition that modern mass media may exert an important psychological, as well as cultural influence, actually affecting the way we think, echoes the work of those scholars who have looked at the consequences of earlier media revolutions and, in particular, at how they have acted to shape the nature and development of religious thought. Both Walter Ong and Jack Goody, for example, have drawn attention to the way in which writing facilitates new modes of thinking.[4] Goody's important analysis of world religions as essentially *literate* faiths is particularly recommended to any reader who is sceptical of Horsfield's emphasis on the likely theological importance of television.[5]

Maintaining the emphasis on the powerful myth-making function of TV and its impact on contemporary culture, William Fore asserts that 'there is no understanding our culture without understanding the media which expresses it'. Such is the power and appeal of the images created by TV that Fore suggests television functions as though it were a religion. However, traditional religious and televisual mythologies are radically out of line (a point illustrated by a comparison of the world-views offered by TV and by Christianity). Fore recognizes that communication is the primary function of all religions. As Christians, Muslims, Hindus or Buddhists are engaged in worship, education or outreach, at the core they are engaged in communication, and there is no way for them to engage in these communicative acts except through culture and its forms. A religious critique of TV and other available media of communication is therefore called for, indeed Fore suggests that there is no effective way to criticize the media without bringing to bear a perspective that transcends secular culture. The importance of stories in religious communication is highlighted and Fore offers guidelines for the effective retelling of stories in terms intelligible to the contemporary media-dominated culture. He also strongly advocates the need for widespread media education to alert people to the underlying symbolic meanings which operate beneath the simple storylines of TV. Such education can, he believes, prevent that illiteracy which leaves people defenceless against the dangers of media manipulation, misinformation and propaganda.

Few would argue with Fore that some measure of media-literacy is desirable. Not only is such literacy likely to be helpful in countering anti-democratic pressures which may seek to subvert the media for their own ends, but increasingly it seems set to become an integral part of any programme of effective religious education. For, quite apart from the question of the religiousness or otherwise of TV itself, the way in which religion is presented by the media raises all sorts of issues about accuracy, bias and omission, which programmes of education in this area ignore at their peril. If they do not want to let the instantly accessible curriculum provided by the media to set the agenda of religious information, educators are duty bound to make some response to it.

The extent to which TV may be seen as being in some sense religious (pseudo-religious? functionally religious? genuinely religious?), inevitably – and usefully – raises the question of how religion ought to be defined. It is famously difficult to define religion satisfactorily, at least in any sort of neat dictionary-type definition.[6] As William James realized, the word 'religion' cannot stand for any single principle or essence, but it is rather a collective name.[7] Building on this kind of insight and influenced by Wittgenstein's ideas about 'family resemblance', scholars now tend to identify a group of characteristics variously manifested by religions, rather than trying to establish some sort of single, invariably present, common denominator.[8] It would be inappropriate to get drawn any deeper into the debate about defining religion here. However, it is important to recognize that the question of television's religiousness is a serious one which cannot be summarily dismissed by referring to some easy hard-and-fast definition. No such definition exists and TV does seem to display many of the characteristics commonly associated with religion.

The opposition between religious and televisual world-views which Fore describes is also recognized by Duncan Forrester, who suggests that Christian communication is essentially against the stream, at odds with the *Zeitgeist*, and that the truth which it seeks to convey is likely to be demanding, confusing and challenging. Such truth is, perhaps, often best expressed through the unexpected and the disturbing. Authentic Christian communication, in Forrester's view, takes place at least as much through drama, news, and documentary programmes as through the formal 'God-slot'. The criterion for such communication, in other words, should not be explicit religious garb, but the ability 'to plumb the depths and reach the heights, to get at people's hearts and wills rather than shimmering over the surface'. Warning of the risk to Christian communication if market forces are allowed to determine content and presentation, Forrester draws on the work of Søren Kierkegaard to underscore the central communicative importance of dialogue, narrative and the image. Stressing that the media highlight and emphasize old problems and possibilities in theology rather than raising any entirely new concerns, he spells out the distorting implications of supposing that truth and its subsequent communication can be neatly separated into two independent categories. Although he is concerned specifically with Christian communication, Forrester points out that this contains some very important general lessons for effective and non-oppressive communication, something which should be borne in mind when reading many of the chapters which follow.

Forrester's point about the way in which Christian communication swims against the current of the *Zeitgeist* is an important reminder of a key element, operative in many faiths, which poses a particular problem when it comes to establishing the relationship between them and a society's media. The fact is that, to a significant extent, religions are likely to subvert many ordinary certainties and be critical of many models of identity and aspiration thought to be adequate – even admirable – by society at large and presented as such on television and other media.[9] As Sallie McFague has put it with regard to the Christian tradition, 'every major reformation within the Church has been sparked by the insight that the essence of Christianity does not support conventional standards.'[10] Since, by and large, television and other media reinforce precisely these standards, it is clear that important aspects of the Christian vision of the world will not fit easily into normal programming. If a religion is radically out of step with the cultural tunes being whistled by a society's media, can we seriously hope for any relationship other than mutual rejection? One is reminded of Malcolm Muggeridge's arguments for Christians to distance themselves from TV.[11]

Eric Shegog considers some of the ways in which the churches might effectively respond to a situation where the media, TV in particular, do so much to set the agenda of accepted values and priorities. Communication of religious truth has, as Shegog acknowledges, always taken place within a cultural framework.

But when part of that framework, namely TV, 'usurped the role previously played by religion as the communicator of myths which embody values and give meaning to life', how can the church communicate the virtues which it believes are inherent in the gospel tradition? Shegog suggests four possible courses of action and spells out the pros and cons of engaging in each. He considers how human dignity, 'one of the most important moral principles inherent in the Christian faith', might be fostered through each of the courses of action he identifies and how it is often undermined by TV. Shegog seeks to alert the churches to their often unrealized potential for influence. He also makes the important point that whilst TV is generally not adept at handling abstract concepts or involved arguments, it is a good medium for telling stories.

As Shegog makes clear, understanding the possibilities and limitations of TV as a medium is an essential prerequisite for understanding how it might handle religious material. This is a point which is touched on repeatedly in the course of the chapters which follow. Naturally, given its impact and audience, many groups, religious, political, commercial and so on, are keen to make their influence felt via TV. Whilst Shegog is no doubt correct about the existence of an often unrealized potential for influence within the churches, the operation of such influence clearly raises a host of questions about who does, and who should, determine what appears on our screens and in the pages of our newspapers. Particularly in a situation of religious pluralism, where members of many different faiths might wish to bring media output into line with their particular outlook and set of values, we would need to proceed with considerable caution in allowing religious lobbies a say on what appears on TV and other media.

Television's storytelling role is further emphasized in the chapter by Jim McDonnell. He notes how, in general, the media shape perceptions. More specifically, when it comes to TV's handling of religious material, this shaping results in an emphasis which many would wish to challenge. For instance, religious stories on TV tend to be stories of social conflict, and the world of TV drama 'finds it natural to present adherence to specific religious doctrines as a problem rather than a personal and social benefit'. Moreover, claims to exclusive religious truth 'are difficult to assimilate in a media system which has elevated professional tolerance and impartiality above nearly every other virtue'. McDonnells's criticisms of the way in which religion is presented on TV are useful in alerting us to the fact that a certain choice of emphasis or per- spective – whether dictated by the demands of the medium, the difficulties of the subject matter or the likes and dislikes of the people concerned – can have wide-reaching implications for the way in which something is seen. Martin Marty once suggested that photographers 'can make anyone look as stupid or as wise'[12] as the photographer (or editor) wishes, simply by choosing one image over and above another. In the same way, the selection of some religious images or stories and the omission of others can pro- foundly affect the way in which religion is seen. Whilst it would be unrealistic to expect TV, or any other medium, to give a *com- plete* picture, it is important to cultivate an awareness of the extent to which media treatments can skew our perspective. Despite their apparent distortions of religious matters and the fact that the media are often held responsible for making people morally bankrupt, McDonnell is at pains to point out their more positive side too. For instance, 'popular films, music and books all speak of a search for transcendent meanings in a fragmented and chaotic world'. Anyone concerned to promote effective religious education in today's media-saturated society needs to be sensitive to the fact that the media are full of what we might term 'implicit' religion.

Examples of such 'implicit' religion in the TV genre known as soap opera (described by both Shegog and McDonnell as the morality plays of modern life) are considered by Neil Simpson and Derek Weber. Simpson draws attention to the role played by soap opera in 'maintaining a kind of popular world-view'. Such pro- grammes, he suggests, serve much the same function in modern times as mummers' plays did in the past. Both 'provide a spiritual framework for life – a kind of primitive sacred canopy'. Though religion may rarely appear in their storylines, the great themes of birth, marriage and death provide their underlying subject matter. Indeed the appeal of soap operas may in part be explained by the fact that 'they strike at the very heart of life's meaning, go for the jugular of our most metaphysical needs'. Simpson suggests that the true significance of soap operas on a religious level is not to be found in the often negative way in which they portray repre- sentatives of a particular faith, but in the contribution they make to 'keeping alive the rumour of God'. Weber likewise stresses that the avoidance of matters spiritual does not mean that there is no theology in such programmes. On the contrary, with their focus on universal life-experiences and their millions of viewers, soap opera constitutes a genre of particular religious relevance. Again, given the claim of programmes of this type to be religious, the question of definition is raised. In studying contemporary religiousness, in attempting to locate and analyse forms of modern spirituality, where exactly should we be looking? If what Simpson, Weber and others are saying is correct, many aspects of TV – and certainly soap opera – would have a strong claim on our attention. It is, of course, easy to dismiss such things as trivial, ephemeral and undeserving of serious attention. But can we afford to dismiss them as such if we are interested in understanding the values and beliefs which animate people's lives and inform popular culture? We are used to religion appearing in particular well-defined media (rituals, books, sacred music, architecture, etc.). Is there any good reason, though, to suppose that its expression is confined to such media?

Given the enormous audience for soap operas, Weber asks 'what is being reflected in ourselves and in our society by the immense popularity of such programmes?' One answer to this question may be 'root paradigms', a concept (taken from the influential work of Victor Turner) which William Biernatzki uses to analyse the intercultural appeal of popular American programmes like *Dallas*. He suggests that the reason why *Dallas* was able to attract audiences throughout the world lay precisely in 'its dependence on themes which relate directly to very general root paradigms – paradigms so fundamental that they may be found in many cultures'. The primordial themes of *Dallas*, he argues, echo those of the book of Genesis. Indeed, people's acquaintance with biblical stories may well have made the themes of Dallas more familiar to them. The resistance of root paradigms to change is remarkable. This is illustrated by reference to the extraordinary use made of TV and video by a group of Laotian refugees in Chicago, in order to support their traditional world-view. Biernatzki is adamant that if we are to communicate religious meaning successfully via the mass media, we need to be thoroughly familiar with the culture in which we are operating and, in particular, to have a grasp of the root paradigms which underlie every culture's values and symbols.

Could TV *change* our root paradigms? Given the pervasiveness and power of this medium, might its fundamental values and pre-suppositions not gradually erode even the most deep-seated outlooks if they happen to be at odds with its vision? Although root paradigms are clearly resistant to change, the long-term effect of exposure to TV is a cultural unknown. Whether media consumption at our present high rates will re-wire the psyche and leave it profoundly altered, or merely wash over or reinforce adamantine and unalterable perspectives leaving them wholly unchanged, remains to be seen. It would be a useful comparative exercise, though, to identify point by point the major root paradigms operative in the world today and match these against the fundamental values on TV.

Of course it is not just in the implicit religion of soap operas that a religious dimension to the media may be seen. Many of the contributors see TV itself as a religious (or pseudo-religious) phenomenon. Looking at one aspect of it in particular, namely television news, Colin Morris suggests that the journalists respon-sible for structuring the bulletins are in fact engaged in a religious activity because 'putting a frame round our experiences', in the way that a news-story format inevitably does, 'is a religious service in the strictest meaning of the word.' Pointing to the limits imposed by the demands of TV as a medium, Morris shows how events are easier to picture than process. So, in terms of television coverage, it is far more difficult to show a tree growing than a tree being uprooted by a tornado. 'Live moving pictures', Morris reminds us, 'have the power to sever the nerve between sensation and meaning, event and context, emotional spasm and deep sentiment, fact and truth.' However, despite its limitations, he enthusiastically endorses the positive role which TV news plays in our lives. Theologically, he suggests it acts to sharpen the 'key questions of the Christian apologetic'. Though it may appear that the outlook offered by TV may render the task of asserting the love of God at work in his-tory more difficult, Morris makes clear that to start from the assumption of a good creation, which he sees as fundamental to the way we understand news, makes a preponderance of so-called bad news inevitable. It is interesting to ask, in light of Morris's comments, if natural theology in the twentieth or twenty-first century (indeed theological enquiry of any kind) could be seriously conducted without making reference to TV.

After all, might our experience and knowledge of the world with and without television, supplemented and unsupplemented by the kind of information it offers, not suggest different views of God? Or does TV just magnify, duplicate, increase (rather than fundamentally change) what we already know? Quite apart from the possible impact of its visual imperative, emphasizing the need for images, is the range and type of information brought before us by this medium likely to have an influence on the outcome of our theologizing?

At one point in the *New Era of Religious Communication*, Pierre Babin offers a striking contrast of world-views which helps to indicate the potential which TV and other media may have to affect our religiousness. To begin with Babin introduces us to the practice among some indian tribes living in the Canadian wilderness, of plugging their children's nostrils and covering their eyes after birth, the better to atune them to the noises of the forest in which they will have to survive. Then, in stark contrast to these 'hyper-auditory' individuals, made alert to the subtlest natural sounds, Babin invites us to consider the modern American adolescent, reared amidst the clamour of competing mass media (such an individual will have logged some 20,000 hours of viewing by the age of sixteen). Is it possible that individuals with such different degrees of media exposure would have similar ideas about God and the transcendent? Could their sense of the holy be thought to follow even remotely similar contours?[13]

Further perspectives on news are offered by John Eldridge and S. A. Schleifer. Eldridge, who provides some interesting criteria for what counts as good and bad news coverage, reminds us that impartiality is inherently problematic. However problematic it may be, though, the alternative is not undisciplined subjectivity. On the contrary, accuracy 'will always remain a bedrock of credibility and newsworthiness'. While Eldridge does not address specifically religious issues, his analysis of the selection, construction and relative truthfulness of news coverage poses vital questions in our debate. Working through a number of examples he shows how news 'occupies a space that is constantly contested, which is subject to organizational and technological restructuring, to economic, cultural and political constraints'. In other words, what emerges to count as the news of the day is itself a cultural construct. In the contested space of news (and indeed other programmes too), what is the role of specifically religious considerations? What constraints govern the way in which religious stories are reported in the news bulletins? The exploration of which religious (and moral) considerations govern the way in which *any* story is covered – and the acceptability or otherwise of such constraints in a secular, pluralistic democracy – takes us back to the issue of influence raised by Eric Shegog and the question of who ought to control what appears on our screens. Stressing again the enormous significance of the media – 'the processes of creating, transmitting and receiving messages', Eldridge argues, 'are not just a secondary feature in modern society, they are part of the warp and woof of it' – he urges the need for an informed scepticism. Such scepticism, he suggests, can act as an important safeguard of democracy.

Schleifer suggests that from an Islamic point of view there are a number of difficulties with impartiality and other ideals of Western journalism. 'The core of modern journalism', he says, 'is as inherently anti-Islamic as the interest-based core of modern banking.' Schleifer also underlines the point that television is intrinsically anti-meditative and has extreme difficulty in handling religious material. He believes that in dealing with people whose spirituality may be strikingly evident in a personal encounter, for example, TV is unable to picture what is there, 'no iconic sense of the inner essence is revealed'. We cannot 'see' the saint via video. Such media can only simulate the image without its invisible aura of spiritual grace. Can *any* medium, though, capture this 'invisible aura of spiritual grace'? The inability of TV to do so may be extreme, but it is not unique. Rather than highlighting a problem faced by television alone, Schleifer has rather identified an instance of what remains the fundamental problem of communicating religious meaning in any medium. Given that, in some important sense, religions involve, touch on, encounter something inexpressible, how is any medium to handle them? Schleifer outlines some of the historical facts which need to be taken into consideration in any understanding of modern Islamic journalism, which he criticizes for its tendency to reduce Islam to a *political* topic. 'Mainstream Muslim society', he says, 'of which the political movements are but a small part, receives disproportionately little media attention.' Given the visual imperative of TV, and the assumption that what is not visible does not exist or is unimportant, Schleifer warns that the increasing power of television journalism poses a profound challenge to any religious outlook. It is, I think, worth asking if the ways in which the media challenge religion demand a different response from each of the different religious traditions. Would an Islamic view of, and response to, such challenges follow similar lines to Christian, Jewish, Hindu or Buddhist views and responses? The moral codes of the major faiths seem to agree when it comes to fundamental strictures governing communication, with a common emphasis on the importance of telling the truth. However, it is unclear if agreement at such a basic non-contextual level could lead to the sort of inter-religiously acceptable codes of media conduct which it will become increasingly important to formulate in a modern pluralistic society.

In my own chapter I look at what happens when communication fails and suggest that important clues about criteria for religious communication can be gleaned from such situations. It is instructive to look at the very radical ways in which communication can fail in time of war. Since war has been described as 'the ultimate failure of communication', examining how media can be distorted in conflict situations can help to identify some of the qualities likely to be needed to safeguard communication from such a fate. My chapter stresses the importance of truth-telling as the most important moral imperative for guiding media use and suggests that empathy and right of reply might be seen as minimum requirements for communication seeking religious sanction. However, though truth-telling is a vital ideal to keep in mind, it is important to recognize that it is an ideal and that it is simply not possible to realize it fully. We cannot hope to tell (and should not expect to tell or be told), the *whole* truth, the *complete* story. As Andrew Belsey and Ruth Chadwick have pointed out: 'telling the truth is not without its problems, for the truth is endless and seamless, whereas the exigencies of time and resources require some selection to be made from the potentially infinite'.[14] Naturally that selection should be done in as equitable a manner as possible. But the principles of selection which we use – 'fairness, justice, democratic significance and avoidance of bias and harm'[15] (religious factors might also be added to the examples Belsey and Chadwick cite) – may not always pull in the same direction.

Although communication failure occurs most spectacularly in times of war, many critics would argue that, from a religious point of view, we are more or less perpetually surrounded by communication which fails to measure up to an acceptable standard. Thus Peg Slinger, Jeanne Cover and Dorothee Sölle all offer robust critiques of media shortcomings, particularly in TV advertising, when this is measured against a Christian scale of values. Again, the enormous social importance of television is stressed. Slinger, for example, suggests that it has changed the daily rhythms of millions of people and as such must be seen as a culturally revolutionary presence. She suggests that analysing advertisements is one way to get at the values and beliefs of the society in which they are broadcast. Condemning as unchristian many of the values and beliefs which her study of contemporary TV advertising reveals, she urges viewers to engage in a careful analysis of the images put forward by advertisers so that they can avoid being hoodwinked into accepting a vision of the world where a small minority of the population is urged to devour a huge amount of its resources while others drown in a sea of poverty. Although advertising undoubtably highlights profoundly unfair distributions of wealth, some might wish to argue that, given its relationship with production and consumption, advertising helps to *create* wealth and employment. Are there situations, then, in which advertising (or at least some advertisements) might lay claim to being theologically acceptable and immune to the sort of questions Slinger raises?

It is interesting to contrast the idea that the media may have some religious quality, whether in terms of the implicit religion of soaps, the story-telling aspect of news, or the idea that in broad social and cultural terms TV now serves certain functions once performed by religion, with the kind of view expressed by Cover when she says that 'the ideology inherent in advertising and the majority of programmes reveals the social sin and collective blindness condemned by Jesus'. She sees much of television's output as something engaged in the desensitizing of our vision and imagination, a desensitizing which also serves to re-order our sense of priorities. She is particularly critical of the fact that 'sacred symbols have been removed from their religious contexts to give a spurious feeling of transcendence and sacredness to a "theology of consumerism".' Cover argues that if the radical transformation of society demanded by a Christian outlook is to be carried out effectively, it is vital that we all learn to be aware of our own role in reinforcing the cultural hegemony served by TV. Again, the point is being stressed that Christian teaching is radically at odds with the main currents of the *Zeitgeist*, as these find expression in advertising and – according to Cover – the majority of programmes. Given the depth and seriousness of the differences between religious and secular outlooks, it is worth considering what (if anything), would remain untouched were a programme of theological censorship to be given free rein. What would media be like that caused no offence to a Christian (Islamic, Hindu, etc.) point of view? Would we still want to watch, read, listen to them?

Dorothee Sölle suggests that consumerism has created an entirely new culture of communication in which the dominant language is the language of television. She is particularly critical of advertising and focuses her comments on Pasolini's analysis of an advertising jingle for 'Jesus Jeans' which appeared in the early 1970s ('Thou shalt have no other jeans before me'). What is blasphemous, she says, is not the use of the first commandment for an advertising slogan, but advertisement as such. In Sölle's view, the new religion is consumerism and it relies heavily for its propagation on the mass media. She voices concern that the contemporary situation is one in which 'we lack a language able to convey something about life's assumed meaningfulness, about the human capacity for truth, about the unconditionedness and totality of existence'. Our expressive resources are being eroded by the language of TV. Linked with this loss of expressivity is the isolation from all forms of transcendence. Advertising attempts to dismantle traditional values and reduces relationships to little more than shared consumption so that 'the icy chill of relations devoid of all longing seeps from the television into every room'. In extreme contrast to life in this dispiriting secular-trivial world, there is the possibility of life lived according to a Christian vision.

Reinhold Niebuhr has spoken of the 'prestige of normality which sinful forms of life periodically achieve in the world'.[16] It seems clear that, according to Sölle, the media would very largely qualify as just such a form of life. Is such harsh criticism justified? The icy

chill of relations devoid of all longing may on occasions seep from
the TV, but is there not a more positive side to its output too?
Can an appeal to the way in which TV comforts the sad, provides company for the lonely, informs the isolated and ignorant,
effectively counter Sölle's devastating critique? Might the way
in which it seems to foster a sense of social solidarity at great
national events – a royal wedding, a presidential funeral – help
to redeem TV from the theological stigma that many believe it
should bear?

Whether we view the media as secular, religious, pseudo-
religious, anti-religious or according to less black and white
categories, it is important to have a grasp of the ways in which
the media handle explicitly religious topics and how religion can
exert an influence on media events. This is the area focused on
in the last three chapters of the book. D. P. Davies offers an
analysis of some aspects of TV coverage of religion in Wales,
focusing in particular on the Welsh-language channel, S4C. He
explains how much of the credit for setting up S4C must go to
individual Christians and the churches in Wales. Ten years after
the inception of this channel – 'the most significant milestone
in the entire history of broadcasting in Wales' – he offers a
review of the ways in which S4C has sought to meet the
needs of the Christian churches in Wales, and the extent to
which it has attempted to broaden religious horizons. Davies
makes clear the difficulty faced by commissioning editors in
having to strike a balance between the apparently conservative
tastes of the viewers and the innovative instincts of programme
makers (a difficulty by no means unique to S4C). Looking to
the future, he calls on those concerned with programmes of
religious worship to address the basic theological and practical
questions relating to the broadcasting of worship on television.
In particular, the visual potential of the medium in presenting
worship needs to be fully exploited and this calls for a readiness
to experiment. His fear is that inadequate financial resources and
lack of theological reflection may lead to programmes that are
little more than radio programmes with pictures. Whilst not
without problems, both in religious and other programming
areas, Davies concludes that S4C should demonstrate to other
minority cultures that a 'local' television service is possible and
worthwhile.

Worship is a key part of traditional religious broadcasting, whether on S4C or some other channel. Worship provides an easy way of picturing religion, offering the camera a wealth of images to focus on. What, though, is its theological status when it appears? Could viewers participate, joining in the prayers and hymn singing? Would the validity or otherwise of their participation be affected by whether the programme was live or recorded? To what extent can the demands of the medium (in terms of time, hunger for colourful images, intolerance of silence, etc.) determine the design of a service without rendering it theologically suspect? As D. P. Davies stresses, the theological questions relating to the television broadcast of worship still need to be addressed.

Rachel Viney looks at religious broadcasting in a wider British context, focusing in particular on independent television. She explains the origins and development of this programme genre and considers how it is likely to change in the future given that – with the advent of cable and satellite TV – the ecology of broadcasting has changed and with it expectations of what broadcasting is about. Viney makes clear the influence of the public service broadcast ethos on TV companies in general and, more specifically, on their attitude to religious programming. She goes on to examine the implications for such programmes of the Broadcasting Act of 1990, which ensures that religious programmes are, for the first time, the subject of rules contained in a legally enforceable programme code (a somewhat ironic situation given the generally deregulatory intentions of this Act). Although the task of addressing the plurality of faiths now flourishing in Britain may not yet have been adequately met by broadcasters, Viney is confident that the future of public service broadcasting is full of potential to explore more deeply what it means to do religious broadcasting which is truly relevant to a plural society. The realization of such potential is, she says, likely to be enhanced rather than limited by the Independent Television Commission, for the range of religious programmes broadcast by ITV and Channel 4 has in no small measure been enabled by the presence of a regulatory body committed to the principle that religious programmes have a proper place in a balanced television output.

Does religious broadcasting have a legitimate role in modern TV output? Before we can begin to answer this question, we need

some kind of definition of what religious broadcasting is. And here
we are likely to run into difficulties which an uncritical usage of the
term in its traditional sense will not have anticipated. For instance,
Quentin Schultze has argued that even if broadcasts are not made for
specifically religious purposes, they may still serve 'the historic
religious function of organizing life around shared beliefs'.[17]
Arguing that popular TV programmes serve a religious function to
the extent that their stories are culturally shared narratives, Schultze
suggests that the term 'religious broadcasting' is deeply misleading
because it implies that other programmes are not religious. If
Schultze is right, do we need to consider 'religious broadcasting' as a
separate category with special regulatory needs? And what criteria
might be suggested for a *successful* religious programme?

Turning from TV to newspapers, Stewart Hoover offers an
analysis of the way in which religion is handled by the American
press. The surveys on whose results he draws call into question
some of the common perceptions held by the press about religion
and religious news. Many widely held assumptions about reader
interest in religion may, Hoover argues, be misperceptions. He
questions whether common journalistic treatments of religion as
a subject of primarily local interest actually fit the reality of religious interest and behaviour in society at large. Despite recent
improvements in the status and quality of religious coverage by
American newspapers, there is still some way to go before reader
expectation is satisfied. Though a majority of newspaper readers
consider themselves to be religious, Hoover's research suggests
that, by and large, they do not read religious publications. The
secular media are increasingly where they turn to to find significant
information about the world of religion. Readers tend to understand religion in a wide-ranging sense, embracing local, national
and international levels and see it as an important dimension
of much of the rest of the news. Yet they do not feel that the
newspapers they read give religion the kind of coverage they
want and expect. They want to see religion mainstreamed (rather
than marginalized) in the papers. If such mainstreaming comes
about who will decide on what is covered? Should the reader,
reporter or editor determine the choice of religious topic and the
manner of its treatment? Given the sheer extent and diversity of
possible stories on our religiously plural planet, what criteria of
selection and omission might be adopted to ensure satisfactory

coverage? If, as Neil Postman has suggested,[18] an entertainment ethic is prevalent in the media, reducing everything to an entertainment format to the extent that we are in danger of amusing ourselves to death, can mechanisms be found to prevent any mainstreaming of religion from simply focusing on what will *amuse* readers?

* * *

H. Richard Niebuhr once suggested that religious currents have often flowed in other than obviously theological or ecclesiastical channels.[19] One of the main questions likely to be raised by reading this volume is the extent to which modern religious currents are influenced by, contained in or thwarted by those mass media which surround us and which exert such a potent influence on modern society. It is clear that we are living at a time which has witnessed enormous, world-shaping instances of media change. Walter Ong may be right to suppose that 'more than any other single invention, writing has transformed human consciousness',[20] but the change from a writing and print to a televisual epistemology has also had profound consequences on the way we think. Many view these consequences as being of sufficient importance to warrant the introduction of elements of media studies or media awareness training into traditional programmes of religious and theological education. Why are media changes so revolutionary? In so far as religions are concerned, Thomas Boomershine has suggested that the reason is no less than the fact 'that changes in communications technology transform the character of the community's experience of God'.[21] However, no matter how significant the advent of writing, or print, or TV may have been for the nature and expression of human religiousness, it is important not to lose sight of the fact that, at the end of the day, *people* are the most important medium of all. As Ninian Smart puts it: 'Ultimately the most important symbols communicating the essence of religion are the people involved – the shaved monk, the village priest, the hermit, the wandering holy man, the preacher, the sober layperson and so on.'[22] Television's undoubted power notwithstanding, this fundamental

insight should not be lost sight of in reading the chapters which
follow.

NOTES

1   William Kuhns, *The Electronic Gospel*, New York: Herder & Herder:
    1969. p.165
2   op. cit
3   Ibid., p. 166
4   See: Walter J. Ong, *Orality and Literacy, The Technologising of the
    Word*, London: Methuen: 1982; Jack Goody (ed.), *Literacy in Tra-
    ditional Societies*, Cambridge: CUP: 1968; Jack Goody, *The Logic of
    Writing and the Organization of Society*, Cambridge: CUP: 1986.
5   Goody, *The Logic of Writing*, Chapter 1, 'The Word of God'.
6   On the problems of defining religion, together with some bibliographical
    suggestions, see Winston L. King's article in Mircea Eliade (ed.), *The
    Encyclopedia of Religion*, New York: Collier Macmillan: 1987, Vol.
    12, p. 283f.
7   William James, *The Varieties of Religious Experience*, (the Gifford Lec-
    tures for 1901–2) London: Longmans: 1928, p. 26.
8   Ninian Smart's ideas about defining religion by identifying a number of
    its 'dimensions', have been particularly influential. See his *The Religious
    Experience of Mankind*, London: 1969, pp. 15–25 for an early account
    of this strategy. A revised model is given in Smart's *The World's Reli-
    gions: Old Traditions and Modern Transformations*, Cambridge: CUP:
    1989, pp. 10–21.
9   On the socially subversive nature of religion and the problems this can
    cause in terms of religion–media relationships, see my 'Tigers: Some
    Reflections on Theological Education and Communication', *Religious
    Education*, Vol. 84, no. 1 (1989), pp. 103–30, especially pp. 122–5.
10 Sallie McFague, 'The Christian Paradigm', in Peter C. Hodgson and
    Robert H. King (eds.), *Christian Theology, an Introduction to its Tra-
    ditions and Tasks*, London: SPCK: 1983, p. 332.
11 See Malcolm Muggeridge, *Christ and the Media*, London: Hodder &
    Stoughton: 1977.
12 Martin Marty, 'Ethics and the Mass Media', in Lee Thayer (ed.), *Com-
    munication: Ethical and Moral Issues*, New York: Gordon Breach:
    1973, p. 189.
13 See Pierre Babin, *The New Era in Religious Communication*,
    Minneapolis: Fortress: 1991, tr. David Smith, pp. 56–7.
14 Andrew Belsey and Ruth Chadwick, 'Ethics and Politics of the Media:
    the Quest for Quality', in Belsey and Chadwick (eds.), *Ethical Issues in
    Journalism and the Media*, London: Routledge: 1992, p. 10.

15 Ibid., p. 13.
16 Reinhold Niebuhr, *The Nature and Destiny of Man*, Vol. 1 [from a passage reprinted in Robin Gill (ed.), *A Textbook of Christian Ethics*, Edinburgh: T & T Clark: 1985, p. 118].
17 Quentin J. Schultze, 'Secular Television as Popular Religion', in R. Abelman and S. Hoover, (eds.), *Religious Television: Controversies and Conclusions*, Norwood, N J: Ablex: 1990, p. 239.
18 Neil Postman, *Amusing Ourselves to Death*, *Public Discourse in the Age of Show Business*, London: Methuen: 1987.
19 H. Richard Niebuhr, *The Kingdom of God in America*, New York: Harper: 1959, p. ix.
20 Walter J. Ong, *Orality and Literacy, the Technologizing of the Word*, London: Methuen: 1982, p. 78.
21 Thomas Boomershine, 'Religious Education and Media Change: a Historical Sketch', *Religious Education*, Vol. 82, no. 2 (1987), p. 275.
22 Ninian Smart, 'Religion', in *The International Encyclopedia of Communication*, edited by Eric Barnouw, New York: OUP: 1988, Vol. 3, p. 443.

2 Media mythologies

GREGOR GOETHALS

The mass media – especially television – have taken command of the power of myth; in live coverage of important ceremonies, television has transformed the temporal and spatial dimensions of ritual. Although the words 'myth' and 'ritual' rest comfortably at home in the scholarly papers of cultural anthropologists, sociologists, theologians, liturgists and philosophers, the real presence of both is found in the electronic media of contemporary societies. Indeed the vitality of myth and ritual is greatest when they are not simply named but experienced as reality.

One role of myth is to situate us, to define the world and our place in it. In the United States various television news programmes perform that function. Myths also enable us to identify values, to discern what is of worth. In those countries where advertising has taken hold, ad agencies and their corporate sponsors define the 'good life'. In addition, traditional myths help us to understand ourselves and provide us with models of human behaviour. Medieval sculptures and stained glass are easily understood visual stories of saints and sinners, heroes, and the faithful who take their place in the story of salvation. However drained of explicitly religious subject matter, television has assumed that iconic role, presenting an extraordinary range of individuals both fictional and actual, from Lucy to Murphy Brown to Anita Hill.[1] Often fiction and reality fuse as heroes and heroines parade across the TV screen and become exemplary figures who cope with life, bring humour, sometimes inspiration, to the tedium of everyday life. The electronic wizardry of television has also enabled millions of persons to escape from ordinary time and space, to 'enter' sacred sites thousands of miles away. Live television coverage has helped to reshape many traditional rituals and has given quasi-ritual dimensions to various kinds of political and sports events. Throughout the world TV draws ordinary individuals into extraordinary occasions, offering what traditional religion once provided: 'pageants, crowds, panoplies, special days marked off by the calendar, something to give form and body to internal fantasy, something external to yield oneself to'.[2] Like traditional ritual, TV's ceremonial coverage of significant events are opportunities for individual feelings and sentiments to be forged into communal, shared ones. Live coverage of events removes the restrictions of space, and rituals once open to only a privileged few become accessible to millions. Through this medium like-minded persons may leap over temporal and spatial boundaries to 'live' in ritual time and space.

The earliest and perhaps most dramatic transformation of ritual by television in the United States is remembered by those who 'took part' in the rites for President John F. Kennedy. As they huddled before their sets, millions of mourners shared the 'real' sacred spaces: the Capitol where a military guard lowered a flag-draped coffin down the steps, the streets through which a caisson bore the body of the slain president, the riderless horse slowly following. Ordinary people in small towns and cities throughout the nation 'walked' with the huge crowd of world leaders slowly and sombrely in the funeral procession. They watched as the young son of the president saluted. Along with those present at Arlington military cemetery, they heard the sombre, ceremonial sounds of the bugle as the body was lowered into the grave; looking above, they saw the military formation of army and navy airplanes and 'Air Force One' fly over in a final tribute to the slain leader. Never before in American history had so many people from all walks of life been able to say goodbye simultaneously in collective sorrow. In his recent study, *Ritual, Politics and Power*, David Kertzer writes: 'Ritual activity is not simply one possible way of creating group solidarity; it is a necessary way'.[3] In one of the most tragic moments of the country's history the medium of television opened up a powerful ritual to countless numbers and drew the nation's many disparate parts into a grieving whole.

A generation later, in January 1991, Americans were in the midst of a very different national crisis: the Gulf War. Like the uncertain days following Kennedy's death, it was a time in which a sense of solidarity was essential. Though it may seem strange to persons outside this society, Superbowl XXV[4] became a significant ritual, an occasion to reinforce feelings of national unity and purpose. In view of the serious concerns of the nation at war, the authorities debated whether or not the Superbowl should be cancelled, but decided finally that it would be good for the morale of the men and women at war, as well as for those at home, to go forward with it. Viewers who tuned in were caught up in the drama of a hallowed sports saga amid the anxiety and suspense of a nation at war. In a spectacular way the televized coverage fused a combination of loyalties – to the nation's war effort in the Middle East, to the favourite teams, and to the American way of life.

Patriotism was the major motif of the game. As if 'hanging' from a blimp high above the field, the viewer looked down on a sea of waving flags and in the next instant was shoulder to shoulder in the stands, holding aloft banners that proclaimed the war effort and those who were serving their country. The opening ceremonies were military extravaganzas that featured representatives from the armed services; cameras moved in with tight shots of their stalwart faces and the vivid colour of their flags. Even more breathtaking, a formation of F-16 fighter planes flew over the stadium to participate in the occasion. Whitney Houston, one of the nation's top singers, then began 'The Star Spangled Banner', ceremoniously signalling that the game would soon begin. She sang with such gusto and passion that it became a great hymn to the American Way. As she sang, the cameras created a moving montage of red, white, and blue, superimposing flag images over fans, the football players and the singer. The presentation seemed to call forth voices across the nation into a mighty chorus. Once the game started, there were the usual commercials, but in addition, there were interruptions for news updates on the war in the Gulf. This great panorama of images – military splendour, the nation's first-rate athletes, heroic action on the field, cheering fans, dramatic music, stunning colour and action, reports from the front, commercials that dazzled the eyes – was a splendid civil ritual.

Later, after a cease-fire had been declared, public television interviewed several humanists and scientists and asked them to give their impressions of the war's effect. A prominent psychiatrist commented on what he saw as a 'tonic' effect on the American public. He noted that the war had transformed America into a real collective identity. We have, he said, been so individualized that the war satisfied a hunger for community and leadership.[5] In view of these reflections, it is important to emphasize that the war was mediated through the media. On that cold day in January, television provided a ritual that gave countless numbers of individuals a sense of at-one-ness, a solidarity of spirit and purpose. Taken collectively, the genres of television – soap operas, commercials, news, and sports, ritualized events – teach us what is 'real' and what we value. In many countries throughout the world people are experiencing competing symbolic orders: those generated by various religious traditions and those shaped by mass media phenomena, particularly television. Do such media mythologies threaten to eclipse the more traditional religious values and world-views? Can traditional religious communities reclaim the power of myth through the electronic media?

Before addressing these questions directly it is important to distinguish between the manifest and latent roles of religion. The manifest, essential role shared by world religions is, of course, redemptive. In various ways they all offer salvation, a way out of human suffering and meaninglessness. Each provides a path – prayers, rites, meditations, rituals – that opens up for individuals a lifelong journey of faith toward an ultimately unknown, awesome mystery. Religion also serves a latent function: providing shared symbols – ways of knowing and communicating, values, and norms. In compact religious societies latent and manifest religious functions are difficult to distinguish. But in highly differentiated societies, marked by secular and religiously plural configurations, the latent function of religion may be assumed by many kinds or orders – scientific, political, economic, cultural.[6] Thus in religiously plural nations the mass media can perform this latent function of traditional religions: to provide an authoritative, mythological order, holding together many competing religious ideologies. For example, images of popular culture legitimate and reinforce certain basic American convictions and values which most religious and secular groups accept. Television offers public, shared symbols which for many Americans answer the questions 'Who am I?' and 'Who are we?' Under a giant canopy of images all denominations and religious traditions are exposed to the same framing of reality. Thus, networks and cable TV, magazines and newspapers combine forces to offer what religious institutions themselves once provided indirectly: images of an ordered world; icons of exemplary individuals, models of what human life can and should be like, and rituals that help to unify people who are diverse – racially, ethnically, religiously.

Media mythologies are inextricably intertwined with the ideals and principles of the nations in which they emerge. Depending upon one's national perspective, the questions raised are answered in different ways. In the United States, mass media symbols blanket the nation with images that celebrate and legitimate the American Way. Hovering beneath this encompassing canopy, religious groups respond in different ways. Sociologist Robert Wuthnow has pointed out that differences among and within church groups today tend to be organized along liberal and conservative ideologies. He also has shown how civil religion itself is similarly polarized. Conservative civil religion is more closely identified with a biblical faith which claims a special place for the nation in the divine order of things, while a liberal view focuses less on a particular country and more on humanity.[7] Diverse attitudes toward culture also reflect persistent ambiguities and tensions between faith and culture, analysed by theologian H. Richard Niebuhr in his classic work, *Christ and Culture*.[8] Some churches, for example, make great efforts to distinguish their beliefs and values while others fuse their symbols with the pervasive myths and civic rituals. In their diversity, American churches are perhaps comparable to those small isolated cults of the pre-Constantinian era which sought to assimilate or to reject the learning and arts of the Greco-Roman culture. The 'televangelists' were quick to embrace the most innovative communication technologies and to blend their own form of Christianity with the dogmas of a conservative public religion. On the other hand, mainline religious groups, uneasy about communication technologies, have generally fitted their own creeds comfortably into a larger framework of meaning – the American Way of Life.

In contrast to both the electronic preachers and mainline denominations, some religious leaders and communities are struggling against an identification of their faith with cultural myths especially evident in commercials, such as the assurance of bliss through perpetual consumption and 24-hour relief from suffering, both individual and communal. At the same time, they take a more positive view of the communication revolution and are trying to appropriate it. They face two challenges. The first is to take an iconoclastic strategy for some mythologies of culture. This means that while performing their priestly responsibilities and addressing the manifest religious needs of people – worship, prayer, evangelism – leaders assume a prophetic role in the larger community, to critique cultural myths in the light of their faith. The second challenge is, in many respects, more difficult: to explore, understand, and use the unprecedented communication technology in a constructive way. Rather than demonize television, they seek to transform electronic and print media and to give traditional myths new symbolic forms. In accepting the first challenge, to develop a prophetic critique of culture, religious leaders frequently find allies among those who have no relationship with church organizations. Some persons simply see an urgent need to critique the goals and values of a consumer society. Others find an essentially secular or humanist basis for their protests. Still others – liberal civil religionists, like many religious leaders, associate their iconoclasm with their faith in the biblical prophetic tradition.[9] Bonded together in a cultural resistance movement, they share a common goal, to critique the framework of symbols constructed by mass media in American culture. While ancient iconoclasts actually smashed images, contemporary iconoclasts attack established principles and institutional authorities through the use of words and images, and they use whatever media is available to them – radio, newspapers, television.

A full discussion of an iconoclastic probe of America's media mythologies is not possible here. That would call for a much closer look at the historical development of clusters of meaning which historian John F. Wilson calls quasi-religious dogmas of an American public religion.[10] In this chapter I will focus on a conviction upon which, I believe, other mythologies depend. The quintessential media myth of American society is the unquestioned assumption that there is a completely open, free flow of information. Although the United States has one of the world's most unfettered communication systems, a critical, iconoclastic examination can only help maintain that freedom. Throughout United States history, public access to information and the right to free speech and press have empowered news institutions to take responsibility for providing shared public knowledge and identifying common concerns. The nineteenth-century visitor to America, Alexis de Toqueville, recognized the ways in which newspapers became a unifying agent in a democracy. The newspaper he says, 'comes to you . . . and talks to you briefly every day on the common weal . . .' He compared the newspaper to a beacon which unites wandering minds. 'Only a newspaper,' he said, can 'drop the same thought into a thousand minds at the same moment.'[11] Shared information, moreover, is vital to ethical decisions and action. As theologian H. Richard Niebuhr observed, our decisions about the appropriate action in a situation depend upon our knowledge of what is happening. At critical times in human history, he says, the decisive question was not '"What is the goal?" nor yet "What is the law?" but "What is happening?" and then "What is the fitting response to what is happening?"'[12] Public knowledge gained through print and electronic media is essential for informed democratic decision. Over generations the American public has expected the press to function as a watchdog so that informed and responsible choices can be made.[13] This tradition of a free press is so deeply rooted that most citizens cannot conceive of news institutions in any other way. This is genuine mythology. In this sense the nation *lives the myth* of a democratic, open information system. Most people in the United States tacitly assume that the most significant events relating to their well-being and participation in society will inevitably be reported. From this deep stratum of myth one can draw out two interrelated dogmas: (1) 'If something important has happened, we will hear about it.' And (2) 'If we don't see it on TV, hear about it on the radio, or read something in the papers, it hasn't happened.'

To explore this basic mythological assumption, church leaders and other cultural dissenters are very dependent upon those who work in the mass media. Mark Hertsgaard, for example, charges that during the Ronald Reagan era news persons did not live up to the concept of a free and independent press. Instead, he says they practiced 'jellybean' journalism and failed to monitor many decisions affecting the public good and to bring to light issues that might affect decision-making.[14] Few journalists of the 1980s questioned the slogan invented for Reagan by a PR firm: 'It's morning in America.' Even as a foggy, midnight darkness descended, no one asked the critical question on which ethical and value choices turn: 'What is going on?' In the 1990s some writers such as William

Greider[15] have begun to recover the watchdog role of the press and to call attention to what journalists of the 1980s seemed to ignore: the declining income of the middle class, the dramatic rise in the income of the very wealthy, and the depth of financial crisis brought about by the Savings and Loan scandal.

One of the most controversial areas that iconoclasts enter is the coverage of a war in which the nation is engaged. The impact of TV images that flooded the United States during the Vietnam War is still being debated. Many credit the reversal of American support of the war to the intense pictures of death and destruction sent back from the battlefield. Clearly ever since that conflict the Pentagon has kept tight control over the images of war – in Granada, Panama, and most recently the Gulf War. Many spokespersons for the press protest today that reporting of the Gulf War – both in images and print – became excessively symbolic. Television, in particular, they argue, functioned essentially to reinforce belief in the administration's actions. Polls taken at the time, however, showed a marked public hostility to the press. And, upon his return, the grand military hero of the war, General Norman Schwartzkopf, echoed a similar suspicion about the freedom of information which Americans have traditionally valued: 'I just think', said Schwartzkopf, 'that in the future when people choose to justify their actions based upon the American public's right to know, they'd better check with the American public first, because the American public has made it very clear to me, in all the literally hundreds of thousands of letters I have gotten, how they feel about the term "the American people's right to know" as it was being used by the people who were doing that sort of thing.'[16] Since news about the Gulf War was so tightly controlled, reports, books and articles continue to probe for information that was not forthcoming at the time. Project Censored, an organization which tries to identify and publicize stories on important issues that have been overlooked or under-reported, announced that the Gulf War issues dominated the censored news list for 1991. For example, topping the list was the story which revealed how news departments at CBS and NBC rejected rare, uncensored footage taken at the height of the air war by two Emmy award-winning documentary producers. 'The footage substantially contradicted US administration claims that civilian damage from the American-led bombing campaign was light'.[17]

While professional communicators are important resources in understanding the symbolic environment, any concerned person can begin to scrutinize the reporting of particular events as they sit before a television set. Even as we watch, we can ask 'What is *really* going on? What is *left out?*' One example of 'What is left out?' still haunts those concerned with ecological issues: the reporting of the *Exxon Valdeze* oil spill. If one reviews the tapes of commercial and public television during the weeks following the disaster, several types of images can be detected: images shot from a helicopter, prolonged interviews featuring talking heads, conversations with oil company officials, members of the administration, the governor of Alaska, interviews with local fishermen, countless charts and maps. What was left out? Images of death: the agony of birds and mammals and the destruction of a pristine environment. Only occasionally, in less that a split second, could one actually see the painful details of a desecrated nature. There was little or no prolonged camera-work that brought viewers deeply into the horror of the creeping crude oil as it smothered rocks and entombed struggling wildlife.[18] It seemed as if anything more than the swiftest glance at such death would have been too evocative, too explosive and would inflame the environmental passions of the public. How could such images be left out? One PBS broadcaster reported via radio that the oil company had contracted with Alaskan fishermen and paid them $3,500 a day not to take media representatives out on their boats or even talk to them. Somewhat later ABC news reported that Alaskans were hired at $16.69 an hour to clean up the environment – with the stipulation that they were not to talk to anyone in the media. And public television, finally allowed into the area, reported that the Coast Guard had restricted the media in the early days of the spill, and in their story gave some glimpse of the unspeakable death that had been reported only sporadically over public radio.

What we perceive about out world in words and images can be reassuring or profoundly alarming. It is understandable, therefore, that various kinds of authorities would be concerned about the constructions of 'reality' formed through the mass media. The responsibility for deciding what information is left out or under-reported is not, however, always easy to determine. A small news item on the front page of *The Wall Street Journal* suggests that certain decisions occur in high places of power:

ENDING PROGRAMS: The Bush budget would terminate Labor Department reports on mass layoffs and the wage and work force consequences of foreign ownership of U.S. operations. . . . They are 'generally good things to do' but ran afoul of budget caps, an official says.[19]

While budget cutting is used to try to justify the elimination of information, it seems naïve to think that this was the only consideration. In a presidential election year the condition of the economy plays a critical role. Any deletion of damaging information about the economy confirms the efficacy of the dogma: 'If I don't read about it or see it, it hasn't happened.' Fortunately, in the United States, the sources of economic information are not limited to Labour Department reports.

Far more difficult for iconoclasts to detect are subtle publicity campaigns fabricated by firms to influence public opinion about policies and people. Righteous indignation flooded the hearts and minds of Americans when hearing that Iraqi soldiers had stormed Kuwaiti hospitals confiscating incubators and leaving newborn infants to die. Even George Bush referred to this incident in several of his speeches. The source of this information was an anonymous young Kuwaiti refugee who had testified to the alleged atrocities before a Congressional caucus. As it turned out, the young woman was the daughter of the Kuwaiti ambassador to the United States and had been coached and rehearsed before video cameras by the public relations firm of Hill and Knowlton, on behalf of their client, Citizens for a Free Kuwait, apparently funded by the Emir of Kuwait. Further investigation by news networks and interviews of Kuwaiti doctors indicated that no such incident had occurred.[20] The successful marketing of political mythologies is also illustrated by an article which appeared in the *New York Times*: The Sawyer/Miller Group, a leading consulting firm for political candidates, announced it was quitting the business of American politics and shifting to corporate and foreign clients, specializing in 'strategic communications consulting'. 'We try to give senior policy makers in institutions, whether governments or business or public institutions, *the ability to change the behavior of their key constituencies in order to carry out policy.*' Examples cited included: work for Drexel Burnham Lambert 'to change the public image of "junk bonds"' and the firm's 'work for the Government of Colombia to convince the American public, through advertising and work with news organizations that the South American nation was seriously trying to combat drug trafficking.'[21]

The American myth of genuinely open communication leads many people to equate media symbols and reality – in the news and all other TV genres. But the pictures of 'reality' which purport to inform, entertain, or persuade us are abstractions: visually and verbally. The picture/word combination serves as a bridge to an unknown sphere beyond our immediate, accessible environment. Functioning as a symbol, it allows people to cross over into another world, one outside of their directly perceived, familiar world of family or neighbourhood. The creation of this symbolic bridge depends upon the principle of selectivity and simplification. Realizing that we live in a highly symbolic environment, the critical question for the iconoclast is: Who is constructing the symbols? Today diverse, specialized groups – corporate sponsors, ad agencies, publicity firms, image managers, network executives – agree upon basic themes and motifs and authorize other groups of gifted writers, artists, and production teams to create symbols that will communicate to the public. Like their ancient and medieval counterparts working in stone and glass for temples and cathedrals, these contemporary symbol-makers attempt to strike a responsive chord in the eyes and minds of believers. 'Believing', in this case, is no longer tied to traditional religions but to something we vaguely perceive as the American Way.

In both Judaism and Christianity the problem of suffering – individual and communal – is paramount. That insoluble, unbearable mystery of existence weaves its way through biblical narratives and the psalms. Have religious communities made a serious attempt to tell these stories in contemporary electronic media? Can there be iconofiers as well as iconoclasts? Are there constructive attempts to use contemporary technology to challenge some of the litanies and mythologies of culture? Many denominations have been repulsed by the techniques and messages of the video preachers. Furthermore, the enormous financial costs of contemporary television technology have further inhibited mainline denominations. Most religious thinkers struggling with media mythologies have thus been more iconoclasts than iconofiers. During the last two years, however, a bold experiment, underwritten by the American Bible Society, was undertaken: an audio-visual translation of a passage from the New Testament, Christ's healing of the demoniac. Along with the video translation is a multimedia, interactive study-guide to the text. While the technology of interactive video is just beginning, this experiment opens up unprecedented possibilities for the communicating of old stories in a daring new way.

The American Bible Society, which has published the Scriptures in over sixty languages, sees the new technology as a way to transform Bible study. Teenagers, selected as the target audience for this project, met in focus groups and chose the story of Jesus's exorcism of the demons from a list of episodes in Mark that biblical scholars had prepared. Following that, the project manager, Fern Lee Hagedorn, and the chief academic consultant, Dr Thomas Boomershine, directed a team of scholars and artists through months of research and adaptation of the passage. The philosophy behind this effort was to find contemporary equivalents for the gospel story. Concentrating upon what the text meant in its own time and setting, scholars began to work with artists and technicians to select the best treatments, images, music, language in order to develop twentieth-century counterparts of the human experience described by Mark. The style of the translation is a music video and the dramatic setting is the city. There is no resemblance here to the old men with beards and bathrobes that typically identify Hollywood's Bible stories. The centrepiece of the project is a music video translation of Mark 5:1–20, entitled 'Out of the Tombs'. Two levels of translations occur. A female voice details the story and thus provides a continuous auditory armature for the video. The images draw the viewer into the mindset of the demoniac – the deranged outbursts and finally the freedom from his madness which comes through an encounter with a stranger who heals him. Since the process of the story unfolds in word and song, the images of the video employ the full range of visual power: tight shots bring the viewer face to face with the tormented young man, drooling, lurching, screaming; abstract, almost painterly compositions of their meeting on a fire escape; surrealist images of the sea, a major motif in the story. Meanwhile the background music and recitation of the story combine with this rushing montage of images into a total sensory translation that neither image nor sound alone could achieve. The total interactive video has three parts: 'See and Hear', 'Explore', and 'Do'. In addition to the music video, 'See and Hear' includes a rap version of the gospel featuring a group of rappers from East Harlem, New York, as well as a translation in the musical form of a chant. The 'Do' section gives those working with it a chance to experiment with images that are programmed to be interactive. The 'Explore' section allows the enquiring viewer to examine background material which puts the Mark story in its historical context. In the 'Evil Spirits' section, for example, one can call up images and texts to find out more about the uniqueness of Jesus's exorcism, other exorcism stories, an explanation of the death of the pigs, and an exploration of the symbolism of the sea. The pilot project, only recently completed, awaits further product and market testing.

Medieval and Renaissance church leaders worked in concert with artists and artisans, using all the resources of culture to communicate the redemptive power of the Gospel. Following the Reformation and the increasing secularization of the modern era, many artists tended to move toward private symbolism and mythology. Others began to drift and become part of the new institutional establishments, such as publicity firms and ad agencies. The experiments of the American Bible Society signal that there can be a revitalized approach to imagery, technology, and the arts. Iconofiers in high and popular culture are searching today for new forms and contexts for images; iconoclasts have been in the trenches for a long time. Although iconoclasts and iconofiers have different tasks before them, they share a conviction about the transformative power of faith in culture. Both understand that in cultural forms, as in all life, is an ever-present possibility of redemption and renewal. While conscious of the destructive dimensions of human creativity, they affirm the goodness of creation and its continuing overflow into human experience.

NOTES

1   The following information may help to dispel any puzzlement which examples cited may cause for non-American readers: 'Lucy' refers to Lucille Ball, a Hollywood comedienne who helped shape television comedy in the 1950s and 1960s and remained a kind of national treasure until she died. The old series, *I love Lucy*, was one of

the most popular American programmes and has been re-broadcast throughout the world.

'Murphy Brown' is a contemporary feminine role model for the 1990s in the United States. The programme, entitled, *Murphy Brown*, focuses on the adventures of a very intelligent, single, female television reporter. The sitcom achieved recent national attention by portraying an adversarial position toward the Bush – Quayle administration. The opening episode of the 1992 series even got a three-minute report on the BBC when the show's heroine fired back at Dan Quayle who had criticized the 'family values' expressed in the sitcom.

Anita Hill is a professor of law who came out of an academic enclave to question the ethics of Clarence Thomas, a Bush appointee to the Supreme Court. Her accusations of Thomas's sexual harassment came to a climax in a nationally televized 'hearing'. Although Thomas was eventually approved by Congress to serve on the Supreme Court, Anita Hill's testimony inspired many women to challenge those elected politicians who consented to Thomas's appointment. At the time of writing, this topic is currently playing itself out in the 1992 elections in the United States.

2   Ernest Becker, *The Denial of Death*, New York: The Free Press: 1975, p. 200.

3   David Kertzer, *Ritual, Politics, and Power*, New Haven: Yale University Press: 1988, p. 62.

4   The Superbowl is the climax of the football 'liturgical year' which begins in the early fall with the Monday-night telecasts of professional football games and ends when the leading teams battle for the position of 'No. 1'. The final play-off game, perhaps the greatest American secular ritual is known as the 'Superbowl'. This takes place usually about the third week of January. It is watched by millions of Americans and is now broadcast throughout the world.

5   Psychiatrist Willard Gaylin was one of the scholars interviewed by *The MacNeil/Lehrer News Hour*, 19 March 1991. Dr Gaylin noted that while the war had a stimulating effect on the people who lead dull lives, it also demonstrated a kind of pathos. The 'tonic' effect showed how desperate people are for community leadership in an over-individualized society.

6   Bryan Wilson, *Religion in Sociological Perspective*, New York: Oxford University Press: 1982, p. 45. See Chapter 2, 'The Functions of Religion in Contemporary Society'.

7   Robert Wuthnow, *The Restructuring of American Religion*, Princeton, NJ: Princeton University Press: 1988, p. 250f.

8   H. Richard Niebuhr, *Christ and Culture*, New York: Harper & Row: 1956.

9   Wuthnow, op. cit., p. 250f.

10 John F. Wilson, *Public Religion in American Culture*, Philadelphia: Temple University Press: 1979. Wilson locates four clusters of meaning

that are central to popular faith: (1) American society understood as perfected and pure, unalloyed and uncompromized. In contrast to the societies of the old world and antiquity, it requires of its members internalized discipline. (2) American society as fulfilment of the dream of the ages, frequently exhibited in historical categories and under eschatological symbols, and held forth in millenarian language. (3) American society as receptive to the deprived and the homeless of the world, and promising them a new life. (4) American society as one of opportunity in which liberty provides the framework for individual and collective development.

11 Alexis de Toqueville, 'On the Relation Between Public Associations and the Newspapers', *Democracy in America*, Vol. 2, New York: Vintage Books: 1958, pp. 119–22.

12 H. Richard Niebuhr. *The Responsible Self*, New York: Harper & Row: 1963, p. 67.

13 See *The People and the Press: A Times Mirror Investigation of Public Attitudes Toward the News Media*, conducted by the Gallup Organization (Los Angeles: Times Mirror: 1986). The survey showed that network anchor persons are considered believable by about ninety per cent of the American population and that people look to the press to serve the public as a watchdog, protecting the interests of ordinary individuals. The survey indicated that Americans trust the press more than politicians or preachers.

14 Mark Hertsgaard, *On Bended Knee: The Press and the Reagan Presidency*, New York: Farrar, Strauss, and Giroux: 1988.

15 William Greider, *Who Will Tell the People: The Betrayal of American Democracy*, New York: Simon and Schuster: 1992.

16 Patrick E. Tyler, 'Schwartzkopf Says Truce Enabled Iraqis to Escape', *The New York Times*, 27 March 1991, A-9.

17 See the 1991 report of Project Censored, page 2. Each year Project Censored publishes a report listing the top ten 'censored' stories of the year. This project was started in 1976 by Professor Carl Jensen in a seminar on mass media at Sonoma State University in California. Every year graduate students, prominent journalists, professional communicators, and analysts research and report on news that is under-reported or not reported at all in the national press of the United States.

18 Ironically the oil-drenched cormorants were permitted on official footage from the Persian Gulf War when it was Saddam Hussein who caused such devastation of wildlife.

19 *The Wall Street Journal*, 4 February 1992, p. 1.

20 *TV Guide*, 22 February 1992, p. 10–16.

21 *The New York Times*, 27 March 1991, C-1 and C-5. My emphasis.

3 Teaching theology in a new cultural environment

PETER HORSFIELD

It has long been recognized that the culture within which the Gospel is communicated influences how the Gospel takes shape and is understood. Assessing the characteristics of culture therefore is an important component of the theological task. Paul Tillich, for example, suggests that theological thought continually moves in a dialetical tension between two poles – 'the eternal truth of its foundations and the temporal situation in which the eternal truth must be received'[1] (although even this statement of the situation hides the reality that even the 'eternal truth' of our theological foundations is culturally embodied). What has not always been recognized, however, is that 'culture' is not a universal, homogeneous phenomenon. In the past few decades liberation, feminist and Asian theologies have been instrumental in reaffirming the reality that culture is specific to particular groups or regions. This recognition has also raised awareness of the extent to which most Christian debate and teaching in this century have been filtered through a very specific cultural perspective, namely that of the Western male academic theologian. While these particular theologies have been successful in explicating other cultural perspectives not addressed by Western theology, there is one important cultural perspective that is still largely ignored in theological thought and theological education, and that is the cultural context being created by national and international mass media.

The mass media, both nationally and internationally, are rapidly becoming not just an aspect of social cultures, but through their increasing ubiquity across cultures, their functional interrelationship, and their place within the international market and economic system, are becoming the vanguard of a new international culture whose web touches and influences almost every other cultural system. The mass media are forming a new symbolic environment within which societies organize and express themselves. In Australia, for example, the environment in which most of the population lives has changed its character in the space of little more than one generation. Australians move about their daily life today within an environment that is shaped less by the need to harmonize with the demands, opportunities and rhythms of the natural world, and more by the rhythms, images and constructions of a mediated consumer economy and its associated mass communication systems. Australians today, particularly those living in urban or suburban contexts, spend almost the whole of their lives in the context of mass-mediated messages. They encounter a constant barrage of visual messages on books and cereal boxes, bumper stickers, posters, billboards, newspapers and magazines. They are enveloped in a panoply of constant constructed sound through radio talk and music in the kitchen, by the bedside, in the car, and even while riding their bicycles. The recreation of Australians is permeated by a highly stylized mythology of contest through such things as mediated news, sports and drama, videos, fun parlours, and computer games. Australian urban and suburban society has become an environment shaped by the scientific and technological method in which God is not only apparently absent but is functionally no longer necessary. The dramatic changes which have taken place in the activities and patterns of people's social lives over the past two generations are of major theological significance in themselves. Of further significance, however, are the changes in the overarching symbolic environment within which these activities are taking place and the meanings which this environment imposes on life's events.

Despite these major implications, the structure, content, functioning and theological ramifications of the mass media remain largely unaddressed in the work of most, theological thinkers and institutions of theological education. Where they do appear, they tend to be relegated to a minor section of the curriculum, tend to be seen as optional rather than central, and tend to be seen as 'soft' rather than 'serious' theology. There appear to be a number of reasons for this. Many, if not most, theologians and theological educators still see the mass media basically as tools for sharing ideas and content. The different media are seen as individual and separate functions, with little connectedness or commonality. Because their own training and preoccupation has focused on the rational discrimination of ideas, the concept of the mass media as integrated power and meaning-generating systems which are actively creating a mythological and heuristic milieu to serve particular social and economic interests is foreign to most theologians. To a large extent the popular media are ignored in theological education because of the dominant media habits and cultural orientations of theological teachers. Most tend to see print as a superior medium for organizing and communicating ideas. Books and journals, therefore, are stock in trade in theological education and comprise almost the entire collection of most theological libraries. While theological teachers may use electronic media such as television, videos or radio for 'elevated' purposes such as news, documentaries, current affairs, 'good' music, or relaxation, 'popular' programming is generally unpopular. While it may have some value in relaxation and entertainment, as a source of theological truth most theological educators would see the popular media as lacking in depth and a waste of time.

The culture addressed and referred to in most theological education, therefore, has tended to be an élite culture, one which is considered by most theologians as more appropriate for the elevated task of theological thought and reflection. The problem is that while such culture may give elevated and cultured expression to theological truth, 'élite' culture does not adequately express or touch the lived situation of the majority of people. If that remains the dominant cultural form within which ministers are trained, then the foundations laid in theological education will be increasingly inadequate for understanding theologically a large part of the world in which ministry will actually be exercised. Complicating this whole process is the traditional discipline structure of much theological education and the inability of that structure to handle the multiplication of information and expansion of ideas characteristic of modern society. Most curricula are already stretched to breaking point by the attempt to include in some way the increasing number of different issues ministers are expected to deal with. Given theological teachers' own perceptions of media, the addition of a further requirement such as media studies is seen as of low priority compared to what is seen as the more foundational discipline of biblical studies, church history, and systematic theology and the rapid increase in information to be communicated in those areas. Seeing the mass media as shaping a new and distinctive cultural environment rather than simply as tools of communication may require a significant conceptual leap for many theologians. When one makes that leap, however, a number of profound implications for the task of theological education and ministerial formation may be identified.

Marshall McLuhan drew attention many years ago to the idea that the form as well as the content of a communication carries meaning. Jacques Ellul in his many writings is one theorist who takes seriously the idea that there is ideology inherent in technology, with the consequence that the adoption of particular technologies has implications for social and religious meaning and expression. Consistent with this strand of thought is the insight that how the mass media function within a society has a strong shaping effect on how a society understands itself. This occurs in two ways. On the one hand, the media shape social understanding and expression by virtue of their nature and organization. Mass communications in themselves are strongly ideological: their messages are highly centralized, largely impersonal, machine mediated, lacking opportunity for user feedback and participation, and restricted by their technological characteristics. This is compounded by the nature of their economic and social function. This ideology which is present in mass media by virtue of their nature and social organization then shapes how they represent social reality through processes of selection and reinterpretation. Studies of mass media indicate that a distinctive and consistent picture of social reality can be identified across the content of various mass media within a culture. These media 'myths' can be seen most distinctively in television, but are common in different ways across most media. While they are rarely explicitly stated, they emerge in dramatic or narrative form in almost all types of fictional and non-fiction programming: news, sports, drama, situation comedies, advertisements, soap operas, and children's cartoons. Extensive studies of the content of American television, for example, have found that television programming repetitively presents a particular and consistent dramatic view of the world and life: what is good and what is bad, what has reality and what does not have reality, what power is and who holds power, how relationships should be conducted, and how one should behave in particular situations. These 'myths' generally serve the ends of those who exercise power within the media or society, not the needs of the broader strata of society.

The important implication of this is that television in particular and the mass media in general (particularly the commercial media) are presenting a consistent and integrated system of belief and social interpretation as a pattern for social understanding and development. This system of belief and social interpretation generally does not reflect the diversity of social reality which exists within the society, but is consistent more with the economic or ideological system which has given it birth and its corporate managers who hold power within the system and benefit from it. These constantly repeated messages have been shown to be effective agents of social change: not so much by producing direct change in individual behaviour, but by slowly affecting perceptions of social reality and meaning which underlie behaviour. Research shows that the more one watches television, for example, the more one will tend to see and interpret events and situations according to the television picture of life. This change in one's perception of life then alters how one subsequently responds and behaves in particular situations.[2] The content of these pictures of reality arising from media culture needs to be taken more seriously as the stuff of theological work, reflection and education and in the work of proclamation and evangelization. In this regard, it is interesting to note the extent to which the media context is beginning to be taken seriously by other professional and educational organizations. In medical care, for example, it is being found that prescribed treatment given by a doctor is often not acted upon by patients because the doctor's diagnosis conflicts with the patient's self-diagnosis which is frequently influenced by media sources including talk shows and even soap operas. In at least one medical school in Australia, prospective doctors are being taught to take seriously the role media might be playing in shaping their patients' self-diagnosis and how this might affect the patient's receptiveness to medical treatment.[3] A prominent hospital in Australia has also found it necessary to run its own media campaign, addressed to doctors, to counter the over-prescription of drugs by high-powered media promotional campaigns of pharmaceutical companies.[4] Theological education needs to take more seriously than it has that the mass media may be having a marked effect on religious faith, not just by the media's presentation of religious issues, but by the influence the media are exerting on perceptions of social reality within which religious faith is understood and experienced.

The development of a media environment holds implications for the contextualization of Christian thought. In 1965, in his book *The Secular City*, theologian Harvey Cox presented a significant challenge to Western theological thought by highlighting the difference which existed between the natural agricultural environment in which biblical thought had developed and the urban social environment of modern life. Cox pointed to the significant work of hermeneutics which needed to take place in order to translate the Gospel message from the biblical rural environment to an urban one. The emergence in recent years of a new media environment which overarches the urban-technological one takes that hermeneutical challenge a step further. Much of biblical thought, Christian theology, apologetics, preaching and church practice is based on an assumed environment of the world of nature. Biblical writers were continually making inference from the environment of nature to nature's God. Much of traditional and contemporary Christian proclamation, apologetics and worship assumes an innate 'suspicion' within people that for the world to be the way it is there must be a greater power behind it – note, for example, Paul's statement to the Romans: 'There is no excuse at all for not honouring God, for God's invisible qualities are made visible in the things God has made.'

The modern environment of the mass media, however, presents a quite different world. It is not a world we have inherited as a gift: it is a world that we ourselves have manufactured and largely control. It is not a world in which the invisible qualities of God are made visible: it is a world of wall-to-wall technological processes in which God is significantly absent and apparently not necessary. It is a world in which the subconscious 'suspicion' of God's existence and presence, on which so much of Christian apologetics and proclamation have depended, may be disappearing. Bishop Bruce Wilson summarized the situation in the following way:

> Everyday life ceases to appear as something manipulated by vast, mysterious forces beyond human control or understanding and becomes a world that is manipulable, predictable, and intelligible ... When you can get by happily enough without God, even if you do believe in him, why bother with him at all?[5]

A further implication for theological eduction arises from the close link that the international mass media have with Western consumer philosophy. The underlying assumptions of consumerism have significant religious overtones: that satisfying one's needs and wants is the desired goal of life; that each individual has a right to have their needs met regardless of the cost to others; and that most needs can be met by acquiring a product or service. Western commercial media are the vanguard in the promotion of this philosophy.

Against such a background, the Christian message of the ultimate supremacy of God, the importance of personal discipline, the postponement of gratification for sacrifice and service, and the limiting of one's own wants and demands for moral reasons can sound jarring, unrealistic, and fraudulent. One Australian prime minister ten years ago received strong criticism and contributed to loss of an election by saying on television: 'Life wasn't meant to be easy!' No politician since has repeated the mistake!

What needs to be explored is the effect this constant conditioning in consumerism is having on the common understanding of what it means to be human, what it means to be religious, and what it means to have faith. At its simplest level, as Colin Morris notes in *God in a Box: Christian Strategy in a Television Age*, the Church in Western societies now finds itself in a totally competitive communication marketplace, vying with the mass media to capture people's attention, time and energy with an answer to their needs. This competitiveness is not restricted solely to the West. A Sri Lankan pastor told me that the time of a church service in his area had to be changed recently because of a conflict with the broadcast of the American television drama, *Dallas*. At a deeper level, as people are conditioned to a consumer outlook, the Church finds itself under challenge to present the Christian faith in a way that meshes with people's desire for answers, and in a more pernicious way for a faith 'product', that will meet their needs with a minimum of effort and disruption. Virginia Stem Owens has suggested provocatively in her book *The Total Image* that Jesus increasingly is being commended, not through proclamation, but through marketing in a subtle way that favourably blends the Christian message with identifiable consumer life-styles.

The ways in which churches are responding to this situation reflect the full spectrum of options suggested by H. Richard

Niebuhr in *Christ and Culture*. What is lacking, however, is a clear and articulated theological perspective to justify the different positions or by which to critique them. The Church Growth Movement, for example, has responded by adaptation, utilizing the technologies of marketing analysis, business administration and mass communication to help churches grow. A principal strategy of the church growth philosophy has been to identify the major demands people are making and to tailor the message and methods of the Church to meet those demands, right down to the type of minister needed, the types of programmes that should be offered, the type of theology to preach, the best places to build, and the most productive market segment to target with one's 'packaged' message. Another example of this approach is the American evangelical broadcasters. The grandeur of their productions, the images of 'success', their 'positive thinking' messages, and their offering of gifts and goods in return for donations, translates the Christian message into an attractive consumer package that reflects a cultural form similar to that of media consumerism.

A range of questions are raised by this phenomenon. Have such churches grasped the new nature of social reality as it has been created in our subconscious by television and the other mass media? What are the theological implications of a change away from the biblical position where God is seen as supreme to the position where people's religious needs are seen as supreme? What are the implications for ministry in an environment where faith is transmuted away from an emphasis on the service of God to one of selection of aspects of faith and churches according to what one perceives one's needs are? Is there a valid integration of the consumer philosophy with the Christian revelation? In what ways must Christian faith accommodate consumerism, and in what ways must it challenge it? Should Christian faith be communicated in consumer terms in order to address people where they are, but nurture them towards the service of God when they are converted from consumerism?

Awareness that there are particular cultural situations rather than a universal culture within which the Gospel takes form raises, of course, the obvious question: what is the Gospel? This is not a new debate. Within Christianity it is as old as Paul's argument against circumcision. It has been raised again more recently in the face of the cultural challenges to dominant Western theological formulations by liberation, feminist and Asian theologians. A dimension which has been missed in this ongoing debate, however, is the extent to which the medium through which the Gospel is communicated adds a cultural dimension which also needs to be considered in discerning the nature of the Gospel. Dimensions of this issue have already been raised by different thinkers. Marshall McLuhan did initial explorations in this in his proposals on how the medium of communication shapes the message and how the dominant media of a society structure how individuals and the society perceive and conceive of truth and reality.[6] Jesuit thinker Walter Ong has identified different ways in which religion is given form because of differences in the media dominant in the society. Jacques Ellul has written extensively on the nature of truth in relation to different media forms.[7]

A number of major issues for theological education can be seen to arise from this debate. A useful starting point for theological educators is a personal one: in what ways do one's own sub-cultural media preferences shape and proscribe one's perception and teaching of the faith? If one grasps the significance of that question, a number of related ones begin to emerge: What then is the Gospel? By what principles can one evaluate the truth of different expressions of the Gospel in different media without confusing differences of truth with differences of taste and without lapsing into an indiscriminate media form relativism on the one hand or an exclusive media form chauvinism on the other? By what principles does one provide a critique of the various media cultures from a standpoint of the Gospel when one's understanding of the Gospel has itself been mediated through a specific media culture? How does one translate truths of the Gospel gained from print sources in theological education to people whose understanding of truth is dominated by oral or audio-visual communication?

A deliberate theological study of the mass media can also give new insights and perspectives to the ongoing theological debate about the contextualization of theology. A simple example may be helpful. There has been ongoing discussion in Australia, as there has in many countries, into identifying characteristics of Australian culture which may serve as a basis for developing a genuinely 'Australian' theology. Many of the characteristics which have emerged in this discussion, however, have not reflected the actual social realities within Australian society, but have increas-ingly reflected some of the media myths about what Australians are really like. The same may apply in other countries: when one seeks to develop theological forms which arise out of 'people's' culture, what sources are being used to identify people's culture and what is the role of the interpretive power of the media in shaping those sources?

The structure and functioning of the international media raise major issues relating to social justice. Most international media systems and news services are Western owned and controlled. News gathering is to a dominant extent centred in the hands of four First World agencies and two major television news agencies. Control of international communication cables and sat-ellites, development of technology, and access to information is firmly in First World hands.[8] The flow of news, therefore, is grossly imbalanced in favour of the West. Even when news does flow from Third World countries it is generally through the eyes of Western journalists. These patterns of control fre-quently make it easier for countries in the Third World to receive news about what is happening in the West than it is to receive news about what is happening in a neighbouring country. The export of cultural products, such as television programmes, is a major item of world trade. Most US pro-grammes are paid for before leaving the US. The price at which such programmes are made available to other countries is gen-erally adjusted according to a nation's capacity to pay, making them much cheaper than local programming and therefore almost irresistible to local broadcasters. In 1980–81, for example, one major Australian broadcaster spent $61.4 million for Australian programmes which comprised 35.6 per cent of programme time, and only $12.7 million for the remaining 64.4 per cent made up of imported programmes.[9]

Other issues relate to national control of the means of social communication. Ownership of Australian media, for example, after being bounced around like a football for the past five years, has become amongst the most concentrated in the world. Television in Australia has become dominated by three corpo-rations, each of which has access to around 60 per cent of the country's viewing population. Rupert Murdoch, who is no longer an Australian citizen, now controls 70 per cent of the total circulation of Australian newspapers and has reduced competition significantly by purchasing major rival newspapers and closing or amalgamating them.[10] Of further interest is the direct effect international media concentration and control may have on the development and extension of religious thought. What will be the effects, for example, of the large number of amalgamations and the growing commercialization of religious publishing in the USA and Britain? Will serious religious thought be displaced by coffee-table theology?

Over the past few decades, occasional articles or books have appeared analysing ways in which people's use of mass media takes on religious characteristics.[11] These analyses, by utilizing a functional definition of religion,[12] indicate different ways in which the mass media are serving a highly ritualized, integrative, value-forming, and community-cohering function similar to that which has traditionally been served by the established and recognized religious faiths. Partly under the impact of constant conditioning in consumerism, people in Western democratic societies increasingly are putting together their own religious belief and life-style packages in order to meet individual needs. The mass media, through their content and in the way they are used, are playing a significant religious role in this process. This is not to say that the mass media would see themselves in such religious terms, nor that people would acknowledge that they see their use of mass media as parallel to participation in a religious faith. But in practical terms the mass media for many people are playing a major role in meeting their needs for integrative ritual, self-transcendence, social integration and shared belief. If one can recognize the vital role which the mass media are playing in this regard and understand some of its major mythologies, exploration of the process and the media mythologies offers rich resources for theological reflection and the cultural contextualization of faith.

Greater emphasis tends to be given in theological education to the analysis and formation of ideas rather than their communication. This factor, along with the largely unquestioned preference for print and the spoken word, has meant that inadequate attention is generally given to other factors which play a vital role in formation and communication of faith, factors such as the way in which the medium used may influence the substance of the message, the potential which exists in media other than print or voice for communicating the Gospel, and the principles which might guide ministers in the most appropriate selection and integration of the different media. The visual arts, music, drama, dance and audio-visual modes of communication are noticeably absent in theological education. Not only does this absence miss a rich potential, it inculcates in future ministers a pattern of communication which is carried into practical ministry. There is a need in theological education therefore to address also the practical and theological questions of media utilization, questions such as: What is the appropriate relationship between inter-personal, group and mass media in communicating the Gospel? What aspects of faith may be communicated by mass means, and what should be communicated inter-personally? What principles should guide one in selecting the different media? What are the practical guidelines governing which media to use, when to use them and how to use them?

NOTES

1 Paul Tillich, *Systematic Theology*, 3 vols., Chicago: University of Chicago Press: 1951–63, vol. I, p. 3.
2 For further elaboration of this concept, see particularly the extensive work of George Gerbner and his associates at the Annenberg School of Communication in Philadelphia.
3 The Newcastle University School of Medicine.
4 Gib Wettenhall, 'A dose of their own medicine', *Australian Society,* May 1987, pp. 25–6.
5 Bruce Wilson, *Can God Survive in Australia*? Sutherland: Albatross: 1983, pp. 34, 41.
6 See *Understanding Media*, Signet: 1964.
7 See Jacques Ellul, *The Humiliation of the Word*, Eerdmans: 1985; Walter Ong, *Orality and Literacy: The Technologising of the Word,* Methuen: 1982.
8 Bill Bonney and Helen Wilson, *Australia's Commercial Media*, South Melbourne: Macmillan: 1983, pp. 48–50.
9 Ibid, p. 89.
10 Paul Chadwick, *Media Mates: Carving up Australia's Media*, South Melbourne: Macmillan: 1989.
11 See for example, William Kuhns, *The Electronic Gospel*, New York: Herder and Herder: 1969; George Gerbner with Kathleen Connoly, 'Television as New Religion', *New Catholic World*, April/May 1978:

pp. 52–6; Gregor Goethals, *The TV Ritual: Worship at the Video Altar*, Boston: Beacon Press: 1981; Peter Horsfield, 'Larger Than Life: Religious Functions of Television', *Media Information Australia*, 47 (Feb. 1988): pp. 61–6.

12 See for example that proposed by Milton Yinger in *The Scientific Study of Religion*, New York: Macmillan: 1970.

4 The religious relevance of television

WILLIAM F. FORE

The religious relevance of television depends upon what one means by the word 'religion'. One of Paul Tillich's greatest contributions to theology was the insight that religion is being ultimately concerned about that which is and should be our ultimate concern. In the Christian tradition, this is what the Great Commandment means when it admonishes us to love God with *all our heart and mind and soul*. All religions deal with the search for that which is or should be of ultimate concern. Christianity claims that the God manifest in Jesus the Christ is the true subject of our ultimate and unconditioned concern. Making this claim – which we call the Gospel – and living according to it is what the Christian church is all about. Congregations are developed to provide places where this claim can be lived out among the faithful. Diverse programmes, from church schools and summer camps for children, to retreats and discussion groups for adults, are designed to encourage the spiritual dimension of life. Meetings and conferences are created to help believers express their faith through programmes and actions in their local communities and the wider society. Theological schools are founded to teach the claim's coherence, substance and credibility to each new generation of leaders.

All these religious activities have in common an essential function: communication. As Christians, Muslims, Hindus or Buddhists are engaged in worship, education or outreach, at the core they are engaged in communication. Some of their communication is focused inward – to allow the faithful to speak to each other in the tradition and language of their faith. But if the religion is to survive, much of their communication must be focused outward – to interact with the culture in which the religion finds itself, to testify, to engage in public testimony, education and mission. This means, for Christians, that *a primary task of the church is to make it possible for the Gospel to be heard in our time.* To make the Gospel known in our time requires three steps. First, it is essential that church members understand what the Gospel is. Second, it is essential that they understand what 'our time' is, in other words, understand the culture in which they find themselves – its values, world-views, myths, and languages. And third, it is essential that they learn to relate Gospel to culture in ways that allow *each to inform the other.* This third step is not easy, because it requires that church and culture, coming from two different perspectives, learn to communicate with one another. But if religion is about that which is of ultimate concern, then the gap between the sacred and secular realm disappears. God is at work everywhere. Communication about God takes place in both sacred and secular places, in both church and culture. Tillich put it this way: religion, understood as ultimate concern, gives substance to culture; it provides culture with its base of fundamental concerns. On the other hand, culture represents the totality of the forms through which the basic concern of religion expresses itself. In short, religion is the substance of culture, and culture is the form of religion.

In communication terms, this means that every religious act, both of organized religion and of individual faith, is culturally formed. Religion comes clothed in culture's language, uses culture's history and its art forms, relies on those common understandings which are supplied by culture's current mythology, and refers to current cultural experiences. There is no other way it can communicate except through culture and its forms. At the same time, every cultural creation contains within it an expression of ultimate concern, even when – perhaps especially when – words such as God, Christ, Saviour or redemption are completely absent and there is no reference to Christian history or theology at all. One only has to recall paintings such as Picasso's *Guernica* or Ben Shahn's prophetic social cartoons, or films such as *The Pawnbroker, The Graduate, Cat on a Hot Tin Roof, Who's Afraid of Virginia Woolf?, Apocalypse Now,* and *Star Wars,* or television programmes such as the *I, Claudius* series or the Bill Moyers interviews with Joseph Campbell, to recognize expressions of ultimate concern throughout popular so-called secular culture.

In sum, Gospel and culture are, and must be, inextricably intertwined as they communicate values and world-views. One cannot exist without the other. God is in the world, but not of the world. Where do the media fit into this? The answer is that the communication media, and television in particular, are the essential expressions of today's culture. These media were created by the same forces that brought our culture into being. Without them, today's culture simply would not be what it is. There is no understanding our culture without understanding the media which express it. And there is no way effectively to critique the media without bringing to bear a perspective that transcends secular culture, that is, a religious perspective.

Let us look at one religious perspective, the Christian Gospel, and ask how this Gospel relates to our current culture, and to television in particular. To begin with, though, what *is* 'The Gospel'? When I ask theological students what they mean by the Gospel, I get very revealing responses. Most start by giving me a definition: the Gospel is the first four books of the New Testament; or the Gospel means 'good news'. Or they get involved in trying to spell out a whole theology. But this quickly becomes boring – to the class, to me, and even to them. Nothing happens. Finally someone says, 'Well, let me tell you what actually happened to *me* . . . how I became a Christian.' And suddenly the air is electric. They begin telling *stories* – stories about their own encounters with the Gospel. They tell about people, places, and events. They tell about mothers or fathers who cared about them, about friends who did not let them down, about trips they took to summer camps, songs they loved to sing, a teacher who unfolded a whole new world of ideas, a memorable sermon or speech or just a quiet talk they had with someone they greatly admired. And they conclude by saying, 'Because of that, I decided to become (or remain, or return to being) a Christian.' This Gospel is *their* Gospel, the news that became good in their lives because of people, places, and events in which they had been involved. The Gospel has always been recreated anew in each new generation out of the life experiences of individuals who say (or testify): 'This news (or experience or story) has profound meaning for me, and I hope that it can have profound meaning for you.' And although the Gospel transcends culture, ultimately people can communicate it only through their culture – through a particular language but also through music, books, movies, history, and every other

aspect of culture as we know it. The Gospel is communicated through the culture of the people of their own time
and place.

We know very little about the culture of Jesus's time, and
even less about the writers of the gospel records. But we do
know that those writers communicated primarily through stories.
Stephen Crites makes a pointed observation about the way in
which truth is communicated by ordinary people – including
those men and women of the first century who experienced
the Christ event in their own lives: 'Honest men try to tell
the truth, but in order to do so they are obliged, like liars,
to tell stories . . . Stories have been told, and told with imagination, in the serious attempt to speak the truth that concerns
human life most deeply.'[1] While we probably have as much information about Jesus as any other historical figure of his time, our
information is sketchy and, above all, filtered through the minds
and the culture of the early Christian community. Good communication theory agrees with religious historian Jaroslav Pelikan:
' . . . the presentation of Jesus in the New Testament is in fact
itself a *re*presentation: it resembles a set of paintings more closely
than it does a photograph.'[2] Our task is no different from the
Christians of the first century, or any century. We must re-present
the Gospel – the meaning of the good news to us – in stories
that connect with the lives of people living in today's culture.
It is not enough to re-tell earlier stories. Those stories belong
to a completely different culture. To reproduce them 'without
note or comment' implies that to us ultimate meaning – the
meaning of God – is found in the past rather than in the
present.

The revelation of God requires communication in today's
culture. H. Richard Niebuhr, in his classic study *The Meaning
of Revelation*, put this idea in the context of religious revelation:

> . . . no universal knowledge of things as they are in themselves
> is possible, . . . all knowledge is conditioned by the stand-
> point of the knower . . . To speak of revelation now is not
> to retreat to modes of thought established in earlier genera-
> tions but to endeavour to deal faithfully with the problem set
> for Christians in our time by the knowledge of our historical
> relativity.[3]

To find meaning, to find God, we have to look to our culture, now. And to communicate our understanding of the Gospel, we have to communicate within our culture, now. The word 'culture' comes from the Latin 'colere' – to grow, to take care of, to cultivate – and today television has become the great cultivator of our culture, the great mythmaker of our time. What is television saying to us on behalf of this technological world-view? To uncover the medium's real messages, we have to look for the symbolic meanings behind its surface messages and so-called 'content'. The underlying symbolic meanings or myths reveal much more than the simple storylines. They tell us what has *meaning* – for example, the meaning of social roles in the society: who has the power, who is the aggressor, who is the victim. They tell us who can do what, to whom, with what consequences. By telling us 'the way things are', they convince us this is the way it *ought* to be.

Elsewhere I have examined in detail some of television's major myths.[4] Briefly, there are four myths which television tells us about the media themselves:

1. That the media tell us the way life really is, that 'seeing is believing'.
2. That information overload is inevitable, a 'natural' price to pay for living in modern society.
3. That the issues of life are simple, and TV helps us identify who and what is 'good' and 'bad'.
4. That there exists a free flow of information; that anyone with a message can 'get on TV'.

And television supplies many more myths about the society in general:

1. Efficiency is the highest good: if it 'works', it is good.
2. Technology is progress, and progress cannot be stopped, regardless of the human implications.
3. The fittest survive, and the fittest are young, white males.
4. Power and decision-making start at the centre and move out, and those at the centre know best.
5. Happiness consists of limitless material consumption. Thus consumption is inherently good, and property, wealth, and power are more important than people.

Television also communicates to us, on behalf of the culture, a complicated set of values. *Power* heads the list: power over others; power over nature. As Hannah Arendt pointed out, in today's media world it is not so much that power corrupts as that the aura of power, its glamorous trappings, attracts.[5] Close to power are the values of *wealth* and *property*, the idea that *everything can be purchased* and that *consumption* is an intrinsic good. The values of *narcissism*, of *immediate gratification* of wants, and of *creature comforts* follow close behind. Thus television tells us that we are basically good, that happiness is the chief end of life, and that happiness consists in obtaining material goods. The media transform the value of sexuality into sex appeal, the value of self-respect into pride, the value of will-to-live into will-to-power. They exacerbate acquisitiveness into greed; they deal with insecurity by generating more insecurity, and anxiety by generating more anxiety. They change the value of recreation into competition and the value of rest into escape. And perhaps worst of all, the media constrict our experience and substitute media world for real world so that we become less and less able to make the fine value judgments that living in such a complex world requires.

All religious world-views stand in opposition to the world-views of the culture and its prime agent, television. Consider, for example, a few of the concerns among Christians for God's love, justice and peace:

1. Christian scriptures tell stories about *freedom*: God leading the people away from the bondage of imperial powers in Egypt, Babylon, Assyria, Rome and Greece.
2. The covenant stories affirm that God will be with all humanity but only if they worship the true God and not *anything* that is less than God – such as possessions, powers, beauty, or success.
3. Parables about the reign of God make it clear that God is not 'out there', but rather a presence within and among us.
4. The stories about Jesus's life tell of a person both servant and Saviour, who through his death and resurrection became the Lord of history, providing hope and reconciliation for all.

Contrast this religious world-view with the cultural/television world-view; the differences are striking. Instead of television's affirmation of wealth and possessions, Jesus tells the rich young ruler to sell all that he has and to follow his way. He makes it clear that wealth has the same chance of entering the kingdom of God as a rope has of threading a needle (Luke 18:18 – 23). As for television's assurance that money can buy anything, Jesus tells the story of the wealthy farmer who decided to build a bigger barn, but then suddenly died, so Jesus asks, 'What does one gain by winning the whole world at the cost of one's true self?' (Mark 8:36). In contrast to television's affirmation of the ultimate value of creature comforts and self-gratification, Jesus affirms that anyone who wants to be a follower must leave self-centredness behind and follow him, which involves taking up the cross (Matt. 16:24). In contrast to television's urging us to look out for number one, the Christian world-view urges us to love our enemies. In contrast to television's emphasis on power that begins at the centre and moves out, Jesus *begins* with the poor and the powerless. In contrast to television's tendency to fragment and isolate people, the Christian world-view encourages the value of creating and maintaining a community of faith in which everyone can be a part. In contrast to television's world-view that we are basically good, that happiness is the chief end of life and that happiness consists of obtaining material goods, the Christian world-view holds that human beings are susceptible to the sin of pride, that the chief end of life is to live in harmony with all of creation, and that happiness consists in creating the reign of God within one's self and among one's neighbours – which includes the whole earth.

Every religious tradition, such as 'the Gospel', has genuine meaning only when we recognize that it comes out of a particular cultural setting and is transformed as it enters into the particular new culture of those who hear it. For 'the Gospel' to be communicated today, we must learn to express its meaning to us in terms of stories which are told within the present culture and its forms, including television. But this confronts people of faith with enormous difficulties, because the culture's world-view is increasingly tied to the spirit of capitalism with its commitment to pragmatism and technology rather than to human values. What can be done lies in three categories.

1. *People of faith should 'use' television, but only with great care that its fundamental connection with the spirit of capitalism does not distort the religious message beyond recognition.* Religious life is a major part of culture, and as such should be seen and heard on television. Religious perspectives on issues should be part of ordinary news coverage. Specifically religious programmes should be available within the diversity of cultural programming. This is an area of great moral ambiguity.

For transcendent religious values are often so much at odds
with society's values that it is difficult (and sometimes impossible) to deal seriously with real issues on radio and television.
Some sensitization through mass media is possible, of that I
am sure. But the dangers of being taken in by the media are
so subtle and so powerful that it is incumbent upon us to
approach every attempt to programme in television and radio
with the greatest caution and theological sensitivity. I believe
that our objective in using radio and TV should be what I
call *pre-evangelism*. You cannot expect radio and television to
take the place of the Church; they simply cannot create the
person-to-person relationships that are essential in any genuine
community. I doubt that you can even give the answers to
serious religious questions satisfactorily on radio and television,
because the media are inherently one-way, and people need
genuine give and take for communication to be most effective.
But you can deal with the right questions on radio and tele-
vision. You can use the media to help people ask: Who am
I? Why am I here? What is the purpose of life? Am I of
any intrinsic worth; if so, why? And this, in turn, can lead
people to communities of faith and to faith itself. For example,
people of faith can use the mass media as *preparation for the*
Gospel. This requires exploring with people what Paul Tillich
calls the 'boundary situations',[6] those places where modern men
and women reach the limits of their human existence. Why do
they sense a lack of personal meaning, a fear of being useless
and of not having worth? Then we can use the media to
affirm people and events that have been able to deal with these
'boundary situations' creatively and with faith. Think of news
stories from Manila and South Africa; biographies of Gandhi,
Martin Luther King, Mother Teresa, Archbishop Tutu. And
finally, we can then point to the Church as being the place
where people can go to begin to work out their salvation, find
community, discover the power of confession and forgiveness.
Christians using the media can help people to understand what
the Gospel message is, and can encourage them to go where
they can get more answers. And that place is, simply, the
Church. For all religions, television should be a signpost, *a*
servant of the local congregation − and never the other way
around.

2. *People of faith, personally and through their organization, must attack the structures of society which tend to make television, and all mass media, subservient to the demands of the capitalist spirit, and thus to cut off the expression of alternative views.* Citizen access to the media of communication, and especially television, should be understood as a right of citizenship. This will require religious institutions to clash with some of the most powerfully entrenched institutions in society. Television creates images of such power and such appeal that in fact it functions as though it were a religion. But it also functions with such centralized economic and political power that genuine competition of ideas in our society is becoming suppressed. One of the tasks of people of faith is to challenge this power and principality, to work towards ways of opening up the communication process in society for the widest possible exchange of views and ideas.

3. *People of faith should develop massive media education programmes in both church and society.* TV illiteracy leaves people defenceless against the dangers of media manipulation, misinformation and propaganda. If people are going to learn how to come to grips with the most powerful single influence in their lives, children must be taught to 'read' TV, beginning in kindergarten. By the time they reach mid-elementary levels, they should be discussing the hidden meanings behind symbols and signs, learning the 'language' of visuals, and producing their own visual statements. While in high school they should learn the more sophisticated aspects of media analysis: who's in control, how media power is exercised, how advertising and profits affect what is covered in the news and what is said in all programmes, how our violence affects us and how our media imperialism affects other people throughout the world. Values are taught, illustrated, and reinforced by media. Schools must help children to understand and deal with the values they experience in the media. American culture includes Shakespeare and Longfellow, but it also includes such new classics as *Silent Spring* and *Catcher in the Rye*. Our educators know this. But somehow they do not know – or admit – that our culture includes *Star Trek* and *MASH* – and that these are classics as well. Such media programmes carry values, yield insights, and have tremendous resonance among both the thinking and unthinking. And even 'negative' programmes on TV – the mindless game shows and *Miami Vice* and Music TV – should

be included in the curriculum, so that students will develop criteria to enable them to separate the good, the bad and the indifferent. The churches should be the *pioneer* in media education. Historically, churches have often moved into those areas of need where the rest of society was not yet ready to move. For example, in nineteenth-century America the churches founded literally hundreds of colleges and universities in response to the pressing need for higher education. Today, media education is a pressing need. Churches could develop the courses – for children, young people, and adults – to help millions of people begin to find their way out of their frustration and bafflement at being confronted with something they do not understand, and consequently something that controls *them* instead of the other way around.

Finally, there is a specific implication for theological education. I believe *that the ability to create (write or produce) and disseminate (print or distribute) religious ideas in the vernacular is central to religious witness, stewardship, mission, evangelism and education.* I often hear colleagues declaim that faithfulness to the Gospel is more important than mere temporal success – success such as, for example, large student followings, impressive book sales, and huge congregations. This is true. In recent years we have seen some monstrous examples of unfaithfulness to the Gospel masquerading in the guise of 'relevance'. The televangelists are only one of many. But faithfulness is not the same as *irrelevance*. Unless church leaders are taught to communicate effectively in their parishes, they fail their congregations. And unless schools of theology begin to grasp the need to understand culture in order to communicate within it, then they fail both the churches and the Gospel. I am talking about applying the principles of communication to the whole range of 'core' academic disciplines. Who will pick up the fascinating theological analysis of culture begun by Tillich and Habermas? Who will apply the canons of Christian ethics to the powers and principalities of today's mass media? Who will rediscover the value of the story and the image for students of homiletics? Who will compare the mythic world of the Old Testament with the mythic world of today's media? Who will recast the parables of the New Testament in ways that work in film and television? Who will write the religious education materials which prepare parishioners to face life in a mediated world? Television is like any other force; it can be used for liberation or for domination. With people everywhere today living under the domination of imperial powers, the situation for Christians is not fundamentally different from that of first-century Christians. Only the culture has changed. The challenge to all people of faith is to apprehend God's presence in their own lives, and then to relate it to men and women in terms of the culture they understand today.

NOTES

1   Stephen Crites, 'Myth, Story, History', in Tony Stoneburner, ed., *Parable, Myth and Language*, Cambridge: Church Society for College Work: 1968, p. 70.

2   Jaroslav Pelikan, *Jesus Through the Centuries: His Place in the History of Culture*, New Haven: Yale University Press: 1985, p. 9.

3   H. Richard Niebuhr, *The Meaning of Revelation*, New York: The Macmillan Company: 1941, pp. 7, 22.

4   William F. Fore, *Mythmakers: Gospel, Culture and the Media*, New York: Friendship Press: 1990. See especially Chapter Five, 'World-views in Conflict'.

5   Hannah Arendt, 'Home to Roost: A Bicentennial Address', *New York Review*, 26 June 1975, p. 3.

6   Paul Tillich, *The Protestant Era*, Chicago: University of Chicago Press: 1948, Chapter 13.

5 The media and theology: some reflections

DUNCAN B. FORRESTER

The modern mass media raise few, if any, *entirely* new issues for theology. But they make some questions that theology has attempted for a long time to dodge, inescapable. The media highlight and emphasize old problems and possibilities in theology. They challenge comfortable and complacent orthodoxies. In a real sense, then, the media are capable of arousing theology from its 'dogmatic slumbers', and hold forth fascinating possibilities of theological renewal and the recovery of long-neglected emphases and insights. It is a dangerous over-simplification to see the media as nothing but a threat to faith and to theological integrity, the trivialization of all that is sublime, serious or holy. And it is naïve to regard the media as simply a new and immensely powerful channel for the communication of the unchanging gospel. If theologians pay any serious attention to the media today, they tend either to see the media as the new Moloch, the modern idol to which faith, truth and human values are being sacrificed; or, alternatively, they treat the media as a powerful and theologically neutral instrument which can be used to get across the message more compellingly than ever before, an opportunity to communicate Christian truth to millions around the world simultaneously. But only too rarely is it recognized that the media are not simply a tool of theology, but an invitation to new things, an opportunity for the deepening and renewal of theology – a challenge rather than a threat.

The older tradition of academic theology insisted that the primary task, the really important and significant operation, was the establishment of the message. Thereafter, attention might be given to technical issues of how to communicate that message effectively. Here the message is understood as something which is eternal, unchanging. Once it is established it is the same for all cultures and ages. The medium, on the other had, is variable in accordance with contextual factors of time, and place, and culture. The establishment of the message is not only an exercise distinct from its communication, but it is the scientific, the academically respectable operation. The communication of the message is secondary – craftsmanship rather than science. The communicator is a technician, transferring a message determined elsewhere. Accordingly, communication, usually in the guise of homiletics, came to have no more than a tenuous toehold in those sectors of the academic theological world which were concerned with professional formation. It had nothing like the significant place that clinical studies have in medicine. It was a kind of postscript to the serious tasks of exegesis and dogmatics, which wrestled with the exploration and elucidation of the message, which was then handed over to the preacher. This was why many of us were unhappy with the notion that communication was the central concept of the discipline of practical theology. It made the subject a kind of 'applied theology', conveying, communicating and implementing truths independently arrived at elsewhere, but not itself involved in any serious way in wrestling with truth. Such an understanding makes practical theology's claim to being an academic subject very tenuous indeed,[1] and also narrowed extraordinarily the understanding of theology as such by making theology-as-theory's links with practice and with communication very tenuous indeed.

This split between theory and communication, and indeed any kind of practice, encouraged strange distortions in the way theology was understood and practised. The assumption that theology was a scientific, academic study which deals with unchanging and ahistorical truths, reinforced a tendency to see its task as the establishment of the original meaning of a text *simpliciter*. Much less attention was given to the possibility that the meaning of the text for today might be different, or to allowing the text to speak afresh for itself. The concern was almost entirely with the original horizon of meaning, and hardly at all with the often very different modern horizon. Exegetes or dogmaticians who gave substantial attention to the modern meaning of the text – Rudolph Bultmann is a good example – tended to see the heart of the message as timeless truths, which had to be translated from one terminology into another – from Paul to Heidegger, for example. In such a process communication easily becomes accommodation to modernity. The assumption is that the kernel of the message, the timeless and universal meaning, may be detached from the husk, the original medium of communication, and then presented in modern form with only the inessentials, the time-bound frame, set aside. Such an approach leads easily to the assumption that the one truth, the universal message, can be packaged and transmitted in various ways, but at the heart we have an objective, universal, truth. This is something that can be exchanged, possessed, sold, or even 'banked' – to use Paulo Freire's term for inauthentic education: 'The teacher issues communiqués and makes deposits which the students patiently receive, memorize and repeat . . . knowledge is a gift, bestowed by those who consider themselves knowledgeable upon those whom they consider to know nothing.'[2] The 'bankers' are the members of an intellectual élite who possess the truth, who control the message, and who convey it to the masses in measured doses, sometimes sugar-coated or otherwise disguised in order to make it palatable. The élite shares its message, at least in part, with the masses. But it also conceals from the people the truths that are regarded as too hard for them, or as likely to prove dangerous in their hands. The élite in fact retains power for itself through its power over the message. And this gives them immense possibilities of manipulation and of ideological control. Here we have the sophists as attacked by Socrates as cynical abusers of truth, the gnostic heretics who despised the masses, the medieval prelates who believed the Scriptures were too dangerous to be put into the hands of the people, the Grand Inquisitor of Dostoevsky, always fearful of allowing freedom to the people, or indeed to Jesus.[3] Here too the place of narrative and of image is usually played down. Rather than being means whereby things hidden from the wise and understanding are revealed unto babes according to God's gracious will,[4] the story and the image become codes to be cracked and then translated into a new academic jargon which is the domestic language of the élite and excludes others.

These tendencies have been struggled against, with more or less vigour and conviction, in the Church down the ages, from the conflicts with the gnostics in the early centuries to the educational methods of Paulo Freire today. Among modern thinkers who have argued that truth and communication must not be separated, and indeed are interdependent, pride of place may be given to the extraordinarily original nineteenth-century Danish thinker,

Søren Kierkegaard. Kierkegaard found key, and very similar, clues to the proper relationship of truth and communication in the lives of Socrates and Jesus. Socrates attacked the sophists, and Jesus attacked the Pharisees, in both cases objecting to a radically distorted understanding of the relation of truth, the message, and communication, the medium. The sophists, according to Socrates, regarded themselves as free to manipulate the message so as to 'make friends and influence people'. Truth was subordinated to their own objectives and goals. It was something they could manipulate and possess, apportion, sell or use to get their own way. The teacher, the communicator, conveyed information to the recipient. Socrates and Jesus, on the other hand, believed in dialogue, in probing and searching together for the truth. For Socrates, any attempt at manipulation, or foreclosing the discussion, or determining its conclusion in advance, destroys authentic dialogue. Truth cannot be imposed by power; it must be freely sought and freely appropriated. Socrates taught and practised a self-involving, probing and practically orientated kind of dialogue which always involved respect for the participants as people. This is a radically open style of dialogue, in this respect different from the traditional Christian catechetical method, where the answers as well as the questions are laid down authoritatively and thus become a form of thought control. But it is surely good to teach people to ask questions, and to realize that their lives and their practice are implicated in the questions and in the answers. The old catechisms were not simply a form of thought control; they encouraged people to question, and gave them basic resources and a model for serious dialectical enquiry.

Authentic dialogue is impossible if it is assumed that one side *has* both truth and power in its hands, is the giver, the authority, the possessor of the truth, and the other side is simply the passive recipient of the communication, of the truth. The powerful prefer this model, and find true dialogue to be profoundly disturbing, precisely because it encourages people to question established certainties. Socrates was condemned for encouraging the young in particular to probe the 'truths' on which power and authority were believed to rest. He was denounced as a traitor and an infidel although he effectively demonstrated his own patriotism and respect for the gods of the city; but his encouragement of questioning was seen as deeply disturbing to the established order of things. Similarly Jesus was condemned to death as a threat to the political establishment, as one who claimed to be the King of the Jews, and as a blasphemer who questioned the place of the temple and the law in the order of things. Both men encouraged people to probe, to question, to enter into open dialogue. And this in itself was seen as a direct threat to the existing powers.

Power, Kierkegaard suggests, always seeks to control communication and regards open, dialogical communication as a threat. And the market, likewise, seeks to package and sell the truth, commodifying communication. This, in relation to Christian truth, leads to various serious distortions. The electronic evangelists, for example, proclaim themselves to be Evangelicals, that is, people who believe in the priority of grace and justification by faith, but their pervasive message is that one can in some sense earn one's salvation by writing in, by asking for prayers, and above all by contributing 'to keep the gospel ministry on the air'. Here there is a subtle but pervasive reversal of the heart of the message encouraged by the pressures integral to the medium. Or consider the following advice issued some years ago to radio and TV speakers by the Protestant Council of New York:

> Subject matter should project love, joy, courage, faith, hope, trust in God, goodwill. Generally avoid criticism, condemnation, controversy. In a very real sense we are 'selling' religion, the good news of the Gospel. Therefore admonitions and training of Christians on cross-bearing, forsaking all else, sacrifices, and service usually cause the average listener to turn the dial. Consoling the bereaved and calling sinners to repentance, by direct indictment of the listeners, is out of place (with designated exceptions) ... As Apostles, can we not extend an invitation, in effect: 'Come and enjoy our privileges, meet good friends, see what God can do for you!'[5]

The medium here is allowed to determine the message in a one-sided way. Or consider how the modern pedagogical orthodoxy can be used to make the message conform to a whole series of fairly arbitrary assumptions about children and their capacity to appropriate complex, disturbing and challenging truths. Ronald Goldman, for example, long a guru of religious education in Britain, argued that young children should not be told the story of the crucifixion of Jesus because they would find it disturbing:

Young children should not be exposed, for obvious reasons, to the painful, horrific and often morbid details of the Cruci-fixion, although they cannot be protected from knowledge of these events ... The emphasis in schools should be emotional rather than intellectual, and it is the Resurrection with its hope, joy and new life which should be the emotional focus.[6]

By way of contrast, Kierkegaard suggests in a passage which is clearly autobiographical that the message which is inherently disturbing and challenging must find an appropriate medium which communicates its authentic challenge. A child, he writes, is shown by a loving parent or a caring teacher a series of pic-tures – remember this comes long before the age of TV and the movies! Here is a knight on a charger; there is Napoleon, leading his troops to victory. Then comes a picture of a huntsman, dressed in green, his bow in his hand staring ahead as he takes aim. That is William Tell. The stories are told to the child as the pictures are shown: the Swiss patriot-hero is taking aim with consummate skill, determined not to harm his beloved son, concentrating on hitting the apple, devoted to the liberation of his people and the welfare of his child. In among the pictures which delight and instruct the child there is one that is different – the image of a man on a cross. This one will puzzle and disturb the child as much as the others delight him. He will be confused by this one, ugly picture among all the lovely ones, by the picture of a criminal suffering torture among all the pictures of heroes in their moment of triumph. He will ask questions: Why does he hang painfully upon the tree? Why is he being executed like the worst of malefactors? Who is he? What has he done? Why do people do this to him? And as he listens to the story which gradually unfolds in response to his questions he will find within himself a turmoil of conflicting emotions and a stream of constant questions about why this happened and the strange meaning of it all.[7]

This tale of Kierkegaard's, about the central Christian image among other images and the dialogue which ensues, raises the issue of the sense in which Christianity can 'belong' in a powerful medium such as broadcasting, which delights and instructs, and broadens horizons, and challenges – and can easily distort or trivialize. Can religious truth and Christian dialogue survive in a medium which amuses and advertises? Kierkegaard's answer, I am sure, would be that Christianity does indeed belong in that

medium, rubbing shoulders with the other images and stories and
amusements and instruction to be found there, like the picture of
the crucifixion alongside the pictures of Napoleon and William
Tell, and heroes rescuing damsels in distress, to say nothing of
the more trivial and violent modern hero figures such as Rambo
or Superman. Its place is there, but it belongs there in a disjointed
and disturbing way. It does not sit easily alongside much that is
displayed in the box of delights. It is inherently different from a
great many of the other things that are to be found there. It belongs
because it points to profundities of the human condition – and if
it abandons that task it no longer has a right to be there. It belongs
because it claims to be true, to be public truth, open to inspection
and examination and discussion, not simply the arbitrary choice
of a declining group in our culture. It belongs because it is interesting and important. It belongs because it interacts, to confirm
and question and be challenged by much else that is on offer. But
if it itself becomes frothy and amusing, the selling of religion that
disturbs no one, challenges nothing, and overlays truth with an
impenetrable layer of candyfloss, we would be better without it.
If it wallows in the razzmatazz and nostalgia of old-time religion,
without any contemporary cutting edge, we should get rid of it as
quickly as possible. If it gives way to the seductions of power and
wealth, so that it can no longer speak the truth to power, or proclaim good news to the poor, or show that God has chosen the
weak to shame the strong, it should be consigned to the dustbin
as quickly as possible as totally lacking integrity.

   Kierkegaard also insisted that the truth is something that is self-
involving. When he reiterated his slogan, 'subjectivity is truth',
part of his meaning was that truth is not something objective,
'over there', to which one can appropriately relate in a detached
way. The truth grabs one, challenges one, demands a response
if it is to be known; the truth is elicited by love, and the truth
is itself to be loved. The truth is not something to which one
may relate in a dispassionate way; indeed for Kierkegaard as
for Christian orthodoxy, the truth is not a 'something' but personal, a Someone; and that Someone is Jesus Christ, who calls to
discipleship, to searching for and following the truth. The truth
that cannot be possessed possesses the disciple. But Kierkegaard
goes further: there is not, he says, a natural and universal tendency to recognize and follow truth. Human beings are in *error*,

turned away from truth, content to live in lies rather than living in the truth. They need to be brought up short, shocked perhaps, caught unawares, surprised or startled if they are to turn towards the truth and be reconciled to that from which they have been alienated. This all suggests some features which should mark Christian communication, in the mass media or in more traditional forms of communication. Its function is not to repeat the conventional wisdom of the age, adding only a religious sugar-coating; it is essentially against the stream, at odds with the *Zeitgeist*. It should arouse passion, not simply a cold intellectual interest. It is challenging, disturbing, unexpected. It calls for decision and for action. It may be consoling, but it is not amusing. It makes a claim and it calls for a response. We should expect many people to turn away from it, to switch channels to something less demanding, confusing, disturbing. So here's a problem for the viewer statistics! And here also is a reminder of how easily Christian communication becomes diluted and attenuated if the market forces of the modern mass media are allowed to determine content and presentation.

Kierkegaard also taught that communication draws people into community, into communion – and only in communion is the fullest and most authentic communication possible, when people speak the truth in love.[8] Both Socrates and Jesus insisted that they could only have as their disciples those whom they loved; only so is the most profound and honest communication possible. Communication of truth creates and sustains community – and destroys the bogus fellowship that rests upon lies. Yet the community does not *possess* the truth, it cannot use or shape or transform the truth as it wills. It stands under the truth, it is sustained by the truth, it passes on the truth. And this truth is an explosive challenge to closed and rigid forms of social structure – and to narrow, complacent ways of being church. Socrates, who sought truth with a total passion, and Jesus, whose disciples declared him to be the truth embodied, each represented, simply by being who they were, an inescapably seditious challenge to the existing social order. For they reveal in their various ways that these orders, which claim to be based upon truth and ceaselessly promote this claim, in fact are founded upon lies, have inherently unstable foundations and will inevitably collapse. Vaclav Havel pointed to a similar situation in the now mercifully defunct dictatorships of Eastern Europe and reflected also, he argued, in the consumerist societies of the West.

The East holds up a mirror to the West. Both systems depend on ideologies, opposed in form but very similar in content, which have the function of providing people 'with the illusion that the system is in harmony with the human order and with the order of the universe'.[9] These ideologies, sedulously fostered by the media, legitimate power by suggesting that 'the centre of power is identical with the centre of truth'.[10] Ideology thus serves to internalize a false reality, to convince people that the lie is the truth, to encourage them to live happily in the lie.

But Havel affirms, and his own personal experience is here very much to the point, that even in a totalitarian dictatorship, even when the media have become an instrument for presenting lies as truth, it is possible for individuals or groups to live in the truth. This means dissent, for living in the truth is inevitably a direct challenge to the whole vast interlocking structure of lies. Hence Havel's call is to all of us, but particularly to those involved in communication:

> It seems to me that all of us, East and West face one fundamental task from which all else should follow. That task is one of resisting vigilantly, thoughtfully and attentively, but at the same time with total dedication, at every step and everywhere, the irrational momentum of anonymous, impersonal and inhuman power – the power of ideologies, systems, *apparat*, bureaucracy, artificial languages and political slogans. We must resist their complex and wholly alienating pressure, whether it takes the form of consumption, advertising, repression, technology, the cliché – all of which are blood brothers of fanaticism and the wellspring of totalitarian thought.[11]

Even the total political control of the media cannot destroy truth if there are some dissenters, some who are striving to live in the truth, around. Even when lies are propagated as truth and power systematically supports falsehood, sooner or later there is someone who, like the little boy in Hans Christian Anderson's story, tells the simple truth: 'The Emperor has no clothes on!' and such simple truths are inherently seditious.

Kierkegaard also stressed the need for what he called 'indirect communication' of Christian truth. Religious and moral truths cannot be packaged up and transferred or sold without distortion of a fundamental sort. These are matters which affect the deepest levels of a person's being. They must be appropriated, welcomed, responded to, and allowed to shape the personality and behaviour. They cannot be imposed by power or transferred as commodities in a market transaction. They must be subjectively appropriated. But truth is often uncongenial; men and women prefer to turn away from truth, and shut their eyes and block their ears. Accordingly Kierkegaard compares the Christian communicator to the Socratic gadfly, stinging people awake, rousing them from their dreams and their dogmatic slumbers so that they may encounter reality, truth. The gadfly's task is to disturb accepted certainties and challenge the received wisdom, allowing people space to engage for themselves with the truth which must pervade their inwardness before it makes a claim to the public domain. Each person must appropriate the truth individually; the communicator's task, according to Kierkegaard (and here again he follows Socrates), is maieutic – the midwife role, assisting to bring to birth, to bring into the open, the truth that the midwife has not created or shaped, and does not control. This all suggests important lessons for the Christian communicator today. The task is to help people to become open to the truth, and then the communicator must step back and allow a direct relationship to the truth to be established. The gadfly role suggests that the truth is often best expressed through the unexpected, the shocking and the disturbing. Authentic Christian communication perhaps takes place at least as much through drama, news, documentary programmes as through the formal 'God-slot'. The test is the ability of a programme to plumb the depths and reach the heights, to get at people's hearts and wills rather than shimmering over the surface.

Kierkegaard is, of course, presenting an understanding of *Christian* communication which is, I believe, both a call to the recovery of Christian authenticity in communication and also has very important general lessons for effective and non-oppressive communication in general. The ultimate model is God's self-communication, which down the ages has taken place 'in many and various ways', but is summed up fully in the person of the Son, who communicates perfectly the reality of God, and to whom people are able freely to relate.[12] Since the truth ultimately is personal and we are called to relate to truth in a personal way, it follows that narrative and image are particularly apt forms of communication. The modern media can play a liberating role here, restoring the centrality of narrative and image in communication and safeguarding against some kinds of theological reductionism, particularly the assumption that the Word, the message, the truth, can be adequately captured in words. Edwin Muir's warning is salutory:

> The Word made flesh here is made word again,
> A word made word in flourish and arrogant crook.
> See there King Calvin with his iron pen,
> And God three angry letters in a book,
> And there the logical hook
> On which the Mystery is impaled and bent
> Into an ideological instrument.[13]

The modern media challenge the wordy didacticism of most theology, and through a renewed emphasis on story and on image help in the restoration of the Reformation insights that while the truth cannot be captured in words, the words that point to it must be in a language 'understanded of the people', and not in some esoteric academic jargon, the modern equivalent of church Latin.

A great deal has been written on the dangers of the modern mass media. The media are not unreasonably presented as for many people fulfilling the traditional functions of religion in a modern consumerist society as well as giving a twist to the practice of religion in its more traditional and organized forms. As an alternative church which presents a kind of world-view which is experienced as coherent and total and which is normally under the effective control of power and wealth, it is not surprising that Christians often find the media threatening and dangerous, a competitor rather than an ally, an idol rather than a place where the truth may be encountered. But there is another side to the matter which I have tried to suggest in this chapter. If Christian communicators do not lose their nerve or compromise with the false values and untruths so often promoted in our society, they may find that the media can trigger and strongly assist important styles of theological renewal, deepening the understanding of the Gospel and the Church, and presenting opportunities of Christian communication in the modern age which are in fact given by God.

NOTES

1   My own university gave the subject intellectual 'respectability' in the 1930s by linking it to a 'recognized discipline', Christian ethics!
2   Paulo Freire, *Pedogogy of the Oppressed*, Harmondsworth: Penguin: 1972, pp. 45–6.
3   F. Dostoevsky, *The Brothers Karamazov*, London: Heinemann: 1912, p. 253f.
4   Matt. 11:25–6; Luke 4:10–21.
5   Cited in W. H. Whyte, *Organization Man*, Harmondsworth: Penguin: 1960, p. 348.
6   Ronald Goldman, *Readiness for Religion*, London: Routledge and Kegan Paul: 1965, p. 99.
7   Søren Kierkegaard, *Training in Christianity*, trans. W. Lowrie, Princeton: Princeton University Press: 1941, pp. 174–9.
8   Ephesians 4:15.
9   V. Havel, *Living in Truth*, London: 1987, p. 43.
10   Ibid., p. 39.
11   Ibid., p. 153.
12   Hebrews 1:1–4.
13   Edwin Muir, 'The Incarnate One', *Collected Poems, 1921–1958*, London: Faber and Faber: 1960, p. 228.

6 Religious communication in the context of soap values

ERIC SHEGOG

Communication of the eternal verities has always taken place within a cultural framework. As Niebuhr pointed out many years ago in his *Christ and Culture*, the church has the possibility of different responses to culture, ranging from complete identification with it to absolute withdrawal from it. The one thing the Church cannot do, as Lesslie Newbigin has reminded us, is to ignore culture[1] – not least because religion is an integral part of it. This means that if the Church's messages are to be effective, they must take account of the cultural and intellectual ambience of the time. As with the Old Testament prophet, we have 'to sit where they sit'. For most people this means literally in front of the television screen. It is here they receive most of their information about the world around them. Indeed it is here they spend an average of over twenty-four hours a week being informed, entertained and educated. And, although the influence of television on the viewer is a complex matter with many determinants, earlier chapters have clearly shown how television has usurped the role previously played by religion as the communicator of myths which embody values and give meaning to life. This view of television is supported by the broadcasters' claim, usually when they are being attacked for an incident which is deemed offensive, that they are not in the business of social change, they are only reflecting what is happening in society.

Given the role of mass means of communication as a purveyor of values, how does the Church communicate the values inherent in the Gospel tradition? Or to put it another way, how can the principles which are embodied in the Church's teaching be reinforced? I raise this not simply to be semantic, but because research shows that viewers place different values on, for example, the principles contained in the Ten Commandments.

In a recent survey of adolescents by the Independent Television Commission, the principle of honouring your parents and not killing was valued higher than the first two commandments to honour God.

Fundamental to decisions about strategy is a theological understanding of the Church's relationship with the world of which mass means of communication are a part. Some religious groups have followed the Johannine stricture that Christians are to 'keep themselves unspotted from the world'. The logic of that position is to steer clear of the media like the plague. Some religious groups feel that because television has a tendency to trivialize everything it touches, it is not an appropriate medium for communicating Christian values. Other groups see mass means of communication as tools to be used for the Gospel – a variation of 'Why should the devil have all the best tunes?' The temptation here is to be so identified with the mores of, say, television, that the Gospel is compromised. The role of the Church is to be in the world but not of it. That is to say, to maintain a tension between identifying with the world and all its sorrows and yet being sufficiently separate to seek its redemption. In Niebuhr's terms it means adopting the stance of 'Christ transforming Culture'. That means being a part of it. After all it is difficult, if not impossible, to change something at arm's length. If this theological position is accepted, then the next question is how to proceed.

There are five potential courses of action. The first approach is to seek to influence those who hold power where television is concerned. This might be government, regulator, programme-maker or those in control of a television channel. The next step is to ask what ways are open to the Churches to do this. One possibility is to lobby, and this can take different forms. The second way is more direct; it is to take what opportunities come our way to present a different set of values. There are increasing opportunities for the Churches in community radio. The requirement for the BBC and the mainstream commercially funded television channels to commission 25 per cent of their output, excepting news and current affairs, from independent producers also offers possibilities. In addition, Church leaders have public opportunities through their speaking engagements, some of which are widely reported by the press, to underline the principles which undergird life in the country. For example, the Archbishop of

Canterbury used a sermon at a service for the Confederation of British Industry to question the morality of a market driven solely by the profit motive. And, we must not forget the possibilities of cable television as it snakes its way round the country. A third and equally important approach is through media awareness training. This is now an integral part of the curriculum in many secondary schools. The Mothers' Union (with the support of the Jerusalem Trust) has piloted this in the Churches, though there is still much to be done. Once people understand the grammar and syntax of television they are able to watch it more critically.

The fourth approach lies in the field of education in general, and in religious education in particular. It is apposite that, as I write this, the Government's White Paper on the future of education in our schools has been published, with its stress on moral values. But clearly, we cannot shuffle off the responsibilities of the home and the religious community onto teachers. It has to be a shared enterprise. A lot of good work is being done by industrial mission and industrial fellowships as they grapple with ethical questions raised by the interface of the Gospel and industry and commerce. But the primary influence in shaping moral values has to be the home. The fifth approach is to affirm those aspects of television or indeed any medium which reflect Christian principles. After all, as recent research by the Independent Television Commission into the values communicated by ITV's top-rated long-running soap *Coronation Street* shows it is not all infidelity and 'get on at any price.'[2]

How would this all work in practice? I want to take each of the approaches in turn and give some practical examples. I shall do this by using the same moral principle for each approach. One of the important moral principles inherent in the Christian faith is human dignity, based on the belief that human beings are made in the image of God and reinforced by the enfleshment of the divine in the person of Jesus Christ. The human personality is a rich and complex concept. It cannot be seen in isolation but only in terms of relationships. It has to be seen in the context of community. If the human spirit is to flower and realize its potential to achieve what St Paul called the fullness and stature of Christ, it needs freedom and opportunity. It also needs a variety of stimuli if it is to understand its true nature. How far does television reflect this understanding of human worth? If a visitor from another planet had to make an assessment, by analysing television, of how society values the individual, I think the impression would be skewed. Gender determines who presents most of the game shows and the main news bulletins. Generally speaking, television stereotypes the role of women in drama and sitcom, though this is changing. The same could be said of the way elderly people or members of the ethnic communities are represented. And the assumption would be that people are mainly interested in being entertained, rather than being informed. After all, apart from news, most of the money is spent on high-rating shows like the soaps and drama. What is more, power is concentrated in comparatively few hands.

How could this situation be influenced using the approaches mentioned above? First, by trying to influence, change and reform the present status quo. One way to achieve this is through political lobbying. If we take as an example the passage of the 1990 Broadcasting Act that came into force in January 1991, we can see how effective political lobbying can be. The great fear expressed by the mainstream Churches when the Government published its White Paper, *Broadcasting in the 90s: Competition, Choice and Quality*, was that quality would lose out to the competition and choice. If the market was to be the determinant, then the consumer, formerly referred to as the viewer, would decide what appeared on the screen. The result would be wall-to-wall game shows and soaps because they would attract the largest audiences and hence the advertising revenue. Documentary programmes, some religious broadcasting (though not all), adult education material and arts programmes would disappear because by comparison with more popular programming their audiences are small. Under the umbrella of the Campaign for Quality Television, the Churches, programme-makers, and pressure groups like the Voice of the Listener, under the leadership of the indomitable Jocelyn Hay, lobbied the minister responsible for broadcasting, first Timothy Renton, then David Mellor, to ensure that the range of programming currently provided by Independent Television would be maintained. They found a sympathetic ear. Not only would applicants have to pass through a quality threshold before sealed bids were opened, but the Independent Television Commission (which succeeded the Independent Broadcasting Authority) was given the possibility that 'under exceptional circumstances', if it felt that an

applicant was offering a programme service that was qualita-
tively better than a competitor who had offered a higher bid,
then it could award the regional licence to the lower bidder. The
end result was that, in spite of the more competitive climate provided by the development of satellite and cable, the mainstream
commercially funded channels still carry a range of programmes.
Sadly, when these are scheduled is determined by the licensee,
with the exception of news and current affairs which have to
be transmitted in peak time. So it will be possible, for example,
to schedule religious or educational programmes at a late hour.
Even so, this means that the value the Christian puts on human
dignity is enhanced. Man and woman do not live by game shows
alone. Their psyche has to be fed, their spirit raised, and their
being enriched by a variety of sources, otherwise, in the words
of Neil Postman's book, we shall simply be amusing ourselves
to death.

On a narrower front, where human dignity is debased by
individual programme standards, pressure can be brought to
bear on programme producers. There are codes which require
standards of taste and decency to be observed. The Churches
had the opportunity to comment on these in draft form. Contrary to popular opinion, letters to producers (particularly if
they are copied to senior staff) are taken seriously. All complaints by telephone are logged. One must also remember that
members of the Churches have considerable economic influence
if they choose to exert it. Letters expressing concern to companies advertising around programmes, where producers refuse
to take notice of legitimate complaint, can be effective, as they
have been in the USA. Fortunately on mainstream channels this
would be a rare occurrence. Where cable and satellite are concerned, however, it might prove increasingly necessary in the
future, given the inability of the British government, under the
European directive, to ban programmes which are approved for
transmission in the host country and received here by satellite. In
some cases, it might be necessary to develop concerted action on
a national scale against particular series of programmes. Sceptics
of the value of this approach need to take account of the impact
of the Action for Children's Television in the USA. This developed out of the moral concern of a few Boston mothers into
a nationwide movement. As William Fore reports in *Television*

and Religion, it organized protests against TV advertising of high-sugar foods for children. It now co-operates with members of Congress for legislation which improves the programme service for children, and it evaluates what programmes are on offer for children, providing the information for parents. Interest in setting up a similar organization in the UK has already been expressed. When you consider the numerical power of the Churches as a pressure group it is quite significant – five to six million people, at least. When you remember how Church members are scattered through the establishment at all levels and are part of many networks, social, political and economic, you will become aware of the often unrealized potential for influence. And remember, attitudes *do* change. The BBC would not, for example, repeat earlier programmes of *Till Death Us Do Part*, featuring a racist, bigoted character called Alf Garnett, because the language this character used would now be deemed unacceptable.

A second and more direct way of communicating the Christian principle of human dignity is to develop programmes which highlight occasions where this is being lessened, or of situations where it is being enhanced. One way of doing this is by alerting editors of programme series to potential topics. *The Heart of the Matter*, and *Everyman* on BBC1, or *The Human Factor* on ITV, are good examples of series which tease out where moral values may be at risk. But it is not only religious programmes which hunt in this moral territory. Documentary-makers, current affairs and drama also highlight different aspects of the human condition. Where we see good programmes which uphold the principle of human dignity we should write in and support them. We need not rest there. There is the possibility of direct entry by offering programmes. The Foundation for Christian Communication, at Bushey near London, has substantial experience of working with both BBC, Channel 4 and ITV. Two one-hour programmes about Jackie Pullinger's work with drug addicts in the walled city of Hong Kong, made by Christians for Channel 4, was a moving tribute to the value in God's eyes of human beings and their worth. This type of programme illustrates the truth that to communicate effectively on television you often have to approach your subject obliquely. While television is not a good medium, on the whole, for dealing with abstract concepts or convoluted arguments, it is a good medium for telling stories. These can be recounted using drama or documentary or seen via news coverage. When the viewer sees somebody wrestling with their experiences of suffering, or frustration, or abuse, it raises questions of meaning and purpose in their own lives.

Increasingly doors are opening up for Christians to have direct access on community radio and cable. There is the slight problem of funding, of course. But these are opportunities to break the monopoly of the experts. If the Churches really do take the principle of human dignity seriously, they can offer the marginalized in society their right to communicate. This is already happening. Wear FM, the Wearside community radio station in the northeast, is chaired by the local rural dean, Granville Gibson. The Anglican deanery has a major share in the station, together with the local authority and local university. Two fundamental principles on which the station operates are to give airtime to community groups, and to provide training possibilities for the unemployed youth of the area. In this way they restore self-confidence and self-worth and at the same time reinforce the value of building community. When this principle of direct access is extended to include the potential of news gathering from Christian news agencies and networks worldwide, there is a possibility of introducing a different set of news values. How often do we hear a Christian comment on a news story? Very often coverage of a foreign news story is constrained by the time available. Foreign correspondents are becoming a rarer breed than they used to be. The Churches have a presence in virtually every area of the world with a potential news-gathering facility as yet undeveloped. In many continents there are Church-sponsored news agencies. With the availability of new technology there is no reason why a co-ordinated news-gathering network focused on the World Council of Churches in Geneva could not become a reality. This could be used to highlight cases where the value of human life is held cheap.

Another major approach open to the Churches is through media awareness training. The study of literary texts through content analysis has, in recent years been extended to television and the cinema. The study of semiotics, a good New Testament word for sign (translated as miracle in John's gospel), is the analysis of images as vehicles for meaning. If we return to the ITC's research on viewers' appreciation of *Coronation Street*, it shows that although the perceived goodness or quality of the characters and their actions were not directly connected with appreciation, the fact that 'there is little in the series that acts as a bad example for any one to copy in real life' was appreciated. This isolated example shows there is a rich vein of material to be mined for use in church discussion groups. Soaps are the morality plays of today. But once people understand the way television and the print media operate, they are not only more aware of their potential influence, their knowledge enables them to plan ways of counterbalancing them.

The third approach open to us for promoting Christian values is through moral education. One in five children of primary school age is in a Church of England school. Add to that the numbers in Roman Catholic schools and you have a significant share of the primary-school-age population. The reinforcement of religious education in the Education Reform Act 1988 (and in the Government White Paper published in July 1992) under-lines the opportunities for all schools. Already the Secretary of State for Education has invited the National Curriculum Council to look at ways of enhancing spiritual and moral education. If Christians are to influence the future moral climate in society, more effort has to be invested not only in schools, but also in our homes and our churches first, to sensitize our young to the moral dilemmas which will confront them. They need the skills to understand moral situations and the encouragement to stand up against the crowd for what they believe to be right. All of this will be counterfeit, however, unless schools, homes and reli-gious communities practise what they preach. In the final analysis human worth has to be expressed in the way we treat each other. You cannot expect a child to respect others if his or her role model does not do the same. 'Do what I say, not what I do,' really will not wash. I recall one of my children coming home from primary school in a highly disturbed state and recounting how a teacher had belittled another child using sarcasm and violence. 'Adults should not do that, should they?' he said angrily.

The final approach is to encourage Christian values by recog-nizing those programmes where they are present. One way of doing this is by writing in, telling programme-makers how much we have enjoyed the programme. Another way is by establishing programme awards. In recent years the Sandford St Martin Trust has given awards for the best religious programmes on radio and television, with particular prizes for local programmes. I know from personal experience how much these awards are valued and appreciated, and the encouragement they give to religious programme makers, (particularly as there is no category for religious programmes in any other national awards). The same is true for the international television awards sponsored by the World Association for Christian Communication and UNDA (the International Catholic Broadcasters' Association), representing the Roman Catholic Church. There is scope, however, for an award for programmes which reflect the Christian concern for human dignity. This award could be open to all programmes and would parallel the awards given by the Order for Christian Unity for journalists who have striven to communicate the truth about a situation, often against great odds.

In the last few years the debate surrounding television has moved through the stage of questioning who provides the programmes and into the whole issue of how they can be financed. The next stage in the process, if we follow the trend in the USA, will be to focus on the content and rationale of programmes. The imperative for the Churches, and for their individual members, is to create environments where moral values are upheld, where the worth of the individual is recognized and enhanced and also expressed in official statements on government policy and on international trends. Otherwise, we shall rightly be accused of cant and hypocrisy. As Churches, we also need to remember that Christianity is not simply 'morality tinged with emotion'. The values and principles we uphold spring out of the tap-root of faith in a God who is at the heart of a universe He created in love.

The dominance of the Enlightenment on the intellectual climate is waning, slowly but surely. The promise of Communism has disappeared with the Berlin wall and the old hierarchies of Eastern Europe. The hopes of material prosperity which were placed in the dominance of a market-led capitalism are increasingly questioned. The time is ripe for the Churches to make a bid to fill the intellectual and moral vacuum that is developing. No one will underestimate the scope of the task. The process by which a climate of thinking in society can be changed is highly complex. There are problems of resources; and how do you raise people's awareness of the need to communicate Christian values? And how do you steer clear of simply becoming the British equivalent of the political force in the USA known as 'the Moral Majority'? The major task, in my opinion, is convincing the Churches that they are like a sleeping giant who can achieve much, once they are stirred.

NOTES

1   See, for example, his *The Gospel in a Pluralist Society*, Grand Rapids: Eerdmans: 1989.
2   J. M. Wober, *Coronation Street – An Anatomy of its Appreciation*, London: Independent Television Commission: 1992.

7 Religion, education and the communication of values

JIM McDONNELL

In 1990, Peter Dawson, of the Professional Association of Teachers, wrote in a newspaper article, 'There is abundant evidence of the destructive influence of television on young people. It makes them illiterate, disruptive and morally bankrupt.'[1] Mr Dawson's view is not uncommon among professional educators in Britain or abroad. His hostility and suspicion of the media is shared widely among people (parents, teachers, clergy, politicians and administrators) who are concerned about education. The strength and pervasiveness of these feelings need to be taken into account in any discussion of the relationship between religion, education and the mass media. As Mr Dawson's remarks make plain, educators have no difficulty in seeing that the mass media are important communicators of values. The presupposition seems to be, however, that the values promoted by the media are overwhelmingly negative. It seems useful, therefore, to begin this discussion by examining some of the reasons why the mass media are blamed for the corruption of values, for making people 'morally bankrupt'.

Part of the reason might arise from almost a sense of betrayal. Though the popular press, the cinema and popular music have always been attacked as agents of cultural decline and moral decay, in Britain, at least, public broadcasting was for a long time seen as a supporter of cultural and, to some extent, moral cohesion. As public broadcasting and broadcasters have moved away from that self-understanding, and as television has both become more commercial and usurped radio as the dominant cultural influence, so it has become harder for educators to think of the mass media as other than rivals to the formal educational system. When radio broadcasting began in Britain under the guidance of John Reith, there was no doubt that public broadcasting was seen as a powerful educational tool which could improve and elevate public taste. That view rested implicitly upon a belief in the permanent truth of certain unspoken values, largely associated with what has come to be called 'high culture', which were considered to be fundamental to the educational mission of the BBC. As late as 1965, Oliver Whitely, Chief Assistant to the Director-General of the BBC, could assert: 'I am a missionary . . . for culture and for the BBC as its discriminating but determined carrier.'[2] But even as Whitely wrote, broadcasting, like society at large, was losing faith in this cultural mission. Broadcasting now held up a mirror, even if a distorting one, to the troubled countenance of a society in which cultural and social mores were changing rapidly. The audience, perhaps for the first time, began to be thought of as plural not only in tastes but also in values. By the time the Annan Committee reported on broadcasting in 1977, the central dilemma of broadcasting in a pluralistic society was clear. The Annan Committee argued that it did not 'doubt that men of good will across the spectrum of opinion would agree on the values which should inspire programmes. But dissension would appear immediately those values began to be interpreted and expressed in a programme.'[3]

Even this statement of the problem was probably too sanguine. It is no longer safe to believe that people 'of good will across the spectrum' can agree on the values which should inspire programmes. Today dissension arises precisely because the cultural values which shape television's output have become both more contentious and less clear and explicit. As the media in general, and broadcasting in particular, have reflected the shifting patterns of public morality and public culture, so has public anxiety grown about the extent to which mass media are active agents of social change. Despite all the academic research which has concluded that it is extremely difficult to prove a direct causal link between the messages disseminated by the mass media and changes in people's behaviour, most people continue to feel that the media do affect the way people act and think. In educational terms the idea has emerged that there is a 'hidden curriculum' in television programmes. This 'hidden curriculum' (which is hard to define, but which is certainly undermining traditional values and beliefs) is felt to be a creation of the broadcasters and outside the control of those formally charged (educators, religious leaders especially) with influencing society's thinking, believing and behaviour.

This notion of television and the mass media in general as rival educators has received some notable academic support. Among the most influential commentators on this phenomenon, particularly in the United States, is the doyen of American communication researchers, George Gerbner. Gerbner claims that the mass media, and television above all, have become the primary socializing agents in modern society. He argues forcefully that 'we have moved away from the historic experience of humankind. Children used to grow up in a home where parents told most of the stories. Today television tells most of the stories to most of the people most of the time.'[4] George Gerbner's contention that television has become society's 'storyteller' allows us to look at the question of the media's effects from a slightly different, and more helpful, perspective. The media do not tell us what to think or how to behave, but they do tell us what to think about. The media shape perceptions. The stories told through the media constitute a variety of frames, or to change the metaphor, a multitude of mirrors which reflect back to us a variety of, more or less distorted, images of our world. The mass media present people with certain ways of seeing and making sense of social reality. In a pluralistic society especially, the media tell many stories from many different, and often contradictory, perspectives. This then raises the question of who is telling the stories (and by what authority) and the related issues of what stories are being told, what values they contain and how they are being received. In relation to religion and education it is illuminating to consider these issues from two different angles. First in relation to the explicit treatment of religious themes in the broadcast media and secondly, as regards the ways in which religious ideas and values are implicitly present throughout the mass media. This examination should help identify some of the core questions which religious educators need to address if they are to function successfully in a media rich society.

The place of religion programmes in the broadcasting system is a good indicator of the place of religion and religious values in society at large. Just as religious groups have always seen the need to have a stake in the formal educational system, so they have also sought to exert influence on broadcasting. The extent of that influence is still evident today in the amount of time which British radio and television, especially public broadcasting, devotes to religious matters. Worship programmes on radio and television are still broadcast on a regular basis. Reflections and short meditations on religious matters are broadcast on a wide variety of stations every day. The very fact of the existence of these programmes indicates that the broadcasting system has not yet become completely secularized. However, the treatment of religious values and ideas in broadcasting has undergone a number of substantial changes over the past two or three decades. There has been a shift away from the direct promotion of religious beliefs towards a more or less detached exploration of religious beliefs, behaviour and values. Religion does not fit easily into the dominant world-view of most contemporary broadcasters who are often ill prepared to deal with religion, being indifferent, or occasionally, actively hostile. For most broadcasters religion is a subject like any other and it is their business to put religious beliefs and behaviour under critical scrutiny.

The stories told about religion tend to be about its institutions, politics and personalities. More often than not, religious stories are stories of social conflict. There are many examples: abortion, the Rushdie affair, Lebanon, inter-communal conflict in India, disputes between Catholics and Orthodox in the Ukraine, liberation theology, women priests, church and politics in South Africa. Many other religious stories are hardly covered: the ecumenical movement, inter-religious dialogue and co-operation, work for peace and reconciliation, the search for spiritual values among the young, the humanitarian efforts of the churches, the religious contribution to art and culture. These stories are, however, less easily resolvable into sharply defined categories or black and white positions. They are, therefore, harder to present in media terms. In addition, broadcasters face a real difficulty in accommodating those religious views which challenge or confront dominant pluralist or secular assumptions. The religious claim to truth, especially to an exclusive truth, is difficult to assimilate in a media system that has elevated professional tolerance and impartiality above nearly every other virtue. The controversy over the *Satanic Verses* and its coverage by the media is a case in point. The degree to which

Muslims feel outraged and upset by Rushdie's book is almost impossible to understand within the prevailing frame of reference.

These attitudes, as well as the more precarious place of religion in an increasingly commercialized broadcasting system, have helped to contribute to an ever widening gulf between the expectations of many believers and the practice of the broadcasters. Many religious critics see the professional commitment of broadcasters to what Sir Hugh Greene called 'healthy scepticism' as a corrosive social force. It seems as if broadcasting is undermining the possibility of any religious values and beliefs being regarded as true and so subtly reducing religious faith to a matter of private taste and emotional inclination. The perceptual frame through which religion is viewed is one which implicitly consigns religious belief to the private sphere and which places religious institutions and groups in the categories of special interests.

Alongside the formal treatment of religion there is another, and equally important, way in which religion and religious beliefs and values are being presented through the media lens. The media are full of what we might term 'implicit religion'. Religion is, of course, a word notoriously difficult to define. For the purpose of this discussion the definition offered by Andrew Greeley will be used. He defines religion as 'the set of answers a person has available to the fundamental questions of the meaning of life and love, answers which are normally encoded in pictures, images and stories (symbols) and purport uniquely to give purpose and meaning to human existence'.[5] The mass media are full of religion, in Greeley's sense. Media 'pictures, images and stories', however, are not always easily recognized as vehicles of religious meaning. Religious broadcasts address a religious public and communicate through a language that presupposes an acquaintance with traditional religious teaching. For the bulk of the audience this language is almost incomprehensible. Most of the audience now professes a mixture of secular attitudes and a certain yearning for an experience of the transcendent which might be described as a diffused religiosity. The mass media are full of folk religion: the half-remembered residue of the traditional languages and symbols. Popular religion is hazy, unspecific, concerned with feelings rather than doctrines.

In his recent book, *Wrestling with an Angel*, Colin Morris puts the point thus:

> The human spirit-life does not wither because official religion is enfeebled. It still feeds on the raw material of religious experience wherever it may be found. And television is one such source which offers a store of stories, images, models and symbols to keep in trim what could be called the human religious muscles – awaiting a higher manifestation of the Spirit on which they might be exercised ... Thus, if the religious muscles of secular man and woman are not exercised by traditional religion, they will be brought to bear on this other world of humanly created meaning, television, for we cannot survive without drama, pageant, play and fantasy.[6]

Ethical and moral issues are the stuff of television and radio drama. One might say that the television and radio serials and soap operas are the morality plays of modern life. Their stories are primarily explorations of personal relationships and their plots are an endless examination of the complexities of family life. At first glance, there seems little evidence of religious values in these programmes. Organized religion is often an object of ridicule or patronizing condescension. The stereotype of the ineffectual vicar is well established in television comedies and drama. When characters are presented who have high moral and ethical standards, these standards are rarely related to specific religious beliefs. More common is the character who acts in a prejudiced or intolerant manner because of a particular religious orientation. There is no doubt that the world of television drama finds it natural to present adherence to specific religious doctrines as a problem rather than as a personal and social benefit. In addition, producers generally take it for granted that the basic social reality within which serials and soap operas operate is one in which an adherence to a particular church or religion is a minority practice with little relevance to the mass of ordinary people. Yet the religious dimension keeps creeping back. Religious values are present but in a diffused or residual form. The staple of soap operas and serials is the battle between light and darkness, good and evil, heroes and villains. The explicit connection between morality and religion has been largely severed but the focus on moral dilemmas, on issues of honesty, integrity, truthfulness, compassion and love, provides a significant point of contact with religious feelings and values.

For many people television drama is where they play out the tensions and problems of real life. The fantasy world of television allows them to explore ideas and meanings that they would otherwise find difficult to articulate. That is why a part of its power to please is its ambiguity; the capacity simultaneously to undermine the very virtues and values it claims to uphold. The most celebrated characters in television soaps are the villains. In the safety of the television experience the audience can taste wickedness, and play with immorality, secure in the knowledge that the world will eventually be returned to rights. Though television genres may not touch the heart of religious experience, their moral dimension provides at least a starting point for further exploration of religious experience. Television is a domestic medium and it tends to domesticate the religious impulse. It is in other media that we find less inhibited expressions of the religious sense. (Though of course television feeds off other media and many novels and films eventually make their way onto the small screen). Many media productions express and explore the development of a kind of mythic consciousness. The immense popularity of fantasy and science-fantasy literature and films is just one example of how people are drawn to these mythic forms of expression.

For many people today, fantasy stories are the place where religious truths are revealed; perhaps because the everyday world has become so bureaucratic and technological that it is hard to discern signs of spiritual reality. Fantasy releases the imaginations of those who find that everyday living has become dull and routine. In the famous opening words of the *Star Trek* television series, fantasy can 'boldly go' into 'space' (inner and outer) which is 'the final frontier'. The realm of fantasy provides a refuge from, and a commentary on, the routines of daily life. Film-makers like George Lucas and Stephen Spielberg and best-selling authors like David Eddings and Gavriel Ritchie Kay are avid builders of imaginary parallel or alternate worlds. Many of them are following in the footsteps of J. R. R. Tolkien's *Lord of the Rings* by constructing detailed fantasy worlds with their own laws and social structures – and their own theologies. Elements from Arthurian legend, Norse legends, the Bible and myths from Eastern cultures are brought together to create new interpretations of human purpose and meaning. The stories and myths which fill the minds and which excite the imaginations of numerous young people are worlds peopled by gods and demons, sorcerers and witches, alien beings, heroes and heroines, hobbits and orcs, and hosts of other fantastic creatures. Under the rubric of science fiction, authors invent fantastic worlds and re-invent dragons and salamanders. Film-makers like Stephen Spielberg or George Lucas in the *Star Wars* series have created new myths – drawing upon Eastern and Western traditions. Popular films, music, and books – all speak of a search for transcendent meanings in a fragmented, mysterious and chaotic world. Mythic structures, whether of the New Age or of the commercial Hollywood story, are frameworks for interpreting messy, confusing reality.

This need to create a framework of interpretation is at the heart of the problem posed for those who wish to promote religious education in the media-saturated world of today. The media offer so many frameworks of interpretation that it is difficult to find a common language within which we can communicate with each other. At the most basic level, the volume of media messages makes it ever more difficult for people to find a coherence in the information that is presented to them. The constant flow of messages, good, bad and indifferent, entertaining, educating and informing, to which everyone is exposed, makes it difficult for us to pick out the significant and discard the irrelevant. Newspapers, radio, television, and advertising present us with a collage of images and words which do not rely on logical relationships. Media experiences are disconnected and fragmentary, linked by association. Corporate experience fragments as sub-cultures proliferate. The host of special interest magazines and newspapers on sale in any large newsagent's underlines the point. As sub-cultures increase in number and as more and more special interest groups create their own media outlets it becomes increasingly difficult for people to cross cultural boundaries. Jonathan Sacks makes the point that frameworks of interpretation require communities of meaning and as different communities of meaning move further apart the potential for shared understanding diminishes. Sacks comments (using a media metaphor): 'We no longer talk of virtues but of values, and values are tapes we play on the Walkman of the mind: any tune we choose so long as it does not disturb others.'[7]

In a pluralistic society, communities of meaning have to find some way of overcoming this fragmentation if we are not to become 'inarticulate in the face of cultural collision'. Sacks argues that we have to learn to become bilingual: 'There is a first and public language of citizenship which we have to learn if we are to live together. And there is a variety of second languages which connect us to our local framework of relationships: to family, and group and the traditions that underlie them.' Sacks goes on to argue that 'Pluralism should not simply be neutral between values. Rather it must recognize the very specific value of Christians, Muslims, Buddhists, Sikhs, Hindus and Jews growing up in their respective heritages. Traditions are part of our moral ecology, and they should be conserved, not dissolved, by education.'[8] This last point brings us back to the problem of the media and their educational impact. For the mass media, as we have seen, are solvents of religious traditions. As Neil Postman puts it, television tends to assimilate every aspect of public communication to its own form – and that form is essentially the form of show business. Television depends upon visual images so stories tend to be dramatized around pictures and personalities. Postman believes that the 'Age of Typography' is declining and the 'Age of Television' is in the ascendant. 'As the influence of print wanes', Postman observes, 'the content of politics, religion, education, and anything else that comprises public business must change and be recast in terms that are most suitable for television.'[9]

The second problem which the media raise is that of religious individualism. The religious communities and traditions identified by Sacks have their place in the mass media but the implicit religious values found in the media are strongly individualistic. A major element in fantasy stories is the quest for meaning and authenticity; but this quest is essentially a solitary, individual quest. The popular media myths are built around individuals – not around communities. The quest is for personal identity; the search for the true self in a world of appearances. The value of religious traditions is not easily understood within this context. Indeed, as Sacks himself recognizes, religious traditions are often seen as an 'assault on personal autonomy'.

If religious education is going to be able to cope with the challenge posed by Sacks it will have to learn to be multilingual rather than bilingual. Religious educators are comfortable with the languages of values and faith, they are less comfortable with the languages of the media. Yet the media form the environment within which people construct their view of social and cultural reality. Too often people tend to assume that this media environment is a kind of transparent window on the world. Religious educators need to help people learn that the media are a constructed reality, shaped by personal, ideological, institutional and economic pressures. Religious educators have to help people discriminate among the messages, impressions and values that the media display. People learn through the media because the media tell them stories. If they are going to be able to consciously and freely construct their own personal framework of interpretation for these stories and to share these with people from other traditions and viewpoints, they will need to be anchored in a community of meaning that is comfortable with stories. As Postman noted, the 'Age of Typography' is on the wane and the 'Age of Television' has arrived. Education, including religious education, has on the whole been comfortable with the language of print and the logical, sequential mode of thinking that print favours. Now that television has become the storyteller of the age, religious education has to find ways to understand and appreciate the non-linear associative mode of making sense of the world. In rediscovering the visual, poetic and storytelling imagination, religious educators may begin to find ways to form a religious sensibility appropriate to all of us who have to live in a media culture. The task of religious educators is to become explorers and revealers of the religious imagination, tellers of tales, and celebrators of the religious dimension to life. The world of the mass media is not an alien world, it is the world of the popular imagination. And if religious education enters that world with boldness it will find that it need not be a hostile world after all.

NOTES

1   *Daily Express*, 26 January 1990.
2   Oliver Whitley, *Broadcasting and the National Culture*, London: BBC Pamphlet: 1965.
3   *Report of the Committee on the Future of Broadcasting*, Cmnd 6733, London: HMSO: 1977.

4   George Gerbner, 'The Challenge of Television', Unpublished paper, 1982, p.8. Quoted in Michael Warren, *Faith, Culture and the Worshipping Community*, New York: Paulist Press: 1989, p. 181.
5   Quoted in Brenden Comiskey, 'Launching Pies or Satellites?' in *Opportunities and Limitations in Religious Broadcasting*, edited by Peter Elvy, Edinburgh: Centre for Theology and Public Issues: 1991, p. 55.
6   Colin Morris, *Wrestling with an Angel*, London: Collins: 1990, p. 175.
7   Jonathan Sacks, *The Persistence of Faith*, London: Weidenfeld and Nicolson: 1991, p. 41.
8   Ibid., pp. 65-7.
9   Neil Postman, *Amusing Ourselves To Death*, London: Methuen: 1986, p. 8.

8 Popular religion on TV

NEIL SIMPSON

In the world of television, soap operas, known also in their various guises as 'daytime drama' and 'continuous serials', are almost as ubiquitous as the mystical presence of God in the real world – or so it seems. From Texas, through Brazil, across Liverpool, to New Delhi, viewers (mostly female, working class and aged over fifty) are entranced (for as much as three and a half hours every day) by the public exposure of private trivia (primarily in the realm of mystery and intrigue, though not exclusively so). The question to be asked is, of course, 'Why?'. What is it about these soaps that so galvanizes an audience and what eternal verities, if any, are they selling? One possible answer is that they strike at the very heart of life's meaning, go for the jugular of our most metaphysical needs. Ever since men and women hit on the idea that it was beneficial to live in some sort of communal relationship, they have been haunted by two questions: 'What is the Meaning of Life?', and 'What are they up to next door?' Soaps appear to offer a vicarious solution to the latter now that 'community' is a thing of the past; do they also, in some highly mysterious way, contribute to an understanding of the former? Do they, in fact, offer their own form of popular religion?

Today, an estimated 50 million people in the US watch at least one soap three times a week.[1] In the UK, soaps consistently take first place on three of the four channels (the fourth, BBC2, does not screen any). In Brazil, telenovelas are shown back-to-back for three and a half hours nightly, and more than eighty countries buy them.[2] In India, when *Mahabharata* was screened from 1989 to 1990, the country came to a virtual standstill each Sunday morning for ninety-three weeks. Everybody, whether they watch or not, has an opinion on soaps. They are a fact of life. People watch soaps, and go on watching soaps, because they offer a storyline which never ends. Here, ideas are not important: feelings are; locations are only the extensions of characters; words, interestingly enough in such a visually dominated environment, are what counts. 'Above all ... [they] must be seamless, endless ... have no beginning and no end, like the universe perhaps.'[3] Within this world, the one ingredient above all others that sells soap, as it does the tabloid newspapers, is 'human interest'. As the audience share 'secrets' with the characters, so subjects for real-life conversations are generated. Neighbourly gossip, once conducted exclusively in an inter-personal manner (i.e. over the fence), can now be mediated before being discussed back in the real world. The very title 'Neighbours', not to mention the sentiments expressed in its theme song (Neighbours, everybody needs good neighbours ... *ad infinitum*), reveal the origin of this genus – and its *modus operandi*.

If close-knit communities are, as many would contend in the Western world, a thing of the past, the need to maintain social integration is not. If religious belief is simply an erratic in the landscape of post-Christian existence (and that is an arguable assertion), values – formerly the exclusive province of that region – are still required. Who better to provide them than our media-constructed alternative to genuine community, the soap opera? Religious dogma may never darken their story-lines, but the great themes of Birth, Marriage and Death frequently do, and, moreover, they provide the staple diet. In dealing with life as it is lived, they not infrequently point beyond the material world to less tangible realms beyond. Their significance on a religious level is not confined to how well (or badly) representatives of the faith are portrayed: rather, their true value lies in the contribution they make to 'keeping alive the rumour of God', how effectively they deal with the drama of life. In this respect, they bear an uncanny resemblance to a folk tradition little known outside Europe, and one to which we now turn.

Consider the following description:

> A group of men enter to stand silently in a semi-circle to the rear of where they are to perform. They are disguised either by a poor attempt at dressing in character or by strips of paper or ribbon sewn to their everyday clothes ... They remain silent and immobile until, when it is their turn to speak, they step forward, declaim their lines in a loud voice devoid of any inflexion, and stand back at the conclusion of their speech.[4]

No, this is not an account of a dress rehearsal for *Neighbours*: rather, it depicts a scene, common enough in bygone rural England, in which villagers re-enacted a drama based loosely on Johnson's 'Famous Historie of the Seven Champions of Christendom' each Christmas. The plots of these plays were highly stylized, featuring (usually) a Valiant Soldier of the Christian army, otherwise known as St George, a Turkish Knight – his deadly Saracen enemy, a Doctor – whose task it was to bring (almost) everyone back to life, and Father Christmas, together with a miscellany of lesser characters. In Swiss tradition, the leading lights might be somewhat different: a Wild Man carrying a whole fir tree as a club, a Fool, a Barber and a Bride. In Romania the plot was expanded to allow for sick children to be laid on the ground so that dancers could dance over them and bring them back to health and vitality. In every case, the underlying theme was that of bringing fertility to all, predominantly through the symbolic dying of a champion on behalf of his community. Precisely how this was achieved varied from place to place, but the *fact* of the vicarious sacrifice was common to all. Literature, the mumming plays were not. Neither were they attempts at sophisticated dramatic art. Rather, their performances were aimed at recreating an atmosphere of magic and mystery which the audience was encouraged to experience first hand, and in this sense the soaps are heir to a number of dramatic traditions. Elements of moral dialectics harking back to Greek tragedy, bardic tribal ballads, and morality plays all have their resonances in soap. What the modern form has done so effectively is to add to tradition a narrative tailored to the needs of the media: the moral drama has indeed come of age.

If soaps inherited from the mummers a need to provide a spiritual framework for life – a kind of primitive 'sacred canopy', they also inherited from the morality play a propensity for moralizing – at least according to some analysts. Proponents of this view argue that, whilst falling short of actually preaching, soaps do have a habit of displaying a remarkably narrow range of moral values associated for the most part with a particular world-view.

> What is traditional morality? It is the puritan ethic militant and triumphant. Goodness is defined by adherence to Biblical precepts. It will always triumph over evil, in the end. It involves devotion

to duty . . . and sacrifices – endless sacrifice . . . Traditional morality is founded on the trinity of Love, Family and Domestic Property. Of these, the last is undoubtedly the greatest.[5]

Thus, in Soapland, sex outside marriage is wrong, offenders are expected to get their come-uppances, and the status quo is firmly upheld. In short, 'the morality of all soap is Conservative, Christian and reactionary.'[6] Julia Smith, creator of BBC's *Eastenders*, is said to consider herself a modern-day Charles Dickens, not only because her product is packaged in serial form, but because she uses a style of social commentary reminiscent of him. The text is frequently built up around topics of current concern – working women, gays, minority rights and old age – and this crusading element is not entirely lost on the viewer who apparently consents to put up with it so long as the overall object of being entertained is not lost. *Neighbours*, on the other hand, offers the audience an insight into antipodean bliss: 'Everything in sun-blessed Ramsay Street is as clean and straight as its schoolkids' teeth . . . here the sermons are simple: do the decent thing; don't take any flak; come straight out with it and stop that whingeing.'[7] Unemployment, alcoholism, racial tension, simply do not exist. How strange then, that this very series should recently come under attack from no less a person than the Moderator of the General Assembly of the Church of Scotland, on the grounds that in this self-same world 'no one ever laughs and life consists of upsetting each other verbally . . . It is as if home life is a constant strain.'[8] Two years earlier, *Eastenders* had similarly come in for criticism – this time for portraying Britain's Brownies (the junior branch of the Girl Guides) as 'lager-swilling shoplifters who go camping with boyfriends'.[9] The complaint, upheld by the Broadcasting Complaints Commission, referred to an incident where one of the characters said of the fictional Walford Brownie pack: 'Two were done for shoplifting before we even left Walford. Three got caught trying to sneak out of a Wimpy Bar without paying.' The BBC's defence, that this was an attempt at humour, failed to satisfy the commissioners.

Can such widely divergent views of soap morality ever be reconciled? Not, it seems, from the critic's perspective. Perhaps all that can legitimately be said is that beauty (and, by the same token, ugliness) is in the eye of the beholder. Statistics, however, do tend to favour the view that soaps *have* changed significantly in content over the years. Their radio forbears' predilection for purity has gone for ever: premarital sex and adultery are commonplace; rape goes unpunished; 'pseudo-incest, bigamous marriages and unmarried couples living or sleeping together are nearly everyday occurrences', at least according to some commentators.[10] Deceit and murder are said to be the most common violations of the moral code but, interestingly enough, there is still a tendency among the script writers to avoid condoning such deviant behaviour. The world might be a more brutal place, but the need for a moral framework is still as great as ever. The status quo is safe, even if there is a tendency to negotiate between competing moralities rather than secure the promotion of a final ethical solution.

At one point in his study of *The English Mummers' Play*, Alex Helm describes a scene from a film made in 1939:

> Then entered the Russian, an obnoxious character, dressed in red rags roughly bound round him, spitting vodka from a bottle and splashing the liquor over the watching crowd ... Behind him was a priest of the Orthodox Church riding in a wheelbarrow and dragging his begging bowl behind him ... The Russian rescued the priest who hobbled off, climbed a nearby roof where, in pantomime, he acted God the Father giving Moses the Commandments.[11]

This tends to support the hypothesis that 'religion on television always takes the form of hypocritical piety or a ceremony you know the participants don't believe in ... [and usually] ... is a stage prop or the butt of someone's sacrilegious humour.'[12] Examples of such parody or near-parody abound. In *Eastenders* we have Dot Cotton – 'chain-smoking martyr to her nerves, survivor of the wickedness of this un-Christian world ... a gossip, small-scale gambler, prissily prejudiced against non-conformists, black people and homosexuals.'[13] Her 'strange moral views and odd religious ideas' rather perversely endear her to the viewers, who perhaps see in her an all-too-human combination of principle and prejudice. In *Emmerdale Farm* (subsequently renamed *Emmerdale*), there was Donald Hinton, vicar of Beckindale. Donald was portrayed as an 'old-fashioned clergyman' – a harmless fellow who lived alone with his books and butterfly collection,[14] quite unlike the earthy Dot and certainly distinct from the lay-preaching, piano-playing accompanist of nightclub-singing Rita Fairclough, Ernest Bishop of *Coronation Street*. Across the Atlantic, accusations of insensitive treatment, by the media, of religious figures, suffered a setback recently, 'When was the last time you saw a character in a situation comedy praying and really meaning it . . . not recently? Try never. At least I cannot recall ever seeing religious faith portrayed that way in a TV series.'[15] Not, that is, until *Sunday Dinner*. At last it seemed that religion had returned to the arena of public conversation, most significantly without the trappings of canned laughter. But, even here, all was not plain sailing. T. T. Fagori, the character who actually prays on screen turned out to be less than traditional in her Christianity, depending rather on New Age and feminist spiritualities, and therefore distinctly suspect in the eyes of more conservative church-going viewers.

In an effort to quantify the explicitly religious significance of soaps, the author recently undertook a preliminary study of British daytime drama: this took in six serials over a period of one week in April 1992, and was limited to the analysis of explicit religious references (defined as 'words or phrases with a clearly religious connotation'), including, as a sub-set, slang/swearwords (profanely motivated ERFs). The results were as follows:

1. Over the programmes watched, there occurred one explicit religious reference (ERF) approximately every $3\frac{1}{2}$ minutes.
2. Within these, there occurred one slang/swearword (SS) approximately every 12 minutes.
3. The programme with the highest rate of ERFs was *Take the High Road* (almost one a minute).
4. This programme also contained the lowest proportion of SSs (one in 13).
5. The lowest number of ERFs occurred in *Emmerdale* (one every 30 minutes).
6. Conversely, the highest proportion of SSs were found in *Emmerdale* and *Eastenders* (one in one), closely followed by *Coronation Street*.
7. These statistics are misleading to the extent that many ERFs were clustered in a particular narrative sequence – hence a conversation in *Take the High Road* about a proposed evening of fortune-telling might account for 50 per cent

of all references in that episode whilst lasting only 2–3 minutes.

8. In these soaps working-class people clearly swear more than anyone else.

9. Religion as such may not feature in storylines very often, but religious personnel (ie. ministers and priests) are still in evidence: personal appearances took place in *Brookside* (a young Catholic priest having to decide between his faith and the girl next door) and *Take the High Road* (a young black minister with a doctorate trying to cope with an outbreak of supernaturalism in a Scottish village), while offstage references occurred in *Neighbours* (the mysterious Revd Richards who spends his time judging baking competitions and worrying about the fabric fund) and *Eastenders* (where the bishop recently visited to wash the feet of Dot Cotton). Only *Emmerdale* and *Coronation Street* failed to provide a church leader.

The above findings, however, mask something that is of far greater significance than simple religious content: research carried out in 1984 at Leeds University has already suggested that, from this point of view, non-religious programmes are more important than overtly religious ones since they contain 82 per cent of all references.[16] What is more interesting perhaps, is the role played by soaps in maintaining a kind of popular religious world-view, something made easier by the above-average loyalty of soap watchers, not to mention their appetite for gossip.

The most outstanding example of brand loyalty in the world of soap within recent years must surely be that brought on by the screening of *Mahabharata* in India. A series inspired by Hindu mythology, its grip on national life was almost absolute for the ninety-three weeks it lasted: audience ratings of 92 per cent were recorded; 85 per cent of viewers interviewed said they watched every episode; 90 million people around the subcontinent tuned in every week – more than one tenth of the entire population.

> People vanished from city streets on Sunday mornings as though there were a bomb scare ... poorer people without a TV set tramped into middle-class suburbs to listen at people's windows ... industrial managers arranged their conventions

around a Sunday morning break ... even wedding ceremonies were suspended so that guests could tune in on portable TV sets.[17]

In Britain, such scenes have not been witnessed since *The Forsyte Saga* succeeded in doing what even two world wars could not – changing the time of the Evening Service. Even so, around 20 million viewers watch *Eastenders* every week and almost as many faithfully follow the goings-on in *Coronation Street* and *Neighbours*. Their plots provide material for conversation, their storylines fuse the familiar and fantastic in a way which heightens viewer involvement, and their highly segmented structure ensures a cliff-hanger every episode. As Dickens found to his own profit, selling by instalments works: the psychology of a supercharged imagination guarantees loyalty. Or, to put it another way,

> ... the audience dreams of their 'union with the Buddha principle of the soaps': the ultimate doctor-dynamic which gently and knowingly fills their expectant recesses [to] guide the powerless safely through the ugly, smelly, bloody vagaries and complications of the life of the human female.[18]

This cathartic dimension is important, both because it seems to help the viewer come to terms with problems (real and imagined) in the relative safety of Soapland, and because it points up once more the inherently religious nature of such a function. Issues of Life and Death, once the province of religion, are now apparently worked out in the public arena of Ramsay Street and Albert Square, far more than behind the closed doors of any church, synagogue or mosque.

If soaps *are* religious in the broadest sense of the word, and there is good evidence that they are, they may be said to perform a function somewhat akin to that of folk mythology – but with one crucial difference. Whereas the latter has its roots (by definition) within mass culture, soaps (again by definition) are precisely controlled artefacts imposed '*from above*' on that culture. Far from being spontaneous, organic, products of the popular imagination, they represent policy decisions of the highest order designed to sell, sell, sell. What they sell is not entirely clear – apart, that is, from audiences to advertisers – but there is no doubt that the shared experience of those who watch is of considerable social significance, and herein lies their true worth.

My own view on the importance of soap is simple. I think it binds us together as a society. In the Middle Ages religion was the glue of society. Today television is the binding agent that helps us cohere. And the sticky quintessence of television (the superglue if you like) is soap opera. To watch soap is an affirmation of social piety, a declaration that we share the beliefs, hopes, fears and prejudices of the rest of Western mankind.[19]

Such a statement is not without its problems, but what cannot easily be denied is that soaps *do* provide one of the few genuinely social experiences left to a generation nurtured on the idea that there is no such thing as 'community' any more. Fewer and fewer people have the opportunity (or inclination) to lean over the garden wall and catch up on what is happening in the neighbourhood; instead, they enjoy the same fruits of the experience, albeit vicariously, by watching the cast of *Eastenders*, *Take the High Road*, *et al* as they engage in just that activity. The *need* for belonging has not diminished; neither has the desire to make sense of the world: what has changed is the method by which people satisfy that need, fulfil that desire. The pulpit has given way to the soapbox, and the Sermon on the Mount has been displaced by the theme from *Neighbours*. In such a world, there is still an awareness of things numinous, still an understanding of the 'urgent magic necessity' of ensuring that life goes on, but it has been sublimated so that there is no longer a clear-cut distinction between mundane and divine: in soap, reality merges into unreality and echoes from beyond find their way into even the most trivial of trivia. If the mummers played out their scripts in order to ensure that summer would follow winter, harvest-time succeed seed-time, the soaps too have their part to play in reassuring us all that life *will* go on — for in the world of soap, it certainly does go on, and on . . . endlessly, like the universe perhaps?

APPENDIX

Results of Programme Analysis: Monday 21 April to Friday 24 April 1992

PROGRAMMES WATCHED

Neighbours	BBC1, daily (Mon. – Fri.), 20 mins.
Take the High Road	ITV (Scottish), Mon. & Fri., 30 mins.
Brookside	C4, Mon. & Wed., 30 mins.
Emmerdale	ITV, Tue. & Thu., 30 mins.
Eastenders	BBC1, Tue. & Thu., 30 mins.
Coronation Street	ITV, Wed. & Fri., 30 mins.

PROGRAMME NOTES

Neighbours, like its counterpart *Home and Away* (not viewed), is an Australian import set in sunny suburbia; its UK equivalent, *Brookside*, lacks the glamour but makes up for it with realism (i.e. bad language and unemployment). *Take the High Road* is the Scottish equivalent of *Emmerdale*: both offer a faintly nostalgic look at rural life in an increasingly urbanized culture. The inner city is catered for by long-lived *Coronation Street* and its London cousin, *Eastenders* – the most popular UK soap of all.

EXPLICIT RELIGIOUS REFERENCES

Programme title	Duration	Viewers	Total References	Slang/Swear
Neighbours	100 mins	17.34m	29	10
Take the High Road	60 mins	0.95m	53	4
Brookside	60 mins	6.49m	23	4
Emmerdale	60 mins	11.55m	2	2
Eastenders	60 mins	20.07m	7	7
Coronation Street	60 mins	19.80m	8	7
Totals	400 mins	76.20m	122	34

NB. Explicit Religious References were defined as 'words or phrases with a clearly religious connotation' – e.g. God, church, Revd, devil, etc.

Slang/Swearwords were defined as 'words or phrases in which

the ERR's are used profanely' – e.g. 'O God!', 'Hell!', 'Poor soul', etc.

Viewing Figures relate to the week ending 22 April 1992. (Source: Broadcasters' Audience Research Board [BARB] and Scottish Television.) Where programmes are repeated audiences are added together.

NOTES

1   Marilyn J. Matelski, *The Soap Opera Evolution: America's Enduring Romance with Daytime Drama*, London: Jefferson: 1988, p. 31.
2   Hilary Kingsley, *Soap Box, the Papermac Guide to Soap Opera*, Basingstoke: Macmillan: 1988, p. 335.
3   Ibid., p. 1.
4   Alex Helm, *The English Mummers' Play*, London: D. S. Brewer: 1981, p. 1.
5   Peter Buckman, *All For Love: a Study in Soap Opera*, London: Secker & Warburg: 1984, p. 26.
6   Kingsley, op. cit., p. 16.
7   Ibid., p. 30.
8   From a report in the *Scotsman*, 1 May 1992.
9   From a report in *The Times*, 6 June 1990.
10 Muriel G. Cantor and Suzanne Pingree, *The Soap Opera*, London: Sage: 1983, p. 5.
11 Helm, op. cit., p. 56.
12 James M. Wall, 'A Show in which Prayer is all in the Family', *Christian Century* Vol. 108 (1991), p. 539.
13 Kingsley, op. cit., p. 238.
14 Ibid., p. 290.
15 Wall, op. cit.
16 See Kim Knott, 'Media Portrayals of Religion', Leeds University (unpublished report): 1984.
17 From a report in *The Times*, 13 July 1990.
18 Matelski, op. cit., p. 127.
19 Kingsley, op. cit., p. 10.

9 Everybody needs good neighbours: soap opera as community of meaning

DEREK C. WEBER

At its height, it was the most popular programme on British television. An Australian import, launching pad for teeny pop mega-stars Kylie and Jason, a true television phenomenon, *Neighbours* became a must see for pre- and early teens. Now somewhat overshadowed by its rival 'Aussie soap', *Home and Away*, *Neighbours* still is synonymous with a genre of television at once reviled as chewing gum for the eyes and fanatically supported as a slice-of-life drama on a human scale. Yet for many media critics the soap opera is television in its purest and most popular form. In Britain it is an event of some note if a non-soap programme even comes close to challenging the rating figures of the BBC's *Eastenders* or Granada's *Coronation Street*. With that Australian import still maintaining a firm third place, these top three UK programmes regularly bring in between 15 and 20 million viewers each showing (numbers scrupulously counted by the audience research group BARB). The only programme to challenge consistently the soap's supremacy is the Oxford-based crime drama *Inspector Morse*, a programme which some call a cop show with soap tendencies, or a soap with cop show tendencies.

The question that comes readily to mind when examining such statistics is, of course, 'Why?'. Why do these programmes appeal to so many? What niche do they fill, what satisfactions do they bring, and what messages do they transmit? Decoding these programmes is a difficult process, one that is increasingly being taken up by media researchers from a variety of perspectives.[1] Soaps are seen as cultural icons, cathartic entertainment, even subversive 'literature' challenging the patriarchal status quo. No longer denigrated as the vast afternoon television wasteland, soaps have taken their place alongside 'serious' programming as worthy of critical study and reflection. Though there is much for us to learn from the more sociological research, our question is a subtly different one: What is the theological significance (if any) of soap opera? But before we can begin to answer that question we must first of all 'name the beast'. What makes a soap opera a soap opera?

Most of us are familiar with the history of the term 'soap opera'. The early US radio serials of the 1930s were sponsored in large part by Procter and Gamble, a well-established soap and oil corporation. In those days there was little restriction on programme content and the sponsoring company was given oversight of scripts and programme plans. Therefore, the term soap opera came to be associated with a melodramatic style of radio serial. Except as archive material the radio soap opera has not existed on the American airwaves since 1960. The long-running programme *The Archers*, a serial about country life, can still be heard daily on BBC Radio 4. Though this has never been sponsored by any commercial enterprise (as yet), it still qualifies as a radio soap. The jump from radio to television was inevitable. Though Procter and Gamble still provide sponsorship to some of these programmes, they no longer have any control over content, except for that extreme action of removing funds if greatly displeased. So even while the sponsorship is much more diverse, the term soap opera has been lovingly accepted by those involved in production and by the fans.

The distinctive qualities of the genre are many. One area that makes soap operas unique is the whole technical side of production which is geared toward speed and low cost. A soap opera is usually recorded on video tape rather than film. This is why they look different from many of the other programmes on television. The primary reason for this is that video is less expensive than film. In a further attempt to save money, a soap will use a set over and over again for years with little change. In addition, most of the soap takes place indoors with little or no location work or outside broadcasting. There have been a few innovations in set construction in the UK worthy of note. When Channel 4 began work on *Brookside*, they purchased all of the houses on a single development in Liverpool. All of their production work could be said to be location shooting because they have transformed the houses into 'television friendly' studios and do post-production work on site. The BBC has taken this innovation a step further. For their new 'Euro-soap' *Eldorado* (first aired in July 1992), they went to

Spain and built an entire village. Missing only a few amenities such as plumbing and sewage, this village is constructed out of brick and stone, rather than wooden façades fronting set pieces. Though extravagant at first, part of a soap's appeal is familiarity, so this set could be used without major rebuilding for as many years as the programme might run. A second distinctive quality of a soap's production is the speed at which cast and crew must work. Particularly with the US soaps, there are few rehearsals, perhaps only a quick run through before the tape is rolling. These programmes appear five days a week for fifty to fifty-two weeks a year, therefore leisure is not allowed. In the US the frequency of broadcast is daily, while the UK and Australia show most soaps two or three times weekly (more with repeats). Following the technical line is the question of broadcast time. Peter Conrad argues that television's genres are determined by their 'time-zones'. 'Programmers superstitiously maintain that an alteration in scheduling can exterminate a show . . . [and the] dreary afternoon is sacred to soaps.'[2] The most popular UK soaps push afternoon a little later, but they still appear earlier than the situation comedies and the drama serials.

These characteristics might be considered external to the soap. They have more to do with how it is made than the content of the programme itself. There are, however, some features of the soap that make it somewhat unique. The first of these is the serial nature of the scripts. A soap opera is an ongoing experience. The purpose of the soap opera according to Dennis Porter is never to end.[3] Indeed even the ending of certain sub-plots proves to be not an end but rather the beginning of a new situation with its requisite tragedies and opportunities. The storylines are complex and convoluted involving a number of people of various relation. This points out the second characteristic of a soap opera: a large cast. Sometimes these casts are supposed to represent whole towns or the entire population of a large city hospital. The people interact through a variety of situations from the domestic (husband, wife, children and extended family) to the business (partners, clients, associates) to the social (friends, lovers, neighbours) to the criminal (victims, enemies, rivals). In fact, it is these relationships that make up the 'action' of the soap. In other words, it is less important to know what happens in a soap opera than it is to know to whom it happens. The action is minimal and is spun out for weeks as each person in the web of relationships discusses how this action affects them individually and through them others. The information about any action is repeated over and over again, 'not just to keep the casual or new viewers up to date, but to further explore relationships. Who tells whom is just as important as what is being told.'[4] Or more important, some would argue. Soaps are not about action, but about relationships. The nature of these relationships subtly different as we begin to explore the international scene. Soaps appear in many different countries all with distinctive traits. Some of the most interesting are the Latin American telenovellas which come out of a particular cultural mindset reflecting both a mythology and a modern political/economic system that is oppressive to the majority of the populace. A few European and Asian countries have experimented with the soap format as well.[5]

Concentrating on the three English-speaking countries we find certain distinctive qualities. The UK has concentrated on what many call 'social realism' in their soap format. The US has opted for melodrama. While Australia attempts to walk a middle line and focuses more on the domestic scene. In the UK the most popular soaps are *Eastenders* and *Coronation Street*. These tend to look at the working-class and lower-income families and individuals trying to make their way in a 'Thatcher economy'. *Emmerdale*, which used to be called *Emmerdale Farm*, has recently tried to change its image from the rural/small-town quiet backwater to gain a more up-market younger appeal. The Scottish soap *Take the High Road* is one of the few soaps that actually tries to transcend class barriers. The cast of characters includes wealthy land owners, business and professional people and those who serve as maids and gardeners. How well this works over the long term, I cannot say, but my brief experience has revealed a sort of *Upstairs/Downstairs* with Scots accents (at least of the workers). In other words, though there is the occasional evidence that even the rich can be caring, the thrust of the programme is to reinforce the status quo. The status quo in American soaps is definitely better off. Except for the occasional lovable rogue type, the cast consists of professionals (doctors, lawyers, media people and business men and women: America's upper class) and those who are striving to be (such as offspring, neighbours and of course patients and/or clients). The titles of these programmes give away the social ethos: *The Bold and the Beautiful*, *General Hospital*, *Santa Barbara* (you won't find a soap named Hoboken, New Jersey). Other titles evoke the emotional ethos: *The Young and the Restless*, *Loving*, *One Life to Live*, *The Guiding Light*. And still others reflect the inevitability of soaps: *As The World Turns*, *The Days of our Lives*, *All My Children*. But perhaps the title that best sums up the ethos of the American soap is *Another World*.

In Australia things are much more pleasant. The cast of *Neighbours* seem terminally middle class, and very young. Not surprisingly, it is the young to middle teens who make up the vast audience for both *Neighbours* and *Home and Away*. The problems, or storylines, seem to focus more on the home life than the business life of the cast. Indeed, many of them don't really seem to have much of a life outside of the home. Though there are problems and as many tearful cliff-hangers in the Australian programmes as in any other, the overall tone of the programmes is less menacing. Perhaps reflecting a more Australian attitude to life, these shows seem to be saying that things will in the end work out. The US and UK soaps, on the other hand, seem to be trying their best to say that there is no possible way that this situation will ever work out, even though it usually does to the momentary satisfaction of most.

Before we begin to ask some deeper questions about soaps, we must address the *Dallas* question. Do the so called 'prime-time soaps' qualify as true soap operas? As with most things there is a yes and no to this. On the purely technical side the answer would have to be no. These programmes have a budget that soaps cannot equal. The once-a-week transmission allows a more leisurely approach, giving more time for retakes and rehearsals. And the time of broadcast brings a different audience and even, some would argue, a different mood. As they are competing with action serials and the like, they are forced to employ a much more active storyline than the average daytime soap. This has direct effects on the type of audience they will draw. This is one reason why the audience for daytime soaps has historically been women. Others argue, however, that it is the nature of the daytime soaps that puts them into a more 'feminine' category. The emphasis on relationship, on talk, on the home and family, makes the daytime soap a programme for and often by women.

However, the prime-time programmes seem to want to emulate their poor daytime cousins in many respects; the large cast, the intertwining, never-ending storyline, the use of 'types', and an emphasis on relationship and dialogue (though certainly not to the degree of the daytime soap). No one would argue that *Dallas* or *Dynasty*, plus various spin-offs, had a definite soap quality. But these programmes are on the wane. Some, like *Dallas*, have disappeared all together. The replacement programmes are a little more difficult to categorize. US programmes like *LA Law* and *Northern Exposure* don't fit the profile as neatly. UK offerings such as *Capital City*, *TECS*, and *Heartbeat* again look somewhat soap-like but cannot meet all the criteria. Perhaps the one that comes closest to fitting the bill is *The Bill*. This programme in its scheduling and format is very much a soap with a police station as the centre rather than the home. Because of the confusion, I would be inclined to take a hard line and exclude all these 'pseudo-soaps' from the discussion. That would enable us to look closely at the genre with definite boundaries. Others may want to argue otherwise and look at the lasting effect of programmes such as *Dallas*, which was a programme with an international appeal (as William Biernatzki explains in the next chapter). Soap operas, as defined here, are much more culturally specific. This does not, however, mute the discussion. Indeed, it rather sharpens the question as to what is being reflected in ourselves and in our society by the immense popularity of such programmes.

A part of the appeal of the soap can be found on the scale between sympathy and distance.[6] On the one hand there is a certain amount of identification with some of the characters in a particular soap. People watch in order to say 'I'm like that'. When we see ourselves there is a certain thrill of recognition. Yet the mirror has an added dimension. The characters with which we identify are able to go beyond our own behaviour. This leads to a certain amount of vicarious viewing: 'I'd like to do that' or even 'I'll try that'. In all of this there is a certain affirmation. On the other hand we watch a soap because the behaviour is alien to us. Sometimes the activity in a soap is so implausible as to stretch the suspension of belief to its limits. A recent issue of *Soap Opera Digest* carries an article on the rapid rate of growth of children in soaps.[7] While pregnancy is a popular plot complication, and babies are often cuddly props to a domestic scene, children are difficult to script for in an adult soap. So, miracle growth! – children born one season are off to college in a few years and getting married shortly after that.

But sometimes the distance is played out by the characters that we 'love to hate'. The scheming woman, or the moral-less man become the anti-heroes of the programme. We enjoy their activities not because we want to emulate their behaviour, but because they represent flirting with the darker side of life. A side that is alien to most of us. *Eastender's* Dirty Den or the Lolita-like Mandy become not role models but rather good bad examples. In all of this, however, some argue that the over-abundance of *risqué* behaviour leads to a tolerance for lowering standards. In fantasy the titillation comes as boundaries are pushed back beyond acceptable limits. But the limits are shifting. Many critics see soap opera and television in general as behind that shift. Or, as some argue, we want to see the bad ones punished, but not too much because they are only acting out our own fantasies.

Despite this dichotomy between sympathy and distance, to many critics the soap opera is an affirmation of morality. Peter Buckman writes that 'soap fulfils the function of folk myth: it deals with the victory of old-fashioned and traditional certainties over the evanescent fashions that assail them.'[8] This brings conflicting desires to the soap viewer, the desire for resolution against the desire for continuation. In fact it might be said that this very cycle of conflict – resolution – further conflict leads to a rather mature expression of reality. Rather than fairy-tale endings where all loose ends are tied up, in the soap there is 'the knowledge that evil will continue to challenge good, no matter how often it is defeated.'[9] The soap is offering the viewer a chance to engage with this on-going battle, to see their own struggles for meaning played out on the small screen by those they come to call 'neighbours'.

Bringing theological questions to the analysis of soap opera may seem to be a contentious exercise. After all, there is rarely any overt reference to any religious sensibilities in most of these programmes. It is worth noting that a few of the soaps, primarily in the UK, are introducing characters that help to break out of the stereotypical representations of religious people. The clergy represented in both *Emmerdale* and *Take the High Road* seem to be whole persons rather than façades. The latter is to be particularly commended for introducing a black actor to play the minister in this small Scottish town. All sorts of stereotypes come crumbling down and all sorts of dramatic possibilities arise. This, however, is only the surface of the theological issues involved. The non-appearance of religious characters, the avoidance of matters spiritual, the lack of mention of deity except as exclamation, does not mean that there is no theology to be found or no theological understanding to be derived. It does mean that we must look more closely and tread carefully when we begin to draw conclusions. It is important to avoid exegesis, or reading in what isn't really there. In order to explore these deeper issues of meaning, we need to look to what John Fiske calls the 'third text'.[10] The first two texts represent first, the cultural environment in which both viewer and programme-makers exist and secondly, the text of the programme itself. How well these first two texts interrelate has a lot to do with the popularity of a programme. A soap that has many cultural referents, that 'speaks' to the issues and moods of the day, will gain an appreciative audience. One that seems out of step or old fashioned will sink in the ratings game.

The third text, however, is the text that the viewer constructs as he/she is involved in the programme. This is at first an individual reaction and understanding based on how any one viewer sees a programme. But then it becomes part of the public space through a variety of means. The first and simplest level is gossip: the casual conversation of two soap fans that replays favourite moments from recent programmes and, more importantly, speculates on future actions of a variety of characters. The programme and the characters become part of the viewer's consciousness in much the same way as the activities of their own family and neighbours. Gossip forms what some call a vital 'social cement' binding together what is a fragmented society and fragmenting medium, i.e. television. This process is then accelerated by such things as fan clubs and various publications. From letters and articles in the *Radio Times* to the total immersion of *Soap Opera Digest*, these publications become sources for further information about the lives of the actors and the plans for the characters. All of these work together to fill out the world of the soap opera, making it seem as complete and as complex as the real world and thereby much more easily incorporated into the real world lives of the viewers.

It is precisely in this area of incorporation that many critics of soap opera begin to get concerned. On one level there is the problem of blurring the lines between fantasy and reality. We

have all heard stories of people who send get-well cards to characters who become ill on a programme, who ask medical advice
from actors playing doctors, and perhaps most extreme those who
carry out aggression against those people 'we love to hate' when
they are seen in the high street. Magazines such as *Soap Opera
Digest* perpetuate this blurring as their stories and photos will
use real names and character names interchangeably. Some writers
question the seriousness of this problem. They argue that viewers
are actually capable of holding together conflicting world-views.
Fiske writes that

> . . . these fans treat the operas as if they were real and sometimes
> relate to their characters as though they were their own family.
> Yet they know what they are doing, they know that their own
> pleasure in reading soap opera as real life is illusory and that they
> are, according to their more normal standards, being somewhat
> silly in doing so. The viewer of soaps can be simultaneously naïve
> and knowing.[11]

Fiske believes that it would be wrong to see gossip as evidence
of the blurring of the line between reality and fantasy. Rather it
is a time of evaluation and active engagement with the issues of
the programme, enabling the viewers to find points of contact in
their own lives. This relates back to the idea that pleasure in soap
viewing comes at least partly from the idea of sympathy. When these
points of contact bring the soap world into the real world then there
is, for some, enough justification for continuing to engage in that
'community'.

Whether or not viewers become completely swallowed up in the
other world of soap opera, there is still a question to be asked
about the content of these programmes. What sort of information
are these 'neighbours' bringing into the community? Some critics
will applaud soaps in their boldness to address current issues. AIDS,
abuse, infidelity, alcoholism and so on have all been plot devices
used to great effect. A certain amount of information and advice
is given out in such episodes. In addition some viewers might find
some solace in hearing that they are not alone in their affliction.
On the other hand, it might be argued that much of the information is not helpful, more along the lines of what not to do.
Taking the AIDS example, though it was brave of the *Eastenders*
producers to tackle the subject, they made the AIDS patient a

heterosexual female (and according to some worthy of our sympathy) and not the more controversial homosexual male (who is only 'getting what he deserves'). *Eastenders* also took the brave step of introducing a black family into their regular cast, but the issue of racism is never mentioned. These are just a few examples of how the subject matter is 'fudged' a bit in soaps so that while it appears they are tackling tough subjects, they are really avoiding the depths of the issue.

The other major issue of contention is how the soaps portray sexual activity. On the surface it would seem that most soaps use sex the way advertisers do, to sell their programmes. The promotion of *Eldorado* calls it 'sun, sand, *sangria* – and sex'. A recent issue of *TV Times*[12] debated the question of sex on soaps and decided that most of them were quite prim in what they actually showed. This is to be expected given the early broadcast times. It was interesting that the concern was on how to avoid showing the actual sexual acts, not about the over-emphasis of sex by inference. In fact, some of the producers were quite proud of how much they were able to say with suggestion. 'Sex is always there', said a *Coronation Street* scriptwriter, 'but you don't have to be rude or crude to get the point across.' Some would complain that the fact that sex is always there is precisely the problem. Others, such as Buckman, see that the soap opera is all about love, losing it, finding it, faking it if need be. But in the end the soap opera is a romance, therefore sex is inevitable as one of the expressions of that love.

We return, finally, to the process of engagement. There is some disagreement as to whether soap opera viewing is fully engaging. Porter writes that the viewers are 'observing unobserved under conditions that titillate but finally leave them untouched'.[13] But Allen believes that 'as soap opera viewers we cannot help but be inside the narrative flow of the text.' It is precisely this insider/outsider experience of soaps that brings confusion. As Allen writes:

> In a very real sense, the better one 'knows' a soap opera, the greater reason one has for wanting to watch every day. Conversely, the less involved one is in a given soap opera's textual network, the more that soap opera appears to be merely a series of plotlines that unfold so slowly that virtually nothing 'happens' in any given episode and the more tiresomely redundant each episode seems.[14]

The soap opera represents a search for community and meaning. For some critics this is an appropriate unifier in a fragmentary world. For others it represents the failure of real communities, such as neighbourhood and church, to meet the needs. But new communities are being formed by soap fans sharing in their common devotion to a story with characters as real as those they meet in the street. 'The purpose of [a soap opera] is a moral one: to strengthen the audience's belief in their place in the accepted order of things.'[15] If Buckman is right, what could be more profoundly theological?

NOTES

1   For a good analysis of the state of soap opera research, see *Communication Research Trends*, vol. 10 (1990) nos. 1 and 2.
2   Peter Conrad, *Television: the Medium and Its Manners*, Boston: Routledge & Kegan Paul: 1982, pp. 144–5.
3   Dennis Porter, 'Soap Time: Thoughts on a Commodity Art Form', in H. Newcomb (ed.) *Television: the Critical View*, New York: OUP: 1982, p. 124.
4   Robert Allen, 'Reader Oriented Criticism and Television', in Robert Allen (ed.), *Channels of Discourse*, Television and Contemporary Criticism, London: Methuen: 1987, p. 81.
5   See *Communication Research Trends*, Vol. 10 (1990) nos. 1 and 2 for more details on the international scene.
6   See Porter, op. cit., p. 123.
7   *Soap Opera Digest*, 23 June 1992, pp. 22–31.
8   Peter Buckman, *All For Love*, London: Secker & Warburg: 1984, p. 38.
9   Ibid., p. 44.
10   John Fiske, *Television Culture*, London: Methuen: 1987, p. 108f.
11   Ibid., p. 91.
12   *TV Times*, 6–12 June 1992.
13   Porter, op. cit., p. 123.
14   Allen, op. cit., p. 86.
15   Buckman, op. cit., p. 90.

10 Religious values and root paradigms: a method of cultural analysis

WILLIAM E. BIERNATZKI

Efforts to understand the ways religion interacts with culture have been plagued by our inability to define either term – religion or culture – in an unambiguous way. Everyone knows what 'religion' is, and most people have some idea what 'culture' is, but even the most sophisticated efforts to grasp their essential elements seem always to slip into grey areas and to give rise to debates among precisely those scholars who have studied the two topics most intensively. In everyday life, these two areas of concern, and other factors, such as 'value', to which they both are intimately related, are too important to become bogged down in unresolvable debates about definitions. Therefore it seems necessary to borrow a tactic from American football and make an 'end run' around them, to concentrate on more immediately critical issues.

Elsewhere[1] I have tried to do this with the question of how to assess the success or failure of a religion moving from its civilization of origin into a new and alien civilization. In the new culture the religion's doctrines may encounter elements which are sympathetic and encourage its adoption. On the other hand, they may meet resistance in the form of contrary and firmly entrenched assumptions about the nature of the world and of humankind which inhibit or prevent the religion's acceptance. Examples of cross-cultural movements of missionary religions are numerous, but the purest examples of the process are mostly in the past. I selected three, from East and South-east Asia, as especially suitable cases for investigation. First was the introduction of Buddhism into China from India and Central Asia during the first millennium AD.[2] Although Buddhism's stress on meditation and escape from the desires and sufferings of this world had an undeniable attraction for many Chinese, the nation's full acceptance of the religion was blocked by many fundamental assumptions of Chinese culture. Among these, one of the most significant was an all-encompassing centralism, which could not allow for an independent class of 'holy men' outside the control of the emperor and bureaucracy. Another was filial piety, reinforced by ideological Confucianism but long ante-dating it, which made no allowance for a celibate clergy failing to continue the family line and its accompanying ancestral rites.

A second example[3] was the spread of Islam into Indonesia, par-ticularly the sultanates of Central Java, where it was accepted with relative ease. However, Central Javan Islam, in contrast to that of Arabia or even Arab settlements in Sumatra and the Malay Penin-sula, was so diluted that it caused little conflict with the pre-Islamic Hinduized and animistic culture of the region. Consequently, many elements of the earlier Javanese culture have continued to coexist with Islam and with it have shaped Javanese life throughout the nineteenth and twentieth centuries.

Christianity was introduced into Korea under various forms which offered Koreans alternatives for the exercise of individual choice unavailable to them in their rigidly structured traditional culture. This phenomenon, centring on the nineteenth and twen-tieth centuries, served as the third example.[4] While the choice of a new religion was an exercise of individual freedom, whichever of the many denominations and sects the individual happened to choose he or she would almost inevitably fall under a new authori-tarianism, usually dominated by a patriarchal figure – whether bishop, minister or sectarian 'messiah'. This satisfied opposing ten-dencies to seek to express individual freedom against suffocating social controls while, at the same time, subordinating oneself to a new structure which would provide a needed sense of security and group belonging.

The method used to analyse these three historical cases was suggested by one of the many seminal concepts developed by the anthropologist Victor Turner, that of the 'root paradigm'. A root paradigm is an unquestioned – and practically unques-tionable – assumption about the fundamental nature of the world and humanity underlying and influencing all social actions within a particular cultural context.[5] Turner found root paradigms in 'social dramas' – intense encounters in which the participants acted out their 'roles' almost as though they were following a script. As the 'drama' progressed they would move through phases towards an almost predictable dénouement. The result might have been foreseen as detrimental to all, but nevertheless was practically inevitable, in view of the prevailing assumptions about the nature of the world which guided the participants' actions. When the continuity of a culture – its transmission, or 'reproduction' from generation to generation – is relatively undisturbed, its root paradigms change very slowly. Often, historical evidence suggests that they may hardly change at all for centuries. Of course, if a society is disrupted to the degree that its culture no longer is learned by the younger generations in an integrated way, even the root paradigms – together with the culture's most deeply held values – may be affected. But in the normal course of events they are almost impervious to change. As an example of a well-known social drama, Turner singled out the conflict between St Thomas à Becket, Archbishop of Canterbury, and King Henry II, which progressed step by step through stages leading ultimately to the murder of the archbishop in his own cathedral in the year 1170.[6] In another example, that of the Mexican Revolution of 1810, Turner[7] shows how even rebellion is guided by root paradigms. Revolutionaries may think they are avant-garde, but the deepest patterns of their revolts and innovations cannot be separated from the deepest assumptions of their culture about how to rebel! Root paradigms function at all levels within a culture, in everyday life as well as in dramatic conflicts. They are most easily discerned in conflicts and intense arguments, however, because the protagonists in such debates are forced to try to influence their hearers' reason and emotions by appealing to the most deeply cherished values and symbols of their culture. These values and symbols, in turn, are founded upon the root paradigms of the culture. The root paradigms themselves are so taken for granted – so 'obvious' to members of that culture – that they are not often directly mentioned but frequently can be revealed to the outside observer through analysis of the arguments, with their statements about values and their accompanying symbols.

Earlier in this century, anthropologists, historians and others concerned with describing societies often tried to do so in a comprehensive way. Thus, Ruth Benedict[8] typified Hopi society as 'Apollonian', because the character types it seemed to encourage in its members resembled those attributed to the Greek god, Apollo: moderation, serenity, etc. On the other hand, she regarded the Kwakiutl people of the north-west coast of North America as

'Dionysian', since the personal traits they appeared to value tended towards those of the god Dionysus: extremes of emotion and unrestrained behaviour. Others used Freudian concepts to describe the 'national characters' of people from various cultures. Earlier, 'culture area studies' had attempted to chart the boundaries between cultures, based largely on evidence from traits of material culture and linguistics. Rather than continue attempting to make such all-encompassing characterizations, a search for root paradigms looks for one underlying assumption at a time, recognizing that it will yield only a partial description of that culture. Each culture is influenced by an indeterminate number of root paradigms. Just because we manage to isolate one there is no guarantee that it embodies the most important assumptions typifying that culture. There may be many more, which may or may not be revealed by looking at other dimensions – different patterns of conflict, etc. – of that culture. The search for new root paradigms can go on and on, and gradually a more and more complete picture of the assumptions underlying the culture will emerge. But there may never be a point at which we can say we are confident that we have found all the root paradigms or that we have a 'complete' understanding of the culture from the perspective of its root paradigms. This approach is therefore both more modest and ultimately more useful in its practical applications than the more traditional 'culture area' or 'national character' descriptions mentioned above.

I started the search for root paradigms in historical cases because the evidence for them is laid out more clearly there than in the booming, buzzing confusion of contemporary life. But they help determine much of what we think and do today, just as the root paradigms of ancient China or medieval England provided 'scripts' for behaviour in those times and places. The search for the root paradigms of present-day cultures can be a rewarding one, because it can reveal some of the underlying reasons for seemingly inexplicable and insoluble conflicts. It can be especially valuable in dealing with inter-ethnic conflicts – which seem to be increasing in seriousness in today's world. It also can be used within a single culture to study the underlying reasons why particular institutional forms are or are not accepted by people within that culture. A thoroughly pursued study along these lines might, for example, yield insights into why particular Christian denominations –

mainstream denominations in America, for example – are in apparent decline while others – Pentecostal sects, for example – are growing. To what root paradigms does Pentecostalism appeal, which the mainstream denominations cannot seem to tap or to which they even seem antithetical? By isolating such points of reinforcement and conflict, research might prepare the declining denominations to revamp and revitalize their preaching and proselytizing. By understanding and conforming more fully to the deepest expectations of the hearers, their efforts to communicate their message might avoid unnecessary obstacles and encourage greater receptivity in audiences. The usefulness of this approach is not limited to religious institutions. In one chapter[9] I used it to analyse the industrialization of Japan during the late nineteenth and early twentieth centuries. The reasons for the success of that secular process – so similar to the missionary expansions discussed in the earlier chapters – lay in the long-established root paradigms of Japanese culture which were eminently suited to the ready acceptance and development of industrial capitalism.

More relevant for the present discussion is the application of this 'root paradigm analysis' to mass media communication.[10] One of the most internationally successful television programmes of recent years was the American 'prime-time soap opera', *Dallas*. During the 1980s, *Dallas* was broadcast in around 100 countries, achieving a high degree of popularity with audiences in most of them. Many reasons have been advanced for this popularity. American television programmes such as *Dallas* are relatively inexpensive 'time fillers' in countries whose television programmers are forced to operate within tight budget constraints. The gross themes of wealth, power and sex also are stressed and are attractive to many audiences. More importantly for the programme's intercultural appeal, however, is its dependence on themes which relate directly to very general root paradigms – paradigms so fundamental that they can be found in many cultures. Among these are some pertaining to the centrality of the extended family, the importance of land to familial identity and security, and the tensions and complexities of role relationships within the family. Audiences might have been attracted to *Dallas* by superficial symbols such as cowboys, big cars, high fashion clothing, etc., but their continuing interest is more likely to have been due to the way the programmes's root paradigms resonated with their own lives and experience.

This interpretation is borne out by the research of Tamar Liebes and Elihu Katz on audience reactions to *Dallas* among several ethnic groups in Israel, the suburban United States and Japan.[11] Popular in the first two countries, the programme failed in Japan. It was used in various ways by Arabs, Moroccan Jews, Russians and second-generation Israelis from kibbutzim, and by Americans. Often they used the story as a springboard for discussing their own lives, problems and experiences. Many did not take it seriously or criticized it according to varying criteria, but enjoyed it nevertheless. The Japanese, however, found it inconsistent and incompatible with their experiences in present-day Japan. Liebes and Katz discern primordial themes in *Dallas* which echo those of the Book of Genesis.[12] Dynasty and family are central concerns, along with power, and many of the personal problems of the soap-opera characters also were those of the Biblical characters. Intimate acquaintance of the Israeli and American groups with the Genesis stories and parallels throughout the Bible may have made the themes of *Dallas* more familiar to them. Lack of such familiarity among the Japanese might have had something to do with their negative response to the programme. On the other hand, Japanese commented that many modern Japanese were consciously trying to throw off some of the same patterns of behaviour, which may have been altogether *too* familiar to them but are regarded as pre-modern. Although recognized as 'primordial', excessive concern with inheritance, in-law relationships, primogeniture, etc., 'are points we want to forget,' according to one Japanese participant.[13]

A root paradigm can manifest itself in many different ways, some even opposed to each other. Even if some of the 'primordial' characteristics Japanese observers resist in *Dallas* are 'traditional,' or 'pre-modern,' the deep assumptions underlying them may be fully operative in the objectors, themselves, in other aspects of their lives, far removed from family and kinship. The modern Japanese businessman has been likened in many ways to the samurai of old, sallying forth to conquer the business 'enemies' of his company much as the samurai did to fight the opponents of his feudal lord. Many of his motivations and attitudes are the same. Only the clothing, tactics, and 'weapons' – a briefcase instead of a sword – are different!

Turning to the application of all this to the communication of religion and values, it seems evident that those who use the media of mass communication in these areas need first to be thoroughly familiar with the culture or cultures in which they are operating. In particular, they should try to penetrate not only to the values and symbols of the culture but even to the root paradigms which underlie them. Communication which is not somehow consistent with the deepest assumptions of its audience about the nature of the world, the nature of humankind and the expectations about human motivation and action which people take for granted, will have little chance of success. Sometimes communicators, including liturgists, will 'modernize' by adopting superficial, transient elements of contemporary culture for religious purposes. That is well and good, but modern forms are not necessarily well articulated with the culture's root paradigms. Superficial elements of western material culture have spread around the world, taken up by people of vastly different cultures without having significant effect on the ways people in those cultures fundamentally understand the world.

One fascinating research project carried out a few years ago illustrates the interaction between modern technology and deeply held views of the world.[14] Many Hmong people from the forests of Laos settled in Chicago after fleeing their homeland in the wake of the Vietnam War. Their world-view included a strong belief in spirits – both harmful and helpful – who inhabited their native forests and were responsible for most sicknesses, accidents and other calamities the people experienced. When they came to America, social workers, doctors, clergy and others tried to persuade them that it is natural causes, not spirits, which bring about such difficulties. Not only was the material and social life of the Hmong thrown into confusion by their move, but these arguments called into question at least one of their root paradigms and confused them even about the fundamental nature of the world, as they had understood it. But the Hmong found support for their traditional understandings in an unexpected place: television. Many horrible incidents were reported in news programmes and re-enacted in dramas and films. The news showed that evil forces were active in Chicago and other places in the western world, just as they had been in Laos. Horror films – which the Hmong obtained from video rental shops and avidly watched on their VCRs – 'proved' to them that horrible spirits do exist and cause trouble. They recognized that the horror films were not documentaries and only re-enacted the horrible events. But they argued that such things were beyond the possibility of fictional invention – people simply could not evolve such fantastic things out of their unaided imaginations – and so they must be based on real events and experiences. In this way the Chicago Hmong were able to restore much of their frightening, but at least familiar, view of the world. In doing so they regained some of their lost confidence in their own identity, in the midst of their otherwise strange new environment.

It may be easier to penetrate to the root paradigms of a different and exotic culture than to recognize those which underlie one's own culture. It is of the nature of root paradigms that they are unquestioned assumptions; so it is understandable that we should regard what they tell us as the way the world 'really is', not merely the way our culture teaches us to *think* it is. But for the sake of full and accurate communication within one's own culture the effort to recognize such assumptions is well worth it. As they become clearer, our messages – regardless of whether they are communicated through speech, handwriting, print or electronic media – can be adjusted so as to complement, rather than conflict with, the root paradigms we have discovered. It is unlikely that we ever will recognize all the root paradigms of our own, or any other culture, but the more of them we discover the more effective our communication can be made. A knowledge of literature may help us isolate our own culture's root paradigms. Successful authors have an ability to penetrate to those deep levels of assumptions which resonate with their readers' own understandings of life and cause them to react to the author's words by saying, 'Yes, that is really true.' The best places in novels to find root paradigms manifesting themselves might be, as Turner suggested with historical and ethnographic evidence, in conflict situations – especially those in which characters are engaged in intensive arguments.

On the other hand, literary works are individual, idiosyncratic expressions, which may manifest the personal insights of an author of genius without reflecting the culture of his or her readers very accurately. Real-life argumentation – records of significant historical conflicts or 'social dramas', barristers' arguments in court, even political speeches – may better embody the assumptions of the culture, since the protagonists are personally engaged in struggling over issues of substantial importance. Consequently they may be much more inclined to use every argument which they think will appeal to their hearers at a deeply persuasive level than the more disinterested author of a novel might be. Working with raw data of that kind may be very complex. A really adequate study of even one topic – the murder of Becket, the speeches of Cicero or Edmund Burke or Winston Churchill, the arguments about evolution of the lawyers in the Scopes trial – could easily become the life's work of a dedicated scholar. Therefore one who is trying to find root paradigms in such material may be best advised to look for them through reputable secondary sources, whose authors will have done most of the painstaking and time-consuming work of sifting through the primary source material. Some caveats should be observed when using secondary sources. The theoretical stance of the author is important, as well as his or her methodology. Many recent students of British culture, for example, have tended to represent a critical perspective, and sometimes a Marxist perspective, which may highlight evidence of some root paradigms while obscuring evidence of others. No matter what the reputation of the authors consulted, therefore, a systematic search for root paradigms in a given case should not rely on one author or even several who represent the same methodological, theoretical and ideological perspective, but should consult authorities on the same subject from a wide range of perspectives.

Richard Hoggart has specified many of the assumptions which guided the daily lives of working-class people of northern England in the mid-century.[15] His work provides a good starting point of a quest for the root paradigms of contemporary Britain. It is one of the hallmarks of root paradigms that under normal conditions they change very slowly – even though they may manifest themselves through more superficial forms which can change quite rapidly. Consequently, if we find any truly *root* paradigms in Hoggart's analysis it is likely that they remain operative today in the same cultural context. But sudden changes, though rare, can occur; so we should also look for recent indications of the paradigms' presence. Hoggart stresses the tendency of the working class to seek immediate pleasures – an evening at the pub or meat on the table – rather than saving for 'deferred gratification' or a 'rainy day' – opportunities or contingencies which may never be realized.[16] In itself, this is probably a result of centuries of oppression and insecurity, rather than an immediate manifestation of a root paradigm, but it ties in with other patterns of behaviour and valuation which begin to reveal the outlines of deeper assumptions. Pleasures may take the form of material symbols of gentility – the 'bit extra' that puts some interest and colour into life: lace curtains at the window, or a rose bush in the garden. Resigned to a humdrum existence, towards the bottom of the social ladder, working-class people make the best of it. But they also harbour a deep cynicism about the political power structure and tend to regard the aristocracy with derisive humour, rather than respect. Hoggart sees this disenchantment, reinforced by a conviction of individual equality and 'almost unlimited inner freedom', extending to values as well.[17] The virtue of tolerance decays into a refusal to recognize any differentiation. This tends to result in a loss of standards – 'It doesn't matter what y' believe so long as yer 'eart's in the right place.'[18]

This very brief dip into Hoggart's insightful book suggests the possible presence of several root paradigms. Ideas of freedom and equality came to the working class, perhaps, through a 'trickle down effect' from the education of the upper classes, with its stress on the Magna Carta, parliamentary government, etc., not to mention more than fifteen centuries of Christian doctrine containing many similarly 'subversive' egalitarian ideas. These resonated with the workers' own sense of being 'as good as anyone', but also of being unjustly treated in both workplace and daily life by a monolithic 'system' run by and for others. Although arising from political conditions, both the workers' sense of equality and the passivity with which they confronted the system might qualify as root paradigms. The system, itself, might almost qualify – at least among a large number of workers, who might tend to accept the monarchy, aristocracy and the capitalist class as 'givens' of society. They might be undesirable 'givens', with unpleasant influence on the workers themselves, but if an assumption exists that society cannot be different, then it comes close to being a root paradigm. Space does not permit the confirmation, here, from other research traditions and more recent sources, which I prescribed earlier; but our look at Hoggart's work will at least provide a suggestion of how to proceed.

In concluding, it seems necessary to mention the role of Christianity in establishing root paradigms in cultures which have long been influenced by it. Any effort to 'revivify' Christian values in a 'post-Christian' society, as Britain is often regarded, will have to take into account the influence the religion has had in shaping that society's culture. Cultural paradigms grow in many ways, but for them to become truly root paradigms a long period seems necessary – long enough, at least, that no one can remember a time, or even a tradition that there was a time, when they were not assumed to be 'the way things are'. Christian doctrine has created root paradigms in many countries where it has been rooted for a long time. It might take a thousand years or more for the cumulative effect of countless prayers, liturgies, gospel readings, hymns, etc., to insert themselves so deeply into a nation's psyche that they can truly be said to have established root paradigms. On the other hand, the final effect of such a long process, provided that it is relatively constant and comprehensive, is almost inevitable.[19] A corollary of that view is that a country which has once been thoroughly Christianized cannot quickly break with the paradigms Christianity has instilled in it. The quick restoration of religion in the republics of the former Soviet Union is a case in point. Perhaps one problem in Britain is that, although the Christian-derived paradigms may still be strong, they are often opposed and, in practice, smothered by a working-class tendency to identify the Church too much with the power structure, a structure which – as Hoggart pointed out – is in conflict with the working-class paradigms of equality, freedom and passive resistance to institutions which cannot be changed. This is only one small corner of the puzzle. Similar analyses of other areas of culture may yield more insights into the obstacles which hinder the broader acceptance of Christian values in the contemporary world.

NOTES

1   William E. Biernatzki, *Roots of Acceptance: the Intercultural Communication of Religious Meanings*, Rome: Gregorian University Press: 1991.
2   Ibid., pp. 47–67.
3   Ibid., pp. 69–83.
4   Ibid., pp. 85–103.
5   Victor Turner, *Dramas, Fields and Metaphors*, Ithaca: Cornell University Press: 1974, pp. 33–42.
6   Ibid., pp. 60–97.

7   Ibid., pp. 98–154.
8   Ruth Benedict, *Patterns of Culture*, Boston: Houghton Mifflin: 1934.
9   Biernatzki, op. cit., pp. 105–23.
10 Ibid., pp. 125–42.
11 Tamar Liebes & Elihu Katz, *The Export of Meaning: Cross Cultural Readings of Dallas*, New York: Oxford University Press: 1990.
12 Ibid., pp. 140–9.
13 Ibid., p. 142.
14 Dwight Conquergood, '"Is it Real?" Watching Television with Laotian Refugees', in *Directions* (programme on Communication and Development Studies, Northwestern University, Evanston, Illinois), Vol. 2 No. 2 (1986).
15 Richard Hoggart, *The Uses of Literacy: Aspects of Working Class Life with Special Reference to Publications and Entertainments*, London: Chatto and Windus: 1957.
16 Ibid., pp. 132–205.
17 Ibid., p. 176.
18 Ibid., p. 178.
19 See David Martin, *The Breaking of the Image: a Sociology of Christian Theory and Practice*, Oxford: Blackwell: 1980, p. 179.

11 The theology of the Nine O'Clock News

COLIN MORRIS

The most widely watched of all television programmes is the News, and the charge most commonly levelled at television news bulletins is that they are endless catalogues of death, destruction and disaster. It's as though television journalists stand the old saying 'No news is good news' on its head and operate on the assumption that no good news is news. What motivates television journalists, and what theological reflections are prompted by the news bulletins they construct? How do they decide in the first place what news is? The base line from which the whole process begins is that of a normal, happy, well-adjusted society – in theological terms, God's good creation, within which much human existence is routine and unremarkable. News is anything fresh and interesting which disturbs this state of affairs (the bad news) and reinforces it in striking ways (the good news).

The reiteration of normality, the assertion that all is well in God's creation, is not news – it is a basic assumption. If it were announced on the six o'clock news that the world is more or less round, this might seem a tedious statement of the obvious. If, however, a person of some consequence, a distinguished scientist and Fellow of the Royal Society not currently in a strait-jacket, were to declare that he had indisputable evidence that the world was flat, that would be news.

Hence, normality is not news, except in an abnormal context. The statement, 'There were no shootings, bombings, muggings or incidents of arson in Milton Keynes yesterday', though reassuring to the citizens of that town, holds little interest for the generality of viewers throughout the rest of the country. But substitute 'Beirut' for 'Milton Keynes' and you have news.

Normality is usually inferred from silence rather than marked by an item in a news bulletin. Some people are old enough to remember the awful ritual of First World War casualty lists in national newspapers. The non-inclusion of a name was a cause for celebration. It was reassurance by silence.

To start from the assumption of a good creation makes a preponderance of so-called bad news inevitable. The bad news, however scarifying, testifies ironically to the goodness and rationality that are inherent in the countless events which go unremarked. Once good news begins to dominate the bulletins, then what is going unnoticed is the normality of a sad, bad world.

Of course, it is open to the sceptic to stand this argument on its head and take as the base line an irrational, evil world. But here we are wrestling with a fundamental moral choice that antecedes any discussion about television news. We have to make a choice. Is evil a powerful intrusion in a good world, or goodness a heroic assertion of nobility against the odds in an evil world? We would be wise to make our minds up about that because, as someone has said, he who sits on the fence in the modern world tends to get electrocuted.

Within the limits of time and cost, the television journalist is preoccupied with a two-pronged question about me as the viewer. What has happened recently which could, however indirectly, affect my life and also intrigue me?

The important and the interesting are by no means the same. The passing of some Common Market regulation about Brussels sprout quotas may affect my life but certainly doesn't interest me to the point where I want a news bulletin to go on at length about it. On the other hand, the antics of a duck riding a skateboard may occupy my mind agreeably for a few moments without changing my life.

At this point we come up against two built-in biases, one in the television medium and the other in human nature. What sort of news both affects and intrigues me? Evil seems to have a decided advantage over good on both counts. The things that could do me and my little world harm are usually, though not always, more immediate, graphic and attention-grabbing than the things that might do me good. The effects of goodness are often subtle, longer-term and occur beyond the camera's range – in the human heart, for instance.

The teenage thug beating the old lady to death makes a gripping story which may also be unhealthily titillating. The saga of that youth's ultimate moral rehabilitation, should it happen, is likely to be long drawn out and outwardly uneventful, even boring. It's an important and cheering thing to happen, but is a process rather than an event: it's the difference between filming a tree growing – imperceptible action – and filming a tornado tearing that tree out of the ground – dramatic spectacle.

There are two properties of television as a medium which bear directly on this issue; the first is its crudity, the second, its vitality. Take the structural crudity of television. The combination of a small screen and a 625-line grid favours the obvious and larger than life: images that are clamant over those that are subtle; emphatic emotions rather than gentle ones. The hatreds and turmoils of human character in a flawed world are highly visible; the camera cannot miss them. Wholesome qualities such as love, kindness and goodness do not shout for attention. Much of their healing work is done in secret. And television cannot cope with secrets; indeed, by definition, broadcasting is in the business of abolishing secrets.

Or take the pagan vitality of television. It seems to generate a life and direction of its own, almost independent of human agency. There is an inherent excitement about the medium that heats the blood of all programme makers. Hence, they are tempted to accept the medium's bare existence as self-justifying – to assume that provided the technical questions are resolved, the value questions will take care of themselves.

Live moving pictures have the power to sever the nerve between sensation and meaning, event and context, emotional spasm and deep sentiment, fact and truth. Because of the immediacy and mobility of modern news gathering, television news editors are confronted in every shift with dozens of tricky judgements in this area which must be made there and then. In my experience, they usually make them with a sure-footedness and sensitivity for which they are rarely given credit, because the public does not see those horrendous pictures that never actually reach the screen.

The medium's built-in bias towards gloom and doom has to be wrestled with so that its visual enticements do not become self-justifying. But human nature also has its built-in bias which exacerbates the problem. Many people find something morbidly fascinating about violence in all its forms. It has an unhealthy hold on the public imagination. People want to know, even though they recoil in horror from what they see. They demand explicitness.

So there is something of the ghoul in most of us, but what about the bad news that cannot be blamed on human beings? The human will, even at its most corrupt, cannot be held accountable for those natural disasters and calamities which take up more and more bulletin time as the techniques of news gathering become swifter and more versatile. Earthquakes, floods, drought, volcanic eruptions and fires – all those catastrophes quaintly described in the old insurance policies as Acts of God – have an added dimension of sheer irrationality which makes many viewers uneasy.

That old question of natural theology – what evidence is there of God at work in his world? – is given a new urgency by what the ordinary viewers can see on their television screens. Simply by reporting disasters and confronting viewers with them in their own sitting rooms as they happen, television news is sharpening the key questions of Christian apologetic.

The cliché has it that the world sets the agenda for any intellectual encounter between the Christian faith and the natural order. Never has the state of the world been so nakedly exposed for all to see, sketching out in flame and smoke the urgent question for the Christian theologian, teacher and preacher, 'Well, what have you got to say about that?'

I doubt whether the faith of serious believers is totally undermined by shocking pictures of natural disasters. They have usually passed beyond any belief in a crudely interventionist God who punishes a recalcitrant world by thunderbolt and lightning flash. But the problem of convincing the generality of the public that God's love is at work in history is made more acute.

The Christian contends that evil in history is at all times fearsome but never overwhelming nor ultimately decisive. And the television news bulletin seems to confirm that view. For if it makes us witnesses of many of the world's agonies, it also gives us glimpses of its glories. The news that exposes us to wounds being inflicted also shows them being bound up. We see not just parched deserts being endured but also cups of water being proffered. Pictures that make us shudder at natural calamity sometimes humble us before the sheer goodness and self-sacrifice of the human response.

We rarely see raw evil depicted in television news, evil out of control, on the rampage. The context is invariably one of challenge and response – gruesome road accident *and* ambulance crews treating casualties; plane crash *and* rescue workers painstakingly picking their way through the wreckage; distraught relatives of violence victims *and* friends and neighbours comforting them.

That parable Jesus told about the wheat and the weeds is bang up to the minute. Wheat and weeds, symbolizing good and evil, grow together in a field, inextricable, nurtured by the same sun, watered by the same rain, woven together to the point where you cannot pick up a handful of one without strands of the other being included. Until the harvest, that is. The television news bulletin is a vivid commentary on that parable – morally ambiguous life in history's field this side of the harvest.

In a curious way, although television news depicts evil extensively, it also puts it in its place, subdues it within a fixed time-frame as though to say: 'We are not going to allow ourselves to be overwhelmed by this awful carry-on in the world. We mark it and feel its impact, but we will not become obsessed by it.'

This unwillingness to permit the grisly side of life to dominate the rest does not make the reality any easier to bear for those enduring it, but it does offer reassurance to the others. The strict time-discipline of the television news signifies the truth that we may have to peep over the edge into the black chasm from which human wickedness and natural calamity bubble up, but we don't have to make a full-time career of it, like witches round a perpetually simmering cauldron. Instead we shall make a cup of tea and get on with the business of normal living.

Such an attitude could be called purblind complacency or sheer escapism, but that is the way human beings have survived and kept their sanity from the dawn of history – by averting their eyes from the surrounding darkness and concentrating on the cheerful flames of the fire.

And there is this much to be said about the rigorous view of life we derive from television news bulletins. At least we know that what we have seen is the sum of the most significant things that might do harm to us and to our personal world. We can be reasonably sure that no greater catastrophe is being kept hidden from us because television news editors have decided we haven't the stomach for it.

Should viewers get the idea in their heads that, for whatever sinister or compassionate motives, unpalatable truths are being left out of bulletins, then the credibility of television news as a reliable information service would be fatally undermined. One conviction that reputable television journalists have burned into their souls is this: as a general rule items should never be left out of a news bulletin because of the effect they might have on those at the receiving end.

This was the ground over which the 'other battle' of the Falklands raged. The BBC and ITN came under heavy fire from politicians for showing footage of the suffering of British service men and women which was judged to be sapping of the national morale. But another of the parables of Jesus is relevant here – the one about the house being swept clean of one devil and left empty to be invaded by seven more. The suppression of bad news does not make the public more prone to think happy thoughts. They don't believe they are any safer in an Eden where bird songs are magnified in order to drown out the serpent's hiss. Human curiosity, like nature, abhors a vacuum; in the absence of hard intelligence it will be filled with rumour, speculation and all the fevered imaginings of people's worst fears.

It cannot be denied that the world is a saner, happier, more law-abiding place than a casual glance at a television news bulletin might suggest. But that is a case the television output as a whole must argue. A twenty-minute news bulletin cannot be expected to offer a comprehensive account of the state of the world.

We are unfair to television journalists when we load on them the whole burden of proving that life is worth living, and then give them only thirty minutes three times a day to do it. Indeed, when journalists ill-advisedly assume the role of Cheerful Chappies and start adding a statutory proportion of happy stories to their bulletins for therapeutic reasons, we just don't believe them. 'Must be short of news tonight!', we snort, as we watch a budgerigar riding a miniature bicycle along a clothes line or listen to the shock-horror disclosure that Princess Diana has changed her hair stylist.

Viewers are not convinced by Mickey Mouse stories planted in the news to raise their spirits, because they know from personal experience that whatever the theologians may say about the world being a good creation, it's a deadly dangerous place through which to negotiate one's way.

Indeed, the public's lust for news originates in a sense of psychic insecurity. Our forebears probably felt more at home in the world than we do, because it was a much more circumscribed cosmos than ours. Unless they were unlucky enough to be living in the eye of the hurricane, happenings way beyond the parish boundary were already merging into history by the time they heard of them. Now, to paraphrase John Wesley's words, the whole world is our parish. No part of it is truly remote as the intercontinental ballistic missile flies or the New York stock exchange fluctuates or the Russian grain harvest flourishes or fails. Cast across our lives is a great spider's web of interlocking forces held in delicate equilibrium – a balance capable of being disrupted at any moment.

This may always have been the case, but now we *know* it, almost instantaneously. The speed of modern communication, besides being a most powerful engine of cultural and social change, also keep us in a state of psychic turmoil. We need to be assured, frequently, that things are holding together in those parts of the big world that could affect our little world. So let's put the news on.

And yet there's a credit side to all this. We viewers are dignified by being invited to share the concerns of a big world – a compliment we might prefer to shrug off, given our natural insularity. When I proposed earlier that the theme of the news is things which might affect me and my little world, I was giving television journalists less than their due. They seek to push back the frontiers of that little world. Because of their efforts, it is a bigger, wider world that bursts into my sitting-room.

Those who construct television news bulletins know what will directly concern and intrigue me. And they know this, not just because they are clever technicians but because they share the same environment. They too are workers, parents, city dwellers fearful of mugging, car drivers nervous about motorway madness, citizens of the nuclear age living in a prime target, threatened by unemployment, worried about the quality of health care or the standard of public education.

Television journalists have little difficulty in engaging with me at the point of my primary concerns. But they also try to do something much harder and confront me with the answers to questions I am not asking. This is the nature of all journalism, of course. Journalists cannot afford to be insular; they scan a more expansive horizon than mine, have a wider range of concerns, trace the complex filaments of my life away into the distance, see connections between this and that which would never occur to me. It's a hit-and-miss business for them. If they miss, the bulletin was a bore, a switch-off, full of foreign stories of no possible interest.

If they hit the mark, I become just a tiny bit more of a citizen of the world than I was before.

I suppose it all boils down to the question: can we trust the television journalists? You will gather that I have much respect for them. Their strengths and weaknesses have been the subject of sustained academic analysis and public debate. The more perceptive of them genially concede the predispositions of their trade, some of which I've already mentioned – the tendency to follow the visual imperative, letting the quality of the pictures determine the worth of the story; the addiction to the cult of the 'new' for its own sake; the assumption that they can record the dilemmas, conflicts and divisions of society without sharing them, as though the television newsroom were a demilitarized zone rather than one more battle-ground; their under-estimation of the extent to which the things which belong to their humanness – matters of culture, education, class and sex – colour their editorial judgements.

All this is just saying that, like the rest of us, journalists are miserable sinners operating in a morally ambiguous world, trying to do the impossible: tell the precise truth using very imprecise tools. Television news certainly offers us refracted images of the world. But then, every representation of the truth has a statutory proportion of distortion in it. No one knows this better than the theologian, pledged to mediate mysterious reality by way of the crude and inexact disciplines of language.

In one of his letters, Paul calls Christians 'true deceivers'. Presumably he meant that, in a warped world, exact truth can only be expressed through symbols which involve a certain degree of deception – as when an artist uses perspective to suggest that parallel rows of houses meet at the horizon. It is deception in the interests of the truth, sometimes at the expense of literal fact.

In this sense, television journalists have no option but to be 'true deceivers'. They are trying to make sense of experience, and if experience were transparent in meaning and could be dissolved without remainder in images and words, we would be infallible. Reflection, judgement, opinion would become redundant human preoccupations. So would faith, since it makes no sense to take someone or something on trust when we *know* beyond a shadow of a doubt. It is the metaphysical wilderness between symbol and reality that all purveyors of truth, whether theologians or journalists, are doomed to wander.

In the Book of Genesis, it is God who brings order out of chaos; in the world of the mass media, it is these true deceivers, television news editors. They subdue into harmony a mountain of telex print-outs, miles of video tape and a pandemonium of ringing telephones. They organize into a coherent picture a riot of impressions, a chaos of events, a bedlam of attitudes and opinions that would otherwise have us scurrying to the hills in a panic. They offer us a view of the world we can live with.

And this is a world-view that does not emerge from endless reflection in the groves of Academe. Aristotle had no six o'clock deadline to meet. Journalists have to put their version of events together at lightning speed, in a welter of almost instantaneous judgements. And I want to suggest in all seriousness that this work of putting a frame round our experience is a religious service in the strictest meaning of the word. For is not the word 'religion' derived from the Latin root, 'religiare', to tie together or to bind? And is not this what the television journalist does when he or she knits together verbal and visual symbols into some semblance of reality?

This television version of reality is distorted, incomplete and never, thank God, beyond challenge, for in a democracy no single account of the truth is sovereign. Television journalists sell their wares in a public market place, with rival stall-holders on all sides bellowing their competing versions. No single source of news has exclusive access to the public ear and eye, though some are more seductive than others. There is balancing power in the multiplicity of news media, in competing channels and even in the variety of perceptions on offer within the same broadcasting organization.

Now, Christians should be accustomed to this synoptic or summary view of the truth. That's after all why we call the first three gospels synoptic, because they offer parallel but by no means identical accounts of the same story.

In one of his regular columns for the *Daily News*, long before the birth of broadcasting, G. K. Chesterton wrote: 'The pedantic decisions and definable readjustments of man may be found in scrolls and statute books and scriptures; but man's basic assumptions and everlasting energies are to be found in penny dreadfuls and halfpenny novelettes.' He might allow me to amplify the quotation by adding that it is from popular journalism, especially in its most vivid, pictorial forms, that believers can quarry a rich seam of parable, discover the raw stuff of their theologizing, and receive a salutary jolt to any sentimental half-baked notions of how God deals with the world.

It is the news which drives most believers, with particular urgency, to penitence and intercession, because it thrusts at them in stark and up-to-the-minute form the perennial questions about meaning, destiny and purpose. That's just a pompous way of saying that the news is the first rough draft of history, and the believer has the task of trying to make sense of it.

12 Ill news comes often on the back of worse

JOHN ELDRIDGE

Living by proxy in the half light,
Items of news slip by like flakes of food in a fish tank.
Between the un-seating of a royal jockey
And the bland insincerities of talking heads
We see, for an instant, the awkward dead
Heaped carelessly at the corner of a street
Like brushwood piled for burning.
This wood is green, unsuitable for firing.
Sap still comes from the stricken limbs of striplings,
Broken boys and girls
With faces made anonymous by death.
Only a tear in the knee of a pair of jeans,
A shoeless foot unnaturally bent,
A rucked up sweat shirt revealing pitiful flesh,
Reminds us that they once possessed a singularity
Beyond the comprehension of the killers
Who stare at the camera lens with eyes
As blank as bottle tops.

'An Item of News', Ewan MacColl

When we in the Glasgow University Media Group (GUMG) called our first three books on television news *Bad News* (1975), *More Bad News* (1980) and *Really Bad News* (1982), we were, of course, being a touch mischievous. The binary contrast good news/bad news is deeply embedded in our history and culture. We are all familiar with the injunction not to blame the messenger for the bad news. But in an age of mass media the messengers are typically contracted to powerful institutions in press and broadcasting. The stories they tell and the how, when, where and why of the telling are an important part of our media culture. In scrutinizing those stories, which are communicated to us day by day, we begin to learn about news values. The processes of creating, transmitting and receiving messages are not just a secondary feature in modern society, they are part of the warp and woof of it. What takes place in and through these processes is, therefore, not simply a comment on social reality but part of it.

The case of television news – a specific form of mass communication – was and remains an important site of study. The reason for this is that one particular value is formally required from news broadcasts: impartiality. Clearly this is different from the press, where editorializing is built into the activity. Impartiality, by contrast, is typically seen as the cornerstone of good public-service broadcasting, so far as news is concerned. The rationale for this is to resist the capture of this news medium by a particular interest group, so that it will not be regarded as partisan or propagandist. This, indeed, is seen both as the guarantee of its reliability and trustworthiness and also the source of its authority and objectivity.

However, I want to argue that the concept of impartiality is inherently problematic. Indeed, however worthy their motives, those who seek to base their claim to credibility by appeal to the concept of impartiality will constantly find themselves immersed in challenges and attacks. Seasoned broadcasters know standard ripostes to some of this: we know our own business and should be left to get on with it; or, since we are attacked from all sides we have got it just about right. Moreover, to replace impartial, objective news with partial and subjective news would surely be to lose one's credibility at a stroke. I want to suggest that there is another way of coming at this which dissolves a spurious dichotomy.

What does adherence to the concept of impartiality mean in practice? Let us recall the way this impinged on John Reith (later Lord Reith) in the early pre-television days of the BBC. In his capacity as first director-general of the BBC he promoted the view that broadcasting could help to develop an informed and enlightened opinion on the issues of the day. His position, while clearly paternalist, was one which explicitly resisted the idea that the BBC was there simply to relay the instructions and views of the government of the day. That was precisely why he favoured the setting up of a public corporation rather than have it working under the aegis of a government department. He wanted the BBC to be free from state interference and political interference. But he also wanted it not to be subject to the normal commercial pressures. Within such a space and within these institutional arrangements public-service broadcasting could, he believed, flourish. So it was, he thought, that a public corporation could serve the public interest with the state's role being confined to the operation of the licensing system. In this regard the public interest was seen as the guiding consideration in contradistinction to private interests.

But from the beginning the worm was in the apple. The BBC was not immune from political pressure as *The Reith Diaries* make clear. In time of controversy and political conflict this is particularly so. At the time of the 1926 General Strike, Reith records that the government was going to set up its own newspaper, the *British Gazette*, edited from the War Office. According to Reith, the editor expected to see the BBC news as an offshoot of that, which Reith characteristically refused to accept. An argument developed within the Cabinet with Winston Churchill insisting that the instrument of radio should be used to the best possible advantage by the government. This view did not prevail in straightforward propagandist terms. Reith's diary entry for 11 May shows a more subtle policy:

> The Cabinet were to make a decision at long last about the BBC. Davidson was going to it. I primed him up with all the arguments and he came to see me at 7.15. As he was smiling broadly I knew it was all right. The decision was not a definite one, but at any rate we are not going to be commandeered. The Cabinet decision is really a negative one. They want to be able to say that they did not commandeer us, but they know that they can trust us not to be really impartial. Davidson came around again at 9.15 and we were supposed to draft a notice defining the BBC position. I wanted the inconsistencies in our acts so far squared up, setting us right with the other side. Davidson, however, thought the Cabinet would only agree to a statement that we could do nothing to help the Strike since it had been declared illegal. This does not seem to me to be straight.[1]

As Reith pointed out, the BBC was in a very awkward position. He was clear that to turn the BBC into a propaganda arm of the government would have destroyed its credibility, and even more so if it had been commandeered. In seeking to resist that he tried in vain to square the circle. His declared sense of loyalty to the Prime Minister cut across his uneasiness that impartiality was a cloak for supporting the government's position − at the very least by keeping other views off the air. What Reith had to come to terms with, albeit with a bad conscience, were the interests of the state in a moment of crisis. The decision on the part of the government as to how to play it was a matter of strategy and tactics.

What does happen when events that take place in the world are conflict-riven and controversial as so many are? We are given in the press and in broadcasting news stories about them. Let us remember that the journalists telling these stories on television share an occupational background with press journalists: they may even move from one medium to another. They attend the same press conferences and relate to one another's output. What emerges to count as the news of the day is itself a cultural construct. In the case of television news a whole range of professional conventions in the presentation operate. These are not unchangeable, as archive film of old news programmes show, but there are established continuities. Let us recall some: the use of music and established iconic forms at the beginning and end of bulletins; the newscaster(s) as providing continuity (sometimes bringing to the programme their own celebrity status); the use of film to delineate the event or graphics to reference it; the use of correspondents to report, describe, interview and interpret what is going on; the use of experts to comment (which nowadays may incorporate the reporter: 'our Economics/Political editor, Peter Jay/John Cole'); the boundary markers – headlines and devices for turning from one item to the next; and the overall 'ordered' structure of the news bulletin.

These activities, complex though they are in terms of organization and technology and often taking place with considerable time constraints, are grounded in professional routines and practices. Indeed, without such constitutive rules by which news of the world can be made meaningful to us – organized, encoded, framed – the daily production of news would be impossible. This output, its nature and significance, not least in relation to the values of impartiality and objectivity is what we have attempted to examine in the *Bad News* and later studies. An important part of the research strategy was to consider, through quantitative and qualitative analysis, what these routines and practices produced to make up the product we know as television news and, more particularly, to look at the treatment of issues which were socially or politically divisive such as the state of the economy, industrial conflict or questions of defence and disarmament.

In 1975, with a Labour government in power, we showed how television newsrooms adopted a number of strategies for concretizing and dealing with economic affairs. Central to this was a constant and ongoing assessment of the government's agreements with the trade-union movement known, in the parlance of the time, as the Social Contract. This was an attempt by the government to set out guidelines for collective bargaining in the period following the previous Conservative administration's attempts to impose an incomes policy. Not only did this concept provide the thematic frame within which stories about the economy were covered, but the containment of wages was presented as the main instrument for the control of inflation. Thus many of the industry wage agreements signed during the first half of 1975 were reported on the news in terms of whether they were within or without the terms of the Social Contract. In 1992 we do not routinely hear about wage settlements but in 1975 all the major settlements were reported within this frame. The identification of these matters as newsworthy is an interesting indicator of a particular social and political climate but it also tended to be from a definite perspective. Whether one agreed with that perspective or not, it was not value-free.

Take for example the case of a wage negotiation between the miners and the National Coal Board. As the reports of the negotiations developed we had the BBC's industrial news reporter telling us that the deal was outside the Social Contract, even though the parties concerned said it was within the terms. And, at the end, the BBC newscaster summed up the position: 'The miners through their negotiators put the Coal Board out of its misery this week by accepting a large pay offer. After some haggling the offer crept pound by pound to the miners' own demands.' (BBC2, 18.50, 15 March 1975.) Employers offered, workers demanded. The employers were put out of their *misery*. The pay offer was a *large* one. The story was told in a particular way. The pay negotiations were presented in the language of battle and as an 'acid test' for the Social Contract. Through the narrative we learn more about the journalists' assumptions about an agreement which saw the advent of a £3,000-a-year basic rate for some miners and £41 a week for surface workers. Analysis of the narrative showed that while some of the participants in the negotiations were able to comment, explain and justify, this was typically within highly structured conventions of interviewing. There were, moreover, more general assumptions about the role of trade unions and the nature of the economic crisis. Thus within the overall frame of the Social Contract was a series of strike stories. The connecting links were about workers and trade unions who were causing inflation, whose disruptive activities were the cause of our economic ills and therefore against the national interest.

The point to be made about this is that news is from a distinct perspective. In so far as this was the dominant tendency in the coverage of industrial and economic questions, not only did it represent a particular ideological view, but also effectively excluded other kinds of explanations – those which had to do with concerns about investment, the role of management, education, training and the structural problems of the economy in a world context, after the oil crisis of the early seventies. Whatever our opinions of these stories they are restricted accounts, given that other accounts were publicly available. In other words our analysis concluded that news accounts were limited and narrow. Such restricted news was, we said, bad news. Not only did it present stories within a dominant interpretative framework, but it did so from a position that laid claim to impartiality.

In his review of *More Bad News*, Raymond Williams commented:

> Let us face it then: the news has been very bad lately. But it is very difficult to be sure how much of this badness has been in the events themselves, and how much in their intense and relentless interpretation by the authorities: a one-sided polemic which I cannot remember being at this pitch since the late Forties ... To be sure, we cannot draw any firm line between events and their presentation. A very large number of the events now presented are in fact interpretations, by a small group of highly privileged voices, directly transmitted or read out by hired celebrities. The privilege of such voices would matter less if it were not also, in the leading cases, the privilege of command of men and resources.[2]

He goes on to point out that as events become the subject of news reports, even when the evidence for their occurrence has been reliably tested, long-standing problems of narration remain, including the identity of the narrator, his authority, point of view, assumed relationship to audience and the possible wider purposes in selecting and narrating the events in the way chosen. In everyday encounters when we hear stories we do learn to ask such questions. 'Yet it seems that we have only to ask them about a broadcasting service or a newspaper to produce outraged cries about an assault on professional competence and independence, or to provoke dark hints, which at least sometimes are surely projections, about a conspiracy to interfere with freedom of news and indeed to manipulate or censor it.'[3]

There are, I think, a number of ways in which the media critic can respond to the media professionals who manifest such concerns. What can we reasonably expect from a television news service in a society which embraces democratic ideals? We expect the information to be reliable and accurate. This, after all, is the *sine qua non* of professional journalism and the touchstone of its integrity. At the simplest level, when the football results are given we expect them to be accurate and have good reason to think that they are. They can be corroborated by many witnesses, whatever their view of the outcome. Any mistake in conveying the results can be quickly corrected. It is helpful to take a simple example since its reminds us that issues of truth are involved. So while, for reasons already touched upon, objectivity in news narratives is problematical, the alternative is not an undisciplined subjectivity where anything goes and one account is as good or as bad as another. Why these facts should be reported raises quite other questions of their presumed significance to the audience. And once these facts become embedded in accounts of matches then we are into a narrative which characteristically will have its judgements, interpretations and sometimes speculation.

If, as the adage has it, journalism is the first draft of history, we can appreciate that, as with historical study itself, selection and interpretation of facts will take place and we are not dealing with unassailable facts marshalled incontrovertibly together but with provisional accounts. Indeed, the epistemological basis on which these accounts rest can vary. We, as readers, hearers or viewers, will not necessarily be aware of this.

In their paper, 'Accidental News: the Great Oil Spill'[4] Molotch and Lester describe how President Nixon visited the beach at Santa Barbara in January 1969 and stated that it had recovered from a massive oil spill. This was duly reported in the national media of the USA despite the fact that there was plenty of evidence, which the journalists could see and smell, that it was not so. In their view this was an example of professional news services being subordinate to political interests. If they are correct then this has the character of cover-up. Unless we are there and have direct experience of that situation – we can see and smell the oil slick – or unless someone, as it were, breaks cover or leaks an alternative version, we have no independent way of evaluating that story.

The above example, if typical, would fit in with a conspiracy view of the media – that they operate as servants of the powerful. As a general theory of the role of the media I think this is unconvincing. But it does draw our attention to the issue of verification. For example, in the Falklands War, ITN lunchtime news showed some film taken by an Argentinian amateur cameraman. The defence correspondent worked on the assumption that all the film was taken on 1 May, when, according to the Ministry of Defence, no British planes were lost. This is what he said:

> But the attack had been concentrated on the airfield [i.e. Port Stanley] where it is assumed these pictures of wreckage were taken. This roundel is not in the colours carried by the British Harriers and may have come from an Argentine plane destroyed on the ground. The variety and totality of wreckage scattered around the airfield suggest British reports of inflicting severe damage to aircraft and military equipment were true. One piece of wreckage which had the word 'Harrier' on it was unidentifiable. Britain says she lost no aircraft during this raid though one Harrier was shot down three days later near the other airport at Goose Green. These would seem to be aircraft wheels, although it's not yet clear what type of plane they came from.[5]

The film actually showed the colours of the roundel which were unmistakeably British, the unique undercarriage design of the Harrier, its name – Harrier – and its serial number. Because the correspondent believed it was Port Stanley and not Goose Green, he is unable to accept this evidence and actually uses British wreckage to stress the success of British bombing! Now this was not a cover up. It was a mistake. Indeed, although there was no apology for it, the evening news used the same film with the following commentary:

> The cameraman was also taken to the Goose Green air-strip where a British Harrier jet was shot down last

Tuesday. The Royal Navy roundel showed through the film of paint.[6]

What was happening? It was difficult to get news let alone film out of the Falklands and there was in practice heavy reliance on Ministry of Defence briefings. They had been stressing the success of the bombing raids on Port Stanley airport. Part of the film ITN received was of Port Stanley and part of Goose Green. Given the success theme, the correspondent cannot believe the evidence before him and actually turns a failure into a success. Ironically, the success theme about the bombing of Port Stanley was to bring other news reporting problems to the surface. The Ministry of Defence stated that the bombing on 1 May had severely cratered the runway at the airport. BBC and ITN news embraced this account. ITN reported: 'The Vulcan's task was to pockmark the runway and it did it with 1000lb bombs, ten tons of explosives.'[7] This was accompanied by a graphic of the runway with the pockmarks circled along the length of it. Yet eventually this was shown to be inaccurate. Gradually another story emerges that the airport was still operational. It is not a simple matter of cover-up news. In *War and Peace News* we came to the following conclusion:

> Once having established a view of the Port Stanley raids – a destroyed runway and cut-off garrison – the news found it difficult to go beyond it. New facts and information were fitted into this framework. The constraint seemed to emanate from the need for broadcasters to maintain their image as purveyors of reliable, balanced and objective information. Journalists found it difficult to admit they had made mistakes. Following the cease-fire, TV news expressed surprise concerning the condition of the airfield. The subject was not considered in any detail. In Task Force South, a BBC production in August, viewers were finally told what British troops had heard before the final push on Port Stanley. In it we see shots of a briefing for troops. A soldier comments: 'The RAF missed the fucking runway ... bombs all around it but there are thirteen aircraft, some of which are definitely Pucara, parked on the aprons around Stanley airfield. There's also another report that they have managed to reinforce themselves from the mainland.' (BBC 1, 12.8.82.) This piece of film was absent from the pictures of the advances on Stanley which were first shown on British TV on 25 June.[8] (GUMG 1985, p. 91)

Our general conclusion about television news coverage of the Falklands War was that both BBC and ITN kept close to official sources. Where, we may ask, does impartiality figure in this? In some respects we get a re-run of the Reith difficulty, discussed earlier. So, the director-general of the BBC told an internal meeting of the News and Current Affairs Committee that he anticipated the BBC would come under pressure, as it had during the Suez crisis to 'conform to the national interest'. He accepted that there was a legitimate point in this but the difficulty was to define precisely what 'the national interest' was. Clearly, he argued, the BBC should be careful not to do anything to imperil military operations or diplomatic negotiations, but it should report accurately and faithfully the arguments arising within British society at all levels. This in practice did not happen. The director-general's remarks were made at the beginning of April; by 11 May the BBC's political editor was telling the committee that 'the BBC was most vulnerable to criticism over its limited coverage of the internal debate in the country, though many Tories would regard any coverage of this as pure speculation because the dissenting views were being kept so private.' Meanwhile another senior broadcaster 'reminded the meeting that the BBC was the *British* Broadcasting Corporation [italics in original]. It was now clear that a large section of the public shared this view and he believed it was an unnecessary irritation to stick to the detached style.'

Nevertheless, as has been well documented, the Tory government was very critical of the BBC's coverage of the war.[9] BBC's *Newsnight* programme was criticized for giving the appearance of being too detached and an episode of the BBC's flagship current-affairs programme, *Panorama*, was the subject of heavy criticism from sections of the Conservative Party. This particular programme, broadcast on 10 May 1982, included some dissenting views on government policy, alongside those of Cecil Parkinson, a member of the War Cabinet. Conservative MPs complained that some of the programmes on the BBC appeared to give the impression of being pro-Argentinian and anti-British, while others appeared to suggest that this was an issue over which the BBC could remain loftily neutral. A senior Conservative, Sally Oppenheimer, referred next day at Prime Minister's Question Time in the House of Commons, to the *Panorama* programme as 'an odious, subversive travesty in which Michael Cockrell and other BBC reporters dishonoured the right to freedom of speech in this country'. In her reply, the Prime Minister indicated that she shared the concern that had been expressed. She continued:

> I know how strongly many people feel that the case for our country is not being put with sufficient vigour on certain – I do not say all – BBC programmes. The Chairman of the BBC has assured us, and has said in vigorous terms, that the BBC is not neutral on this point, and I hope his words will be heeded by the many who have responsibilities for standing up for our task force, our boys, our people and the cause of democracy.

The difference between this situation and the Reith episode over the General Strike was that it was much more exposed to public view. The *Panorama* programme was called 'Traitorama' by the *Sun* newspaper (echoing some of the comments in the House of Commons). After a stormy meeting between the chairman and director-general of the BBC and the backbench media committee of the BBC, Alasdair Milne (then director-general) told the *London Standard* in an interview on 12 May 1982:

> The notion that we are traitors is outrageous. There is no one in the BBC who does not agree that the Argentinians committed aggression. But this is not total war. One day we will be negotiating with the enemy so we must try to understand them. We at the BBC have re-examined our broad policy and will not change it. We have no sense of guilt or failure.

What was also significant about this episode was the strength of feeling that was generated and how specifically government hostility was directed at the BBC. In *The Fog of War*, Mercer, Mungham and Williams cite a member of the War Cabinet who told them:

> At a war cabinet meeting there was a general hate of the BBC whom we reckoned to be biased, and pro-ITN whom we reckoned were doing much better. One minister said: 'Well, you know we give all this information to the bloody BBC and what do they do with it? We don't help ITN enough and we ought to help ITN more.'[10]

What emerges from all this is not a conspiracy theory of the media but rather the consequences of a professional set of practices which, while valuing the principle of independence, relies heavily upon official sources for its news. In some respects the very mark of its professionalism is that it has access to these sources. The controversy over the *Panorama* programme was a sharp reminder of the tight limits on dissent that were regarded as permissible in time of crisis, which the Falklands conflict undoubtedly was. It was, after all, the government that had left the Falklands undefended in the first place and it was in jeopardy of falling as a result.

The government's hostility to the BBC was to have further ramifications. When the United States bombed Libya in April 1986, Norman Tebbitt, then Chairman of the Conservative Party, produced a report of the coverage comparing the BBC unfavourably with ITN.[11] He accused the BBC of carrying Libyan propaganda uncritically. In his letter to the BBC accompanying the report he questioned 'whether an increasingly confrontational style of BBC news coverage is appropriate for a public-service broadcasting system, funded by the taxpayer, required to emphasize impartiality, objectivity and factual reporting'. The BBC offered its own detailed reply. Nevertheless, Alasdair Milne had been forced to resign as director-general by the end of 1987 by a board of governors that had become increasingly politicized. Before his successor was appointed the offices of BBC Glasgow were subjected to a police raid. The government was unhappy with two programmes prepared by the journalist Duncan Campbell in a six-part series entitled *Secret Society*. One of these was on the procedures surrounding the financing of the Zircon satellite, which Campbell argued had been irregular; the other was on the operation of secret Cabinet committees, which, among other things, produced evidence of the government's campaign against the peace movement in 1982 – 3. No charges or arrests were made but the pressure on programme producers and journalists was clear enough. The Zircon programme was eventually screened and the Cabinet programme re-made for Channel 4. This is a sharp reminder that those in positions of power will certainly make attempts to control the media, but the concern for independence is a journalistic value that is genuinely striven for and embraced by many journalists, even while they are aware that they can sometimes be restricted, censored and constrained by the powerful.

But impartiality as a journalistic value becomes almost a will-o'-the-wisp phenomenon: now you see it, now you don't. In time of war or national crisis the governmental concern with broadcast (and other) news is not 'are you impartial?' but 'which side are you on?' If, in other instances, the broadcasters say we cannot be impartial about apartheid, they will find themselves criticized from the right. Norman Tebbit, for example, in the report on the Libyan coverage, took a side-swipe at the BBC, because its assistant director-general had said that they could not be impartial over apartheid. The report stated that this was in breach of the BBC's constitutional duty. (Conservative Party Central Office, 1986, p. 12). This from the same Norman Tebbit who, in an Open University programme on the media, was to state that impartiality was very difficult and that the problem was of balance rather than impartiality. This, he pointed out, was a matter of judgment in practice.[12]

In the end, if we take account of the conditions under which news is gathered, it is difficult to apply concepts of objectivity or impartiality to it. The question of accuracy is and will remain a bedrock of credibility and trustworthiness. However, where there are grounds for doubt or uncertainty on factual accuracy, this needs to be indicated. In the Gulf War, Martin Fletcher of NBC spoke from Israel on the second night. Wearing a gas-mask he reported that Israel had been hit with a chemical weapon. This was relayed on BBC news where the source for the story was claimed to be NBC's monitoring of police radios in Tel Aviv. However, the BBC's veteran reporter in Washington, Charles Wheeler, urged caution: 'Everybody here's getting in a dreadful panic.' As the programme went on, more uncertainty about the missile attack seeped through. Towards the end of the bulletin we hear this exchange:

> Martyn Lewis: So that report from NBC could well be wrong?
> Charles Wheeler: A lot of reports could well be wrong.

It is precisely that kind of scepticism that is important and in my view is a more effective way to judge the quality of news reports than an appeal to impartiality. After that we can ask questions about the framework within which the facts are presented. To understand that these frameworks are not determined by the events themselves is the beginning of wisdom and incidentally provides a solid reason for media studies. The general point has been nicely made by Robert Manoff:

> Narratives are organizations of experience. They bring order to events by making them something that can be told about; they have power because they make the world make sense. The sense

they make, however, is conventional. No story is the inevitable product of the event it reports; no event dictates its own narrative form. News occurs at the conjunction of events and texts, and while events create the story, the story also creates the event. The narrative choice made by the journalist is therefore not a free choice. It is guided by the appearance which reality has assumed for him, by institutions and routines, by conventions that shape his perceptions and that provide the formal repertory for presenting them. It is the interaction of these forces that produces the news, and it is their relationship that determines its diversity or uniformity.[13]

So I want to suggest that television news, like other journalism, occupies a space that is constantly contested, which is subject to organizational and technological restructuring, to economic, cultural and political constraints, to commercial pressures and to changing professional practices. The changing contours of this space can lead to different patterns of domination and agenda-setting and to different degrees of openness and closure, in terms of access, patterns of ownership, available genres, types of disclosure and range of opinions represented. Although it is intrinsically difficult to theorize about the complexities which are implied in this formulation, the implications of the empirical outcomes of the struggle over this terrain are crucial for the ways in which they help or hinder the democratic process. For this reason journalists and their audiences when they first hear news should always ask the irreverent question: 'says who?' This may be bad news for the official managers of society, but it will be good news for democracy.

NOTES

1   Lord Reith, *The Reith Diaries*, edited by C. Stuart, London: Collins: 1975, p. 96.
2   Raymond Williams, 'Isn't the News Terrible?', in Raymond Williams, *What I Came to Say*, London: Hutchinson: 1980, p. 114.
3   Ibid., p. 115.
4   Harvey L. Molotch and Marilyn Lester, 'Accidental News: the Great Oil Spill', *American Journal of Sociology*, vol. 81 (1975), pp. 235–60.
5   ITN Lunchtime News, 12.00, 9.5.82.

6   ITN News, 18.50, 9.5.82.
7   ITN News, 21.55, 1.5.82.
8   Glasgow University Media Group, *War and Peace News*, Milton Keynes: Open University Press: 1985, p. 91.
9   See, for example, Glasgow University Media Group, op. cit.; Robert Harris, *Gotcha! The Media, the Government and the Falklands Crisis*, London: Faber: 1983; Derrik Mercer, Geoff Mungham and Kevin Williams, *The Fog of War*, London: Heinemann: 1987.
10 Mercer, Mungham and Williams, op. cit., p. 134.
11 Conservative Party Central Office, *The American Raid on Libya: a Comparative Analysis of its Treatment on the BBC 9.00 O'Clock News and ITN News at Ten*, 1986.
12 Open University programme D103, *Society and the Social Sciences*.
13 Robert Carl Manoff, 'Writing the News (by Telling the "Story")', in Robert Carl Manoff and Michael Schudson (eds.), *Reading the News*, New York: Pantheon: 1986, pp. 228–9.

13 An Islamic perspective on the news

S. A. SCHLEIFER

In Islam the word is paramount.

It is not so much that Islam is iconoclastic, simply that its icons, its representations of the sacred inner essence of all things, are aural rather than visual. The calligraphy that adorns traditional mosques, tombs, schools and homes is not just some sort of alternative decorative motif in a religious culture that rejected the medium of figurative art. On the contrary, these calligraphies depict words that are the aural components of The Word. So too the calligraphic representation of whole sentences from the Qur'ān (again a dominant motif in public and private buildings) serve to represent God. The words contain The Word.

The principle of the word as Word (i.e. sacred calligraphy as aural icon) informs this important medium of Islamic expression. The most favoured Qur'ānic passages, whether for recitation or calligraphy, are invariably the more mystical passages in which the names of God figure with such intensity. The rituals required of the ordinary Muslim for the recitation of the Word, particularly in formal or canonic prayer, could be likened to the sort of ritual preparation or purification required of both the priest and the communicant in the Christian Eucharist. Indeed, precisely because The Word has been made word in the Islamic tradition, most intensely so as the Beautiful Names (The 99 Names) of God, it is the preferred methodology or Way for the mystic's quest to know or experience God. The idea that God is mysteriously present in His Name is a concept that is not limited to the Islamic Tradition but it most clearly colours or, perhaps more appropriately, perfumes Islamic spirituality. Thus one might say that the equivalent of the miraculous substances in the Roman Catholic Communion – which has a material or pictorial representation in the form of wine, wafer or bread – is The

Word, whether as a Qur'ānic passage pronounced in formal prayer or as one of the names of God pronounced with intense concentration in the Sufi practice of *dhikr* (the invocation-remembrance of the Name whereby the invoker experiences the presence of the Invoked).

Of key relevance to our discussion of the paramount significance of the word (as Word) in Islam, is the fact that the word (the Qur'ān) itself refers Muslims to the Prophet and his ways, as the explanation of its passages. In other words, the Prophet, his life and words, becomes the sacred commentary of the sacred text. In daring language, which nevertheless is contained within Islam's orthodox canonic literature, the Prophet is The Qur'ān. Now this could be profoundly troubling to the typical Muslim or, more accurately, to the typical modern educated Muslim, given Islam's powerful and unequivocal denunciation of 'associating' any thing or person with God, but it is there in traditional orthodoxy, which always (it seems in all traditions) has the capacity to handle sacred ambiguities. Given this view of The Prophet, whose life is at the very least a sacred commentary on the Qur'ān, it became imperative to accurately assemble canonic collections as to every certified statement or act of the Prophet. The collection of these reports, or news about the Prophet, *Ahadith* literature, quickly became a major branch of the religious sciences of Islam in the earliest formative centuries, along with Qur'ānic recitation and Qur'ānic commentary. Indeed, containing as it did the sacred commentary that had to be the ultimate source for all subsequent commentaries (of which there are tens of thousands) and in turn for all the other religious sciences, one could safely argue that *Ahadith* studies are the core of the Islamic sciences.

Certainly the collection of canonic texts, their circulation from one end of the Muslim world to another and their use as primary texts in any Arabic Islamic education beyond the most primitive level was, along with Qur'ānic memorization, and the elaboration of an Islamic law that owes much to *Ahadith*, a major factor in the amazing degree of religious and even cultural unity within a universal religious community drawn from such diverse cultures as the Arab, the Berber and other African peoples, the Persian, Turkic, Indian and Malay peoples, not to mention the Muslim Slavs (Bosnians) and Albanians. To have a sense of the centrality of *Ahadith*, or sacred reporting, to Islam, we can consider the formal prayer, undertaken five times a day. The time, the manner of the prayer and the content has not varied since the lifetime of the Prophet. An American Muslim can parachute into the most obscure village in Sumatra and be able immediately to join and either follow, or even lead, canonic prayer. It is an example of how profoundly 'catholic', conservative and ritualistic Islam is, revolutionary and modernist Muslims notwithstanding. It is Qur'ān that defines regular prayer as the most incumbent duty for the Muslim after declaration, or 'witnessing' the famous Creed ('There is no divinity but The Divinity'). But the time, manner, content and various postures of this ritual are only known to the Muslim and universally practised as such, because of the sacred reports on the subject found in *Ahadith*.

What is relevant to us, is that this canonic text is perceived as *sacred news*. And since in a theocentric culture (such as that which characterized Islam up until a century or so ago) political and social disputes are all acted out within a religious vocabulary, then *Ahadith* (i.e. 'reports' sourced back to someone reputable who actually heard the prophet say such-and-such-a-thing, or saw him do such-and-such-a-thing), were most vulnerable to forgery for the sake of political expediency. The task of sorting out the false from the true fell to the Traditionalists, scholars devoted to the Traditions (*Ahadith*) of the Prophet, who developed an extraordinary criterion for determining veracity. The key lay in what modern journalists would describe as sourcing – tracing any given *Ahadith* back to the prophet and the person who actually heard the Prophet speak, through a chain (*isnad*) of reputable sources, along with other rigorous technical criteria. It is *hadith* which in turn authenticated respectable histories of the Prophet and his Companions in Islamic literature. The history of earlier prophets which are based on canonically acceptable material is designated as *qisas* – story-telling – and while such combinations of legend, fantasy and derivations from Old and New Testament accounts were accepted as spiritually edifying, they were never accorded the prestige or honour of the sourced sacred reporting of *Ahadith*. To falsify *Ahadith*, in other words to falsify sacred news of the Prophet and his Companions, is considered an act of self-damnation and the pious recorders of *Ahadith* first ritually bathed and then prayed before committing *Ahadith* to memory and to paper and they did so in fear and trembling.

Of course all of this discussion presumes that Arabic language and Islam are synonymous, which they are not. The overwhelming majority of Muslims in the world do not know Arabic; many may know the alphabet, but they can neither read for comprehension nor speak Arabic in either its classical and most sacred mode, or in the modern literary Arabic of the press, derived from the classical, or in the various local colloquial patterns that approximate the relationship of romance languages to Latin in the European medieval era. But what matters, and again it has to do with the Word becoming word, is that the idea of Arabic is central to that vast world of nearly one billion Muslims; all of whom recite formal daily prayers in Arabic, even if many would be hard pressed to accurately translate the liturgy into their own native tongue. And many can read the text of the Qur'ān in Arabic, and be beneficiaries of spiritual grace by virtue of that reading even if, as in millions of cases, they do not know the meaning of the words they read. This centrality is fixed geographically by the location of Mecca as the obligatory centre of pilgrimage in the heartland of Arabian culture. Al-Azhar, Cairo's thousand-year-old university-mosque, has been the centre of Islamic scholarship for the entire Sunni Muslim world for many centuries and the greatest Shi'a shrines are to be found not in Persia but in Iraq (i.e. all within the domain of Arabic speech). The Arab world is not the *demographic* centre of Islam (there are more Muslims in Indonesia or the subcontinent of India than in the Arab world) but it is central in the *cultural-spiritual* sense, for The Word did not become the word of just any language, but of Arabic. Only the Arabic Qur'ān can be used in formal prayer and only the Arabic of the Qur'ān possesses intrinsic spiritual grace.

With all of this as background then, one might assume that the practice of journalism in the Muslim world, and particularly in the Arab core of the Muslim world, would be the model of soul-searching honesty, decency and above all of painstaking accuracy and sourcing, inspired by indigenous values. On the contrary, modern Arabic-language journalism is in most cases at best no worse than any other journalism. In certain ways it is better in that scandal for its own sake, the invasion of privacy for its own sake – i.e. for a 'good story' – tends to be practised not at all or rarely. (When it is practised, it is not as some principal practice of a 'modern free press' but as a clearly partisan – and therefore limited – practice intended to injure an enemy of the publisher or editor.) Arab journalists' gut-sensitivity, or residual traditional sensibility, is to personal private honour, particularly family honour, in a religious culture in which family life is central (the Prophet's Mosque, the prototype mosque, was in fact his home). Such family life has always been sealed off from public view and it is interesting to note that the domain of women, the domain of the sacred and the domain of the forbidden all have the same root in Arabic. That the veil and the *mashrabiyas* (a perforated screen allowing air and softened light into a room but barring visibility) are metaphors for traditional Islamic life, likewise indicates the opposition of such life to the norms of a modern free press.

For the same reasons, i.e. basic residual values or fear of popular fury (as most noticeably in the Salman Rushdie case), newspapers and magazine editors in the Arab and Islamic world – however secular or even closet-atheist they may conceivably be – do not blaspheme God or His Prophets. And aside from the polemical Fundamentalist press (where that press is tolerated) editors do not blaspheme the other 'heavenly religions', the Egyptian establishment's phrase for Christianity and Judaism and by extension all other religious traditions, which are protected by traditional consensus from blasphemy. But it is precisely in the area of accuracy, of reliable sourcing, of the veracity of information, that the Arabic-language press can be scandalous. At best it is often indifferent to these qualities (which are so important in Anglo-American journalism). At worst it has nothing but cynical contempt for them, dismissing them as merely time-consuming concerns. There is an important dichotomy here. On the one hand there is an authentic cultural tradition, which is a living tradition – *Ahadith* literature, particularly the canonic collections, remain bestsellers, outselling any of the 'popular' modern Arab novelists. And, on the other hand, there is modern journalism in the Arab world. This dichotomy arises in history and in particular in the history of the printing press and its arrival in the Arab world. We can only speculate about why the printing press was introduced at such a late date in the Muslim world, but it was certainly *not* because of any inherent objection to adaptation and synthesis by Islam and the world civilization it produced. Prior to the colonial epoch and the post-colonial modern secularist epoch – epochs that share the experience of imposed, artificial and subversive cultural synthesis forced upon

Islamic civilization, Islam is recognizable as the great universal religious phenomenon that it is *precisely* because of its characteristic of racial and cultural synthesis.

From a traditional Islamic perspective, just as the last Prophet confirms all past prophecy so this last and most universal sacred civilization salvages the residual knowledge (including *technique*) of the ancient worlds. To this sweeping generalization should be added two qualifications. First, that the synthesis was always in the service of an aware (and comfortably triumphant) Islamic consciousness, which was quite capable over a historic period of time of discriminating between those natural and philosophical sciences that lent themselves to Islamicization and those that did not (like tragic theatre or naturalistic art for example). Secondly, the ancient worlds, however much they may have differed in dogma from Islam, shared a sense of the sacred and any adopted/Islamicized forms or techniques, if not purely Islamic, were nevertheless never intrinsically demoralizing. Thus the difference between the inescapable impact and ultimate Islamicization of Byzantine or Persian dynastic political forms on one hand and that intrinsic revolt against Heaven and denial of God known as the French Revolution on the other. The first Muslim writers to observe and comment upon the French Revolution were universally convinced that it was *fitna* (subversion, seditious dissent and corruption.)

As Elizabeth Eisenstein has so clearly documented, the printing press can be a potent weapon for subversion (witness the use made of it by the plethora of sects which splintered the religious unity of Europe during the Reformation). But I can only suggest that there was more to Ottoman distaste for the printed word than fear of subversion, and when printing in Turkish and Arabic finally came to Istanbul, it was first in the form of an official press. Rather, we might consider that The Book, and thus by metapoetic understanding the archetype of all books, as mentioned before, is to the Muslim, the Uncreated Word of God. Transmitted to the Prophet and then reproduced as sacred speech by the Prophet's voice, to be preserved in its entirety in the memory of the earliest Believers and, as a religious necessity, preserved (however modestly) in the memory of every Muslim for use in ritual prayer until the end of time, it was only committed to scribal manuscripts in the formative years for fear that the memorizers were being killed off in civil wars. Certainly there has never been a century in the fifteen centuries of

Islamic history when the written or printed text of Qur'ān has been as cheaply and massively available as the century we now live in. But I cannot imagine even the most enthusiastic revivalist characterizing this century, in contrast to any of the preceding ones, as notably an age of faith and unity. In Afghanistan, where the Muslims waged one of the most extraordinary examples of popular resistance in defence of the faith against outrageous odds, the number of printed Qur'āns in circulation until only a few decades ago was barely more than a handful; the extent to which the Qur'ān was contained within the memory of the typical Afghan is as extraordinary as the *jihad* waged for its sake.

With this as context we can appreciate why the traditional Muslim would stop and examine any stray piece of paper that he passed by, in the event the paper contained one of the names of God and as such was subject to desecration by dirt or any ritual impurity. *Fikr* (jurisprudence) tells us how to dispose legally of paper containing the Names. Consider this aspect of traditional Islamic life; reverence for God and the importance accorded to His Revelation which that reverence reflects and reinforces. Then consider the implications of a modern Arabic-language or Urdu- or Persian-language newspaper containing in all its varied (and vocally sacralizing forms) the names of God, whether as direct reference to Allah or as spiritual *adab* (good manners) that continuously invoke God in what is still utterly conventional social formula – Inshallah (God Willing), *Bismillah* (in the Name of God), *Mashallah* (God so Intends), *Subhanallah* (Praise be to God), *al-Hamdalilah* (Thanks be to God) – or in the customary forms of Muslim names e.g. Mr Abdur-Rahman, Mr Abd' Allah, Mr Abdul-Karim (literally Mr Slave-of-The-Merciful-One, Mr Slave-of-God, Mr Slave-of-The-Most-Generous.)

The oral opportunity for self-purification that each of these occasions promises – invocation of the Name, spiritual *adab*, and addressing by Name our brother-in-submission to Him – becomes displaced in the context of fast offset printing presses capable of producing a quarter of a million copies of a ten or twenty page Arabic-script newspaper. Such presses might be seen as processing plants for the desacralization of The Word (and most particularly of the Names). At the very least, such a situation leads to indifference to the Name by virtue of its mass and impersonal vehicle; at worst, it means the desecrating use of millions of pages of daily newsprint for fishwrapping and treatment as trash. Whatever one may make of such matters, the fact remains that pre-colonial Islamic civilization, which never hesitated to seize upon any new weaponry developed in the West, ignored (or perhaps was spiritually appalled by) the printing press. When it came, it did not do so within an organic development, as one might suggest was the case with Protestantism and the development of the printing press in Europe. Rather it was colonial conquest – Napoleon's brief but profoundly important defeat of the Mamluk dynasty and his conquest of Egypt. Napoleon retreated but the printing press remained and for the Muhammed Ali dynasty that succeeded Turkish-Mamluk rule in the wake of Napoleon's retreat, the idea was established of France as the gateway to modernity, or at least to the technology needed for survival in the contemporary world.

Conceivably an organic development into an authentic Arab-Islamic journalism might have arisen in the wake of the late-eighteenth-century *Ahadith* Revival that swept the Muslim world. The Revival was particularly noticeable in Egypt given Cairo's prestige as a gathering place for scholars clustered in and about Al-Azhar. The *Ahadith* Revival, like the late-eighteenth-century Sufi reform movements, was a religious and spiritual response from within orthodoxy to the sclerotic condition of a religious culture in such a state of tensionless equilibrium that degeneration was inevitable. The *Ahadith* Revival had direct linguistic implications. It was a spiritual protest against corrupted language, perhaps an inevitability in societies dominated for several centuries by non-Arabic-speaking ruling military élites. And it reasserted the direct and clear speech of the Prophet and his companions as something preferable to the two dominant linguistic modes. First, the overly formal, overly stylistic, overly embellished court Arabic of the pre-Islamic court traditions in Byzantium and Persia. And secondly, the highly rhetorical language of the pagan pre-Islamic poets who survived into the Islamic epoch by virtue of their usefulness in teaching Arabic. But the *Ahadith* Revival had barely begun when the Napoleonic Conquest occurred and any number of scholars who, prior to the conquest, would have been drawn into the ranks of *Ahadith* Revival, now attempted instead to come to grips with the religious implications of military defeat.

With religious thought in disarray and the technology of the printing press in place, this nineteenth-century void was soon to be filled largely by Arab Christians from the Lebanon and from Syria who were in contact with modern French culture and who out of anti-Ottoman sentiment rather than Islamic reform, adopted the cause of reviving Arabic (and with it a secular Arab nationalism in which Arabic language rather than religious identity would define nationhood and first-class citizenship). So the first great newspapers of the Arabic world were to an amazing degree founded by non-Muslims. And because of this particular phenomenon and the aggressively *laic* if not agnostic quality to the nineteenth-century Parisian press, the secular mode of thought that prevailed in this ersatz *Nahda* (the Revival or Renaissance of Arabic letters in the middle and late nineteenth century) drew upon an alternative literary tradition to the real, but stillborn, *Nahda* of the *Ahadith* Revival.

Instead of *Ahadith,* with its rigorous insistence on sourcing and accuracy and its almost impersonal quest for objectivity, the secular and usually non-Muslim pioneers of Arab journalism were drawn to the *belles-lettres* tradition of Arabic literature which had more to do with literary flourish and subjective self-expression, with opinion and with literary stance, than with such prosaic concerns as accuracy and sourcing. Indeed this tradition had little respect even for the facts of the event itself, as opposed to the writer's opinion of them. This tendency was deeply reinforced by the French-Continental perception of news as a vehicle for analysis – and very often a most partisan or ideological analysis – rather than news or information as an objective in itself. This tendency is in stark contrast to the ultimate Anglo-American model which sought accuracy and objectivity (if only for utilitarian reasons due to its mercantile origins). From the merchant's perspective there was a need for fast, accurate information about shifting prices of commodities or political conditions affecting trade and stability. It simply paid to get it right. Such a utilitarian perspective operated on a very different dimension to the search for veracity for love of God and in fear and trembling, but in the end it would have married better, if only due to the coincidence of outward form, to the mainstream *Ahadith* tradition in Muslim consciousness. But by the time the British assumed first partial and then full colonial authority in Egypt (in the late nineteenth century) French cultural domination was secure and the unique character of the Arabic-language press was already defined. Of course, even if history had worked out differently, (which from an Islamic perspective is almost a forbidden form of speculation, for it reeks of the denial of destiny) it would be naïve given the intrinsic metaphysical or spiritual problems posed by modern mass communications to assume a happier – from the Islamic perspective – ending.

So, much of the acceptable canon of modern journalism, in the 'objective' school of Anglo-American journalism as well as in the adversarial or partisan press tradition that has flourished particularly in France and elsewhere on the Continent, remains unacceptable to Islam from a basic ethical perspective. This would be apparent to anyone in the Muslim world who consciously thought about it. Instead, as I indicated earlier, most of the reservations about modern journalistic practice stem from intuited sense, gut response, residual inhibition, rather than from deliberate intellectual scrutiny. The core of modern journalism, that the public has 'the right to know', amounts to a right to subsidize the invasion of privacy, to appeal to idle curiosity, to accept 'public opinion' as sovereign and to circulate discomforting news. This is as inherently anti-Islamic as the interest-based core of modern banking (perhaps not surprising since journalism emerges as a child of the same desacralizing forces in Western history that spawned finance capital). It is significant that 'the father of modern journalism', Pietro Aretino, publicly distributed journals containing reportage and commentary on his times. These were flavoured, according to all accounts, with insults, slander and obscenities generally directed at the Pope, the monks and the priesthood. Aretino's journals were popular precisely because they invaded privacy and agitated an emerging Western 'public opinion' as the printing press replaced the pulpit as the source of 'news' and 'opinion'.

What is 'news'? What is 'newsworthiness'? Peace, stability and continuity are not news, but conflict, contention and disorder are. Respectability and moral conformity (which is an Islamic virtue, however unfashionable the idea of conformity may be in modern times) are not news. Erupting scandal on the other hand, is. Many of the accepted modes and techniques of modern journalism must be acknowledged as particularly repugnant from an Islamic perspective. Spying and seeking to confirm suspicions (i.e. most investigative reporting) are forbidden by Qur'ān and *Ahadith*, as are slander and backbiting. Slander is not simply a legal error or an occupational hazard; it is a great sin. In numerous *Ahadith*, Muslims are forbidden to publicize their own and others' faults.

On the contrary, the Muslim is urged to cover up or hide faults. There are, of course, exceptions to all of these prohibitions, but the exceptions concern military affairs and the specific requirements of administering justice, not the needs of an enterprising reporter.

In the case of television news the problem is more subtle and perhaps for that reason more pernicious. Al-Ghazali defined religion as belief in the Unseen World. From the perspective of Islam's articles of belief (God, angels, heaven, hell, destiny etc.), or the articles of belief of Judaism and Christianity, that definition is hard to fault. But spiritual grace (*baraka* in Arabic) does not 'track'[1] – however apparent it may be to its recipient. However obvious and almost palpable it may be to those vast outpourings of the faithful on pilgrimage to sacred centres or at miraculous sites, *baraka* cannot be recorded electronically on video tape or for 'live' transmission. Television may induce trances, but it is intrinsically anti-meditative. Even the itchiest of us can sit for many minutes drinking in a beautiful sunset or the play of moonlight upon a stream or the grandeur of a desert and its sandscapes. The Muslims believe these are signs – *ayat* – from God, Who asks us to remember Him by meditating upon these, His signs. But put these same scenes on video, even high-definition TV, and after a few seconds they pale and we become bored. The electronic recording that is video simulates the image without its invisible aura of spiritual grace. I have met holy men. Some I have known; some I have sat with. The feeling of *baraka* was almost palpable. But take their picture with a videocamera and usually what we get is the image of some nice old guy with a pleasant friendly smile, or maybe someone who is a little weird looking. No iconic sense of the inner essence is revealed. We cannot 'see' the saint via video.

When I was working in highly competitive situations as a television producer or reporter and calling in our coverage to my New York or London news desk, nobody ever asked me if I had the story. Instead, I was always asked if I had the picture. If there was no picture, then in that special television sense of reality, of what would be put on the air for two or three minutes and what would not, if there was no picture it did not exist. If religion in the traditional sense of the word is the source of enduring and transcendental (rather than situational and worldly) ethics, and if, by *technological definition*, the unseen does not exist on TV, then the increasing power of television journalism poses a profound

challenge to any religious outlook. If God, the angels, heaven, hell
and spiritual grace are not visible, then in a tele-technological
understanding of ontology, they do not exist. Sex and violence,
however, certainly do. Again, what fascinates me are processes at
work that are beyond intention just as they are beyond ideology.
Objects in movement and obvious visible emotion track best. They
are the most easily 'read' or assembled in the sense that we 'read'
or assemble a picture out of the poorly defined dots of colour on
the screen into an identifiable image.

The television signal, a spiral of electronic energy, is never
stable. Unlike film, we can only 'freeze frames' on our video
editpacks with the most expensive of equipment. Its instability is
a metaphor for TV's morally destabilizing capacity, since the preferred image (movement, intense visible emotion) is, by definition,
always changing. 'Good picture' and sleazy morals coincide. Sex
and violence make good pictures. When combined, particularly
when combined with artistic flair, they are almost addictive, in
that same sense that men and women may become addicted even
to a substance that they know abstractly is harmful, because the
effect is so attractive.

What then are Islamic criteria for the practice of modern journalism? First, necessity; the entire Muslim world is rapidly being
incorporated into an international secular culture based on mass
communication – newspapers, magazines, television, radio and
film – that is breaching the cultural forms that have traditionally protected Islamic consciousness. Islamic journalism can surely
attempt to offer alternative mass communication experiences to
those destabilizing experiences contained within the typical news
messages. For example, it might concentrate on stories that call
attention to, and encourage participation in, what remains of traditional, direct, personal religious systems of communication, such
as Qur'ān recitation, circles of *dhikr*, and lessons delivered in the
courtyards of the great mosques as well as traditional sermons.

Unfortunately, the news media that has arisen as part of the
'Islamic Revival' rarely concerns itself with the rich fabric of traditional Islamic life that still remains (for all modernity's unravelling
of the social fabric). It is precisely in its practice, in reporting on the
world of Islam, that 'Islamic journalism' is too often disturbingly
similar to the very same secular press it theoretically confronts –
similar both in its self-perception as 'the scourge of princes' and

in its perception of the world of Islam. All too often Islamic journalism displays a willingness to assume the 'rights' of the journalistic licence that violate those very limits that Islam imposes on our practices. As to the perception of the world of Islam, it is here that Islamic journalism almost monotonously substitutes the life and activities of various Islamic political movements for the life and activities of a much broader, yet Islamically conscious society. Mainstream Muslim society, of which the political movements are but a small part, receives disproportionately little media attention. The reduction of Islamic phenomena to narrowed-down Islamic political phenomena is a form of *reverse secularism*, and it is ironic that a journalism largely inspired by Islamic movements, which are devoted to combating secularism, is itself party to it. For if secularism insists that religion has nothing to do with the political domain, the reverse secularism of Islamic movement journalism insists that religion is worthy of reporting only in the political domain, and the more confrontational that domain, the better.

NOTES

1   To 'track' is to record a sound or picture electronically on tape for reproduction.

14 Learning from failure: towards a rationale for religious communication

CHRIS ARTHUR

If I had to pick a *single* book to add to theological reading lists in order to alert students to the importance of communication and media, I would choose *The First Casualty*, Phillip Knightley's masterly study of the war correspondent from the Crimea to Vietnam.[1] It is in no sense a theological work, religion is scarcely mentioned in it, but it illustrates in a very powerful way the importance of obeying that most basic of moral directives concerning communication, namely: *tell the truth*. The significance of this fundamental imperative, and the consequences of ignoring it, are sometimes lost sight of, or simply taken for granted as being too self-evident to need attention. Yet such truth-telling surely provides the foundation for any theology and for any acceptable rationale for religious communication.

It may seem perverse to begin by focusing attention on war. My reasons for doing so are similar to those expressed by the author of a recent study of arctic peoples for focusing his attention on such a *geographical* extreme. 'I write about the far North', Hugh Brody explains in *Living Arctic*, 'in the belief that we can best discover who we are by going to what we think of as the margins of our world.'[2] War provides a margin against which we can measure certain fundamental standards of communication practice and media ethics. It is a far north of human experience in whose bloody climate we can see growing to educative extremes those aberrations of communication whose everyday occurrence may appear deceptively harmless in the gentler climes which normally prevail. As Michael Traber has suggested, war can be seen as the ultimate failure of communication.[3] Going to the media margins marked out by war and looking at some dimensions of the failures which occur there will, I hope, help us to learn something about ourselves as communicating beings and provide some pointers to what any rationale for religiously sanctioned communication might regard as acceptable and unacceptable behaviour.

Commenting on the work of Roger Fenton, one of the first war photographers, Knightley remarks that his pictures of the Crimean War established an axiom which still holds good today, namely: 'although in most cases the camera does not lie directly, it can lie brilliantly by omission.'[4] Fenton's pictures showed a comfortable, efficiently organized war with well-dressed officers and men. The disease, equipment shortages and appalling lack of facilities for the sick and wounded simply did not find their way into the photographs he took. In the valley where the Charge of the Light Brigade had taken place, and where many of the fatalities still lay unburied at the time of his visit, Fenton did not even bother to unpack his camera.[5] Such omissions establish a gulf between actual conflict and reports of it. The mediated versions of war's savagery tend to offer a partial and inaccurate picture.

To sustain such cosmetic perspectives, such alternative, mediated realities, involves careful selection in what is pictured and written. Of course every medium of communication will inevitably impose its own limitations. In the same way that a black and white photograph cannot but fail to do justice to a peacock's spectacular plumage, so every medium is bound to leave something out. It is not such automatic, implicit shortcomings which should concern us, however, (though it *is* important that we are aware of them[6]), but the *deliberate* and *avoidable* ways in which communication may be used to convey an untrue version of events. Umberto Eco once described semiotics as being the study of every medium which can be used to lie.[7] A religious perspective on communication must, I believe, have a similarly wide-ranging remit in terms of the range of activities over which it seeks to exert some influence.

Just as Fenton's photographs of captured forts in the Crimea were taken *after* the casualties had been removed,[8] so in the First World War, the artist Paul Nash complained that he was not allowed to put dead men into his paintings.[9] In the Second World War, the German Propaganda Corps established a rule of never showing pictures of German troops who had been killed in action,[10] a strategy that the Allies too seem to have operated as regards their own war dead. As Jeremy Isaacs remarked in the 1988 Huw Wheldon memorial lecture, he saw a grand total of five corpses in all of the contemporary newsreel which he watched in doing background research for the series *The World at War*, a television history of the Second World War.[11] Phillip Jones Griffiths, one of the few photographers to concentrate on portraying how the Vietnam War affected Vietnamese civilians, had great difficulty finding an outlet for his work in the United States. He was told that his pictures were 'too harrowing' for the home market.[12]

Instances of lying about war could be endlessly continued across every medium that has been used to report it. Accounts of battles which never happened, incidents faked for the camera, invented atrocity stories, authentic film shown with fabricated narrative, scenes of appalling suffering and cruelty edited out ... the examples are legion.[13] Each instance helps to reinforce Knightley's main thesis that in war truth is the first casualty. A key task of religious communication would seem to be one of preventing truth from becoming a casualty and providing a robust and effective antidote to any act of communication in which it does suffer such a fate. As such, religious communication is almost bound to come into conflict with political utterance, for as George Orwell put it, 'political language is designed to make lies sound truthful and murder respectable'.[14]

Of course there are all sorts of arguments about keeping up morale, confusing the enemy, or not wishing to shock, outrage, desensitize or alarm which can be used to justify *not* accurately communicating the full horror of war, whether in a news report or in a film like Peter Watkins's *The War Game*.[15] The fact remains, though, that insisting, for whatever reasons, on a cosmetic perspective means that it is necessary for the camera, the reporter's pen, the war artist's brush, whatever medium is being used, to be silent or selective or to lie – and the distinctions between these different modes of non-communication can become very blurred indeed.

It is instructive for anyone trying to map out the margins of communication which can be created by war, to consider some observations made by Hannah Arendt about the alternative realities constructed by the Nazi's communication policy. All official correspondence referring to the slaughter of the Jews, for example, was subject 'to rigid "language rules" ... it is rare to find documents in which such bald words as "extermination", "liquidation", or "killing" occur. The prescribed code names for killing were "final solution", "evacuation" and "special treatment"'.[16] Treblinka, Auschwitz, and other concentration camps were referred to as 'Charitable Foundations for Institutional Care'.[17] What actually happened in them was masked by a deliberately euphemistic vocabulary, in every word of which truth became a fatal casualty. Communication was fundamentally compromised and all the media it used, from the shower signs which pointed the way to the gas chambers to the communiqués between the senior bureaucrats involved, created a grotesquely untrue version of events, an alternative reality beneath which appalling inhumanity was perpetrated.

Not telling the truth, though often apparently innocuous, can have some disastrous consequences which affect message and medium, sender and receiver. The whole delicate continuum of communication may be put at risk once we stray too far from the ground rule of trying as best we can to be truthful.[18] In fact George Steiner has suggested that the most basic medium of all, the very fabric of language itself, can actually be damaged if used to communicate in the terrible way exemplified by the Nazis.[19] The currency of evil can rend a massive tear in the fragile ecology which allows honest relationships to criss-cross and sustain the human community. Truth may be the first casualty, but if its wounds are fatal and it is allowed to perish then many other essential components of our humanity are likely to die alongside it: trust, love, compassion, pity and so on.

In a world where techniques of communication (and of deception) are becoming ever more sophisticated[20] and where the various mass media, television in particular, seem to dominate public life, it is imperative that the technology of mass communication and the political and commercial forces behind it do not lose touch with basic religious and moral values. For example, it is surely a matter for profound disquiet that 'When Abby Mann's film *Judgment at Nuremburg* was scheduled for transmission on American TV, the American Gas Association succeeded in having any mention of Nazi gas chambers removed from the script'.[21] I am not suggesting that there is any single, 'true' picture of the world which may be arrived at via 'complete objectivity'. Obviously there are many ways in which to view and communicate about even the simplest scene. At the same time, however, *without* asserting that there is only one correct view of every situation, it seems uncontroversial (but important) to point out that some views are more truthful than others. 'Complete objectivity' is, of course, a fiction, but this does not excuse us from the effort of *trying* to be fair and accurate in whatever we picture, say or write.

If I were allowed to recommend *two* books for inclusion in the communications / media section of the theological bibliography, my second choice would be Sam Keen's *Faces of the Enemy*, a fascinating study of the psychology of enmity.[22] Where Knightley concentrates on the war correspondent, attempting to report in the midst of conflict, Keen focuses more on the psychological factors, especially as they affect media and communication, which lead up to, and are in his mind largely responsible for, such conflict breaking out in the first place. *Faces of the Enemy* carefully documents the way in which we dehumanize other peoples in what we say about them and how we picture them. In the illustrations which Keen has gathered together, we see human beings portrayed as faceless automatons, savage barbarians, or as animals or monsters. Such images invite their audience to treat the people so caricatured as something less than human. Harking back to the Confucian idea that if we named things correctly we could live in social harmony, Keen suggests that 'peace begins with the rectification of terms'.[23] Seeing the murderous potential of some of the terms used, both in the propagandist's art and in common parlance, the notion of a genesis for peace in communication has a certain plausibility. If religious communication is concerned with peace (as it is surely bound to be), then it must ensure that we do not impose an enemy's face upon innocent countenances.

I hope that by looking at these extreme situations, which occur most obviously in time of war (or in what Keen terms the 'hostile imagination', which seems always to be with us), some basic requirements for religious communication will have begun to emerge. For many of the situations described by Knightley and Keen provide models of 'irreligious', 'godless', 'loveless' even 'demonic' communication, communication, no matter what adjective you choose to describe it with, which would be resistant to any but the most questionable theological justification. Such models show, more clearly than an analysis of current media output could, just how serious the consequences can be when, as is all too often the case, our communication contains elements which fail to measure up to any decent standard.

A common element which emerges from communication in which other people are presented as less than human is a complete failure to try to see things from their point of view. Interestingly, Hannah Arendt viewed this failure as the key to much of Adolf Eichmann's complicity in the Nazis' genocidal racial policies.[24] Empathy, then, the ability and inclination to stand in someone else's shoes and see how the world looks from that perspective, would seem to emerge as one important minimum ingredient in religious communication.[25] (This on the assumption that 'religious communication', however we choose to define it in detail, will be fundamentally opposed to the appalling failures of communication which occur most obviously in time of war).

Some sort of right of reply, a space for a response, would seem to be another minimum requirement. Such provision for listening to what the other person has to say is invariably disallowed when truth is dispensed with and we allow dehumanizing images currency in our media. Of course empathy and listening are very much interrelated, both may, indeed, be seen as practical expressions of valuing other people sufficiently highly to want to listen to them and to ensure that such listening is effective. It is encouraging to note, incidentally, that these minimum requirements find support in policy approved by the World Association for Christian Communication and the World Council of Churches.[26] Moreover, further substantial backing for the fundamentality of empathy and dialogue in communication comes in the psychotherapist Carl Rogers's analysis of what qualifies as 'good' communication.[27]

A strong candidate for the most misleading media proverb of all time must surely be the saying: 'sticks and stones may break my bones, but words will never hurt me'. Of course words cannot wound *directly*, but they are invariably behind the sticks and stones which do. It was words, after all, which were behind the appalling fate of Europe's Jews when the Nazi vocabulary seeped its poisons into the German spirit. Although today we may rarely hear anything so self-evidently evil, our careless use of words does little to ensure that such inhumanity will not be repeated. When some massive armaments deal has been clinched in Britain's favour, for example, the news is often reported entirely in terms of economic advantage. It seems less than honest to allow our words to hide what is being manufactured and what it will be used for. Words which lead us to see whole nations as 'the enemy', and which make us think of the creation of horrendous weapons in terms of job opportunities, may well illustrate the wider truth of another media proverb (which began its life as a Ministry of Defence jingle in the last war), namely: 'careless talk costs lives'. When the sticks and stones of a vocabulary of hatred could render dumb the whole globe, it is imperative that whatever religious perspectives guide our outlook on the world, they make us look to our every utterance and ensure that we communicate with care.

Any rationale for religious communication which wants to guard against our going down the sort of paths mapped out by Knightley and Keen, must emphasize the need for caring communication. Careful talk, and the moral extends to any medium – careful photos, films, paintings, broadcasts, which have a reverence for life. Portraying others as inferior to us, as monsters, faceless automatons, savage barbarians, or whatever other motif of hostility we care to mention, communication which displays neither empathy or right of reply, cannot be granted theological credence.

Abandoning truth seems inevitably to involve a sickening of communication. A central task for religious communication lies in trying to prevent such sickening from occurring and treating it whenever it does occur, no matter how much this may bring it into conflict with other interests.[28] Empathy and dialogue seem to be essential ingredients in that innoculation of our communicative practices which can prevent truth from becoming an early casualty. However, just because such characteristics may occur does not mean that the medium involved is religious, or that it will be true. But if such characteristics are altogether missing, it is hard to see how the communication in question could be granted religious sanction, no matter what other features it might display.

Empathy and the right of reply might be seen as constituting minimum requirements for religious communication, for communication in which the other person is valued and treated with respect, as a thou rather than an it. But might it not be objected that there is something highly paradoxical about suggesting that religion should concern itself with caring communication at all? For it remains a sad fact, amply borne out by history and by current affairs, that the world's religions have often been deeply implicated in wars and

violence, their communications practice following, indeed sometimes enhancing, the contours of aggression and hatred, rather
than displaying even the bare minimum of caring interchange.[29]
If truth is the first casualty, the hands of religion often seem
deeply stained with its blood. How can we then propose as the
minimum requirement of religious communication that it acts to
protect truth from harm and that it insists on empathy and dialogue in all its communicative endeavours?

I do not want to embark on an analysis of the reasons for religion's
frequent connectedness with violence. Fascinating though such an
investigation might be, it is clearly not something to undertake in
a brief chapter such as this. A comment of Gurdjieff's serves to
throw some interesting, if obvious, light on what yet remains a
puzzling paradox and points in the direction in which I *do* want
to go here. Warfare, according to Gurdjieff, consists of thousands
of sleeping people killing thousands of other sleeping people – if
they woke up they wouldn't do it.[30] Although the religions of the
world seem often to lead people into ever deeper nightmares of
violence, I believe this is more frequently an aberration, a failure
to understand religious teachings or to apply them consistently
to the conduct of life, than an accurate expression of the fundamental communicative thrust which lies at the heart of almost
every variety of human religiousness. An important part of that
communicative thrust has to do precisely with the sort of *waking
up* which Gurdjieff saw as vital to peace. This characteristic has
profound implications for any communication which attempts to
remain faithful to some form of religious inspiration.

Clearly, in trying to establish any guiding principles for religious
communication, a lot will depend on how you *define* religion to
begin with. Such definition is notoriously difficult, and rather than
attempting it here I want instead simply to focus on waking up
(metaphorically understood, of course) as one thematic thread
in this massive area of human experience which has some crucially important consequences for communication and media. The
most obvious consequence for religious communication, if we view
religion in terms of its involving a waking from sleep, is that in order
to fulfil this role it must be shocking rather than soporific. Pierre
Babin has suggested that the only useful material for effective religious education is that which contains an element of shock value.[31]
I would suggest that the force of his argument extends to much of

religious communication too, demanding that it is startling and awakening, that it opens our eyes to certain fundamental truths about ourselves and the world we live in which may be obscured by everyday discourse.

If this sounds rather far removed from much of what we normally associate with religious broadcasting or religious literature, then perhaps, as Dennis Potter has suggested, much of these endeavours merely offer us 'little pellets of sweetness'[32] that have very little to do with religion. In just the same way that we tend to get cosmetic pictures of war emerging in reports of it, so we often tend to get cosmetic pictures of life emerging via the media (even – indeed often *especially* – in its religious output). Yet if it is to be successful when assessed according to the criterion of religious waking, communication must act as John Crossan says the parables of Jesus act, to 'shatter the deep structure of our accepted world . . . remove our defences and make us vulnerable to God'.[33] Instead, it often seems that TV, radio and the press encase that vulnerability in a veritable armour of indifference, courtesy of a thousand asinine games shows, fatuous comedies and endless commercials.[34]

Alternative, mediated realities in which truth is a casualty often act as what might be termed 'spiritual soporifics'. At their most extreme, they can help to implicate us in what Gurdjieff saw as war's terrible sleepwalking tragedy, where communication fails altogether and killing takes its place. But although it is in war that we can most clearly see how communication and media may help to blot out the sort of wakefulness which religious teachings endeavour to secure, it would be misguided to imagine that it is *only* during war that we sleepwalk according to the contours of a mediated, alternative reality in which basic religious truths are lost sight of.

Alas, George Orwell's grim concept of 'newspeak', where language itself is brought under political control and is used to dim wakefulness about issues which might be embarrassing to Party ideology, is not confined to the realms of fiction.[35] Nor is its occurrence in history restricted to the Nazis' distorted vocabulary. More recently, for instance, the American military authorities resorted to something not unlike newspeak in their press briefings during the Vietnam War. Thus 'to deprive the enemy of the population resource' was used to describe the bombing of civilian villages,

and 'circular error probability'[36] was used to account for accidental destruction, while the ecological devastation of vast tracts
of land using defoliants was referred to as 'an environmental
adjustment'.[37] Such language would suggest that if truth is not
already on the casualty list it is certainly under very heavy fire
indeed.

Even when such cumbrous terminology is not used, media clichés
can exert the same sort of deadening effect, dulling our conscious-
ness of what is going on and paralysing our concern for others.
Robert Fisk, winner of the 1987 Valiant for Truth Media Award,
has pointed out the way in which clichés give us a distorted view
of things. As a small example, he cited the way in which, in the
Western press at that time, Syria was almost invariably tagged
'Soviet backed' and Kalashnikov 'Russian made', whilst Israel and
M-16 were rarely if ever accompanied by 'American backed' or
'American made'.[38] The clichés which resound in news reports
and headlines (in *both* sides of any conflict) are, Fisk believes,
'becoming a real danger to our task of understanding what is
going on in the world'.[39] Religious communication needs to root
out the dead metaphors and stultifying jargon which infect language and dull the understanding, and provide in their place a
shocking syntax of caring in which clichés find no voice, a
vocabulary in which respect for others is unfailingly implicit.

Fisk's point about the way in which lazy, unreflective communication can mislead, is further developed in an interesting
analysis of the language used by contemporary British media
to report on nuclear weapons.[40] Its authors identify a similar
avoidance of truth by utilizing a distancing, cosmetic, clichéd
vocabulary. Such 'nukespeak', as Paul Chilton dubs it,[41] is filled
with terms like 'deterrence theory', 'mutually assured destruction',
'Polaris', 'Trident', 'ground-launched cruise missile', and so on.
Such terms, by their mere familiarity, have grown dangerously
cosy. It is easy to forget that they refer to genocidal weaponry.
Nukespeak, according to Richard Keeble, constitutes a 'horrendous
linguistic deformation'[42] because of the horrors which, through its
vocabulary, are being eased into public acceptance and moral legiti-
macy. This dangerously insidious process is largely being carried
out through the uncritical communication which often tends to
characterize the mass media, and so comes to affect interpersonal
communication too.

There are many sorts of sleep which can afflict our communication and, if such communication is conducted via media of the massive potency of modern TV, radio and press, then we can expect the effects of such soporifics to be widespread. Some varieties are relatively easy to spot as such, others are not. Thus considerable vigilance must attend any religious communication that seeks to be wakeful and awakening. Edward Said, for example, has suggested that the Western media tend to give a highly distorted picture of Islam.[43] His extensively substantiated charges must be a matter for serious attention. Likewise, many have voiced concern at the invasive commercial perspectives which advertising seems to propagate, in which every problem is solved by purchase and where worth is assessed merely by possessions.[44] As Henry David Thoreau once remarked, 'all moral reform is the effort to throw off sleep'.[45] If our religious communication is to be adequate to the promises and perils of our modern media potential, it is imperative that it act to throw off the sleep which can so easily infect the way in which we communicate. We can as little afford to poison our rivers and seas as we can allow soporific, uncaring communication to course through the veins of the various media we use.

In a book which suggests just how deep and pervasive the slumber may be through which religious communication will have to break, Daniel Boorstin has shown how, as he puts it, 'we have used our wealth, our literacy, our technology, and our progress, to create a thicket of unreality which stands between us and the facts of life.'[46] In particular, he draws attention to the formative role which the media plays in 'the new kind of synthetic novelty which has flooded our experience',[47] namely the 'pseudo-event'. 'The American citizen', he concludes, 'lives in a world where fantasy is more real than reality.'[48] Echoing Boorstin, the memorably named Jerry Mander has argued that the United States has produced the first culture 'to have substituted secondary, mediated versions of experience for direct experience of the world',[49] a substitution in which the media plays a crucial role. Mander believes that: 'As humans have moved into totally artificial environments, our direct knowledge of the planet has been snapped. Disconnected, like astronauts floating in space, we cannot know up from down or truth from fiction.'[50] Such a profound disorientation is bound to have serious religious implications. After all, as R. T. Brooks has suggested, a first step in religious communication may simply be 'to make people more aware of the facts and workings of the physical world' in order that they become 'more sensitive to its spiritual significance'.[51] But if we are living in artificial environments, if we are surrounded by the alternative realities created by media, such a step will be rendered much more difficult. Brooks believes that 'we need to look at the actual world as something to be contemplated with wonder'.[52] I would suggest that until we do so religious communication is almost bound to fail. The pseudo-events described by Boorstin, the artificial environment of which Mander complains, the faces of the enemy which Keen identifies and the various casualties of truth which Knightley brings to our attention, all act to dull the shock of wonder which is central to any religious outlook. When media are geared to such soporific ends we are in profound need of a religious awakening to vivify our communication.

One of the most frustrating aspects of modern mass media is perhaps the sense of helplessness which tends to be engendered by the massive amount of information to which we are now daily exposed via the channels of TV, radio and press. We are acquainted with injustice, tragedy and catastrophe worldwide, but are often powerless to do anything about it. In contrast to such a sense of impotence, there is a great deal that can be done by every individual to counteract the alternative realities in which uncritical, uncaring communication may result. Writing in his *Introduction to a Theological Theory of Language*, Gerhard Ebeling argues that: 'Since language is so intimately associated with life, something of the necessary reverence for life should be carried over to the way we use language.'[53] Those who complain that our language contains elements of 'nukespeak' are surely moving on a course similar to that suggested by Ebeling when they insist that rather than repeating the atomic catechism unthinkingly, we should translate its terms into plain talk, so that instead of '100% mortality rate', for example, we have 'everybody dead'.[54] Likewise, instead of viewing another nation indiscriminately as 'The Enemy', we might keep on our mantelshelves a photograph of an ordinary Argentinian, Iraqi, Iranian (or whatever) family — to remind us that it is people like ourselves, and the way in which they communicate, which constitute the human community of any nation. On a much larger scale, the proposals made for a New

World Information and Communication Order by the International Commission on Communication Problems, contain many recommendations for reform which are undergirded by a fundamental reverence for every human being's right to free expression.[55] Sam Keen shows how we might begin to put into practice the sort of communicative ethic which Ebeling spells out, when he suggests that we should start to curb the hostile imagination and its morally somnulent vocabulary 'by a small but radical reclaiming of language, by ceasing to sanctify blind obedience to authority with the honorific "duty", or call the willingness to kill an unknown enemy or die in the attempt "courage", or baptize the spirit of revenge with the name of "honour".'[56] This is something we can all do, and of course it is not only language, but all forms of communication which have an intimate connection with life and so deserve a careful reverence in their use.

It is also important to bear in mind the enormous *positive* potential of modern media. From Live Aid to soap opera, from newspaper columns to blockbusting films; from radio phone-ins to telethons, from *The Hitch Hiker's Guide to the Galaxy* to *Heart of the Matter*, the media can help to inform us about what is happening in the world, to waken us into action, to create a sense of community, to enrich popular culture and to make us laugh. Though I have focused very largely on what can happen when communication fails and media sours, it would be absurd and erroneous not to acknowledge the many benefits which the media bestow on the modern individual's life. However, I have assumed that such benefits are self-evident and sought to further the cause of good communication by warning of what happens when it goes wrong, rather than dwelling on its many obvious achievements.

It is important to remind ourselves (to wake up to the fact) that however powerful and impersonal the mass media which surround us may seem, they do not exist as some sort of independent third party. On the contrary, every film, piece of propaganda or truthful reporting, every constitutive image and utterance on TV and radio, every newspaper story, has a moment of genesis in an individual human mind and is received by individual readers, viewers and listeners. That is why codes of conduct for fair reporting, impartial news coverage, for advertising which is 'legal, decent, honest and truthful', are doomed to failure unless they are accompanied by a personal sense of responsibility in every individual's approach to his or her own communicative activities. The fact that such individual genesis can, through modern technology, be magnified and disseminated so that an audience numbered in millions may be addressed and influenced, makes it particularly important that such a sense of responsibility is properly developed. Can such development take place without some concept of caring communication, which is in turn dependent on perceiving the world and other people with the sort of wonder and reverence which Brooks and Ebeling talk about?

I think a convincing case can easily be made for putting communication skills and media education pretty near the top of almost any curriculum, and certainly of any theological curriculum. After all, as Peter Meggs put it, not only is communication *the* critical issue of our age because of the state of international relations, but it is, quite simply, 'the purpose of all life'.[57] The problem lies, not in demonstrating the importance of communication, but in convincing institutions to reform themselves accordingly. There are already some promising developments at school level, though by and large they focus on media as such, rather than fostering any kind of individual communicative responsibility which begins from the premise that people are the most important medium of all. Addressing the American scene, William Fore has suggested that media education is 'just beginning to take hold in the public schools and is almost altogether missing in the churches. Yet teaching people to understand what media are doing to them . . . could scarcely be more important to educators and church leaders.'[58] The situation in Britain seems very similar. Some encouraging work is of course being done – the activities of the World Association for Christian Communication and of the Centre for the Study of Communication and Culture are particularly noteworthy, whilst the television awareness training scheme, pioneered by the Media Awareness Research Centre in America and now being run in this country by the Mothers' Union is a first step towards more widespread media literacy.

Marshall McLuhan has suggested that in the future education will become 'civil defence against media fallout'.[59] In the present situation, with satellite TV becoming firmly established, with computers and video creating new contours in the media environment of every home, with continual advances in communications technology, it would be easy simply to take the view that things are in such a state of flux that any recommendations made are likely to be rendered speedily redundant as the technology changes (Alvin Toffler has even proposed the possibility of direct mind-contact between individuals as the point towards which media development is moving[60]). In such a situation I think it is important for theologians, along with broadcasters, educationists and anyone involved in communication, to keep abreast of new ideas – but also to try to work out some fundamental ethic for communication which will not change merely according to the changing technologies. We do not know what message we shall eventually communicate to history, we can only hope that it will not constitute the sort of fallout which requires remedial education to handle.

As Wolfgang Bartholomaus once observed, 'one cannot *not* communicate'.[61] The trouble is, what is communicated in our buildings, the way we dress, the investments we make, our choice of action in scores of decisions made every day, often does not fit in with the communicative ideals which an awakened and awakening religious perspective might suggest. It is all very well counselling the need for empathy and dialogue, and the saner sense of priorities they would result in. But if the way we act does not also display these qualities then our communication will be an affair of media only. The message will go no deeper than the medium. The real challenge of religious communication is that it calls for *transformation* rather than dealing uninvolvedly in impersonal exchanges of information or ideas. It seeks a situation where the message is embodied in every aspect of the life of the communicator, rather than merely in what he or she happens to say or write or broadcast on TV. Perhaps we cannot legitimately use the mass media for religious ends at all until we ourselves have become effective *personal* media of whatever message we are seeking to communicate. As John Bluck has remarked, writing from a Christian perspective, the most powerful statements about that faith,

> are usually not the self-conscious attempts we make through the mass media ... We speak more clearly through the style of our church buildings and the use we put them to, in the way in which we invest our money, the modesty of our lifestyle, our choice of careers and clothing, our presence among people who hurt most and whose voices are least able to be heard.[62]

It remains an important theological task to try to chart with care and detail the waters of communication in which we all live and move and have our being, marking in as clearly as we can prevailing winds, currents, reefs, shallows and so on. Too often, religion seems merely to be communicatively adrift and sometimes unaware of the messages it is beaming out. This chapter has been a crude attempt to take some basic soundings and plot the rudiments of a course. I am fully mindful of the need for much more detailed navigational studies in this area.

I would like to end with two brief stories recounted by Idries Shah in *Thinkers of the East*. Both help to stress important points about religion and communication. In the first, a Muslim holy man is asked by a student how he feels. The holy man replies: 'Like one who has risen in the morning and does not know whether he will be dead in the evening.' Puzzled to hear so apparently ordinary a reply coming from one who was widely famed for his wisdom, his questioner complained rather disappointedly that this was surely the situation of *all* men. To which the holy man retorted, 'Yes – but how many of them really *feel* it?'.[63] It is, I believe, an important test of the adequacy of religious communication to ask whether or not it helps to keep us mindful of such fundamental truths about the human situation, or if it merely provides little pellets of distracting, soporific sweetness. The second story again involves a question put to a holy man.[64] How, the sage was asked, did you reach your present heights of spiritual attainment? His answer deserves to have the last word:

> Through making the heart white in celestial contemplation, not by making paper black with writing.

NOTES

1   Phillip Knightley, *The First Casualty, from the Crimea to Vietnam: the War Correspondent as Hero, Propagandist and Myth Maker*, London: Andre Deutsch: 1975. Knightley quotes as epigraph to his study the words of US Senator Hiram Johnson (spoken in 1917) that 'The first casualty when war comes is truth'.
2   Hugh Brody, *Living Arctic, Hunters of the Canadian North*, London: Faber: 1987, p. xiii.

3   Michael Traber, in John Bluck (ed.), *Beyond Technology, Contexts for Christian Communication*, Geneva: WCC: 1984, p. 66.

4   Knightley, op. cit., p. 15. For a fuller discussion of some of the limitations of photography which Knightley's axiom is getting at, see Michael T. Isenberg, *War on Film, the American Cinema and World War I*, London & Toronto: Associated University Press: 1981, Chapter 4, 'The Myth of the "Objective Camera": a Critique of Film reality'. At one point (p. 59) Isenberg remarks: 'The motion picture camera is a mechanistic tool which, no matter what the intentions of its operator, restricts and distorts reality as defined by the human eye and mind.'

5   Knightley, op. cit., p. 15.

6   According to Robert Liebert, for example, (writing in *Religious Education*, Vol. 82 no. 2 (1987)) the majority of viewers are unaware that television news bulletins owe their form to a series of editorial decisions, let alone to the intrinsic limitations of TV as a medium. Many simply accept news as a straightforward documentary record which describes the most important events of the day.

7   Umberto Eco, *A Theory of Semiotics,* Bloomington: Indiana University Press: 1976, p. 7. As quoted in Robert C. Allen (ed.), *Channels of Discourse, Television and Contemporary Criticism*, London: Methuen: 1987, p. 24.

8   Knightley, op. cit., p. 15.

9   Ibid., p. 99.

10 Ibid., p. 226.

11 Jeremy Isaacs, 'How to Make History', the 1988 Huw Wheldon memorial lecture, hosted by the Royal Television Society, London, and broadcast on Channel 4, 17.5.88.

12 Knightley, op. cit., p. 390.

13 Many such examples are described in the course of Knightley's book and in Sam Keen's *Faces of the Enemy* (see note 22 below).

14 George Orwell, 'Politics and the English Language', reprinted in *The Collected Essays, Journalism and Letters of George Orwell*, Vol. IV, 1945–1950, London: Secker & Warburg: 1968, p. 139.

15 On Peter Watkins's *The War Game* see Michael Tracey's 'Censored, the War Game Story', in Crispin Aubrey (ed.) *Nukespeak, the Media and the Bomb*, London: Comedia: 1982.

16 Hannah Arendt, *Eichmann in Jerusalem, a Report on the Banality of Evil* (revised and enlarged edition), Harmondsworth: Penguin: 1983, p. 85.

17 Ibid., p. 109. It is worth noting that there still exist mediated 'alternative realities' which attempt to deny that six million Jews were slaughtered by the Nazis. For instance, *Holocaust News*, published by the Centre for Historical Review, suggests that 'the allegation that more than six million Jews were deliberately exterminated in gas chambers or otherwise, as part of a campaign of genocide is a preposterous propaganda fabrication which daily becomes threadbare.' (This undated issue of *Holocaust News*

was supplied by the Anne Frank Centre in Amsterdam, whose touring exhibition Anne Frank in the World seeks to counter precisely such dangerously misleading 'alternative realities'.)

18 On the difficulties of truth-telling, of 'seeing what is there' and 'telling it like it is', see my 'Tigers: Some Reflections on Theological Education and Communication', *Religious Education*, vol. 84 no.1 (1989), pp. 103–30.

19 In *Language and Silence* (London: Faber: 1985, p. 69) Steiner writes: 'The possibility that the political inhumanity of the twentieth century and certain elements in the technological mass-society which has followed on the erosion of the European bourgeois values, have done injury to language is the underlying theme of this book.' The essays 'Silence and the Poet' and 'The Hollow Miracle' (both contained in *Language and Silence*) are particularly interesting in this respect, though Steiner admits (p. 15) that the 'prophecy of lasting linguistic decay and sterility' voiced in 'The Hollow Miracle' has 'proved erroneous'.

20 On the increasing sophistication of techniques of deception see, for example, Paul Lester's 'Faking Images in Photo-journalism', *Media Development*, Vol. 35 no.1 (1988), pp. 41–2. Some further interesting material is to be found in *Media Development*, Vol. 33 no.3 (1986), in a special issue devoted to the subject of 'Lies and Lying'.

21 Colin Morris, *God in a Box, Christian Strategy in the Television Age*, London: Hodder & Stoughton: 1984, p. 87.

22 Sam Keen, *Faces of the Enemy, Reflections of the Hostile Imagination: the Psychology of Enmity*, San Francisco: Harper & Row: 1986.

23 Ibid., p. 96.

24 Hannah Arendt, op. cit., pp. 47–8.

25 In advocating empathetic communication, it is important to bear in mind Allan Bloom's critique of some aspects of such 'openness'. See his *The Closing of the American Mind* (New York: Simon & Schuster: 1987). Some remarks which may help to defend empathy against such criticisms are contained in Chapter 6 of my *In the Hall of Mirrors, Some Problems of Commitment in a Religiously Plural World*, Oxford: A. R. Mowbray: 1986.

26 *Christian Principles of Communication*, published by the World Association for Christian Communication, (WACC), paragraph 3. For the WCC's endorsement of empathy see John Bluck (ed.), op. cit., p. 88. WACC's *Christian Principles of Communication* are reprinted at the end of this volume.

27 Carl R. Rogers, 'Dealing with Breakdowns in Communication – Interpersonal and Intergroup' in *On Becoming a Person, a Therapist's View of Psychotherapy*, London: Constable: 1967, pp. 330–7.

28 It is important to remember that there is a very real sense in which religion is subversive and destructive. As Sallie McFague has put it with regard to

the Christian tradition, 'every major reformation within the church has been sparked by the insight that the essence of Christianity does not support conventional standards' ('The Christian Paradigm', in Peter C. Hodgson and Robert H. King, *Christian Theology, an Introduction to its Traditions and Tasks*, London: SPCK: 1978, p. 332. Bringing this insight to bear on communication, Duncan Forrester notes that the function of Christian communication 'is not to repeat the conventional wisdom of the age, adding only a religious sugar-coating; it is essentially against the stream, at odds with the *Zeitgeist*' (see his 'The Media and Theology: some reflections', Chapter 5 above, p. 74.

29 Many examples could be cited, I will confine myself to one short news item which appeared in the *Guardian* on 14.5.85 and seems to illustrate something of religion's potential for hostility: 'A High Court judge in New Delhi yesterday dismissed a petition calling for a ban on the Koran, after protests about the case in India, Pakistan, and Bangladesh. The petition, filed by two Hindu Indians in Calcutta High Court, provoked violent demonstrations in Bangladesh and a furious reaction from the Pakistan Government. Crowds also took to the streets in Srinagar, capital of India's mainly Muslim northern state of Jammu and Kashmir, throwing stones at traffic and shops. The suit said that the Koran should be banned because it preached hatred and violence and was inimical to the country's majority religion, Hinduism'.

30 Quoted in P. D. Ouspensky, 'The Life of Sleeping Men', *Parabola*, Vol. 7 no. 1 (1982), p. 77.

31 Pierre Babin (ed.), *The Audio-Visual Man, the Media and Religious Education*, Ohio: Pflaum: 1970, pp. 155 and 159: 'A document is apt for religious education to the extent that it expresses a deep human situation which forces one to question the meaning of his life . . . A document that has no shock value is of little use'.

32 Dennis Potter in discussion on BBC 1, 25.8.87, following a screening of his *Brimstone and Treacle*. Potter makes some further elucidating comments along the same lines in an interview with Mary Craig in *The Listener*, 13.5.76, p. 613.

33 John Dominic Crossan, *The Dark Interval, Towards a Theology of Story*, Illinois: Argus Communications: 1975, p. 122.

34 Edward Robinson, in *The Language of Mystery* (London: SCM: 1986, p. 81), identifies what he terms 'Acquired Immunity to Mystery Syndrome' and reminds us that it is not just the TV camera or journalist's pen which can create alternative realities that may encase our 'vulnerability of God'. Art too (or, rather, bad art) can also act in this way: 'Bad art does not just fail to tell the truth; it substitutes a lie. When Christ is portrayed as a characterless figure of sentimental benevolence surrounded by cuddly lambs in a romantic landscape, what effect does such a representation have on the prayers, let alone the theology, of those for whom he is a

focus of worship?' (p. 62). The language of mystery is, in other words, sometimes *stifled* by religion.

35 For George Orwell's concept of 'Newspeak' see his famous novel *Nineteen Eighty Four*. Bernard Crick relates newspeak to the modern media situation in the edition of *Nineteen Eighty Four* published in 1984 by the Clarendon Press, Oxford, which contains his critical introduction and annotations. See, in particular, pp. 59–60.

36 Knightley, op. cit., p. 421. Barry Zorthian, head of the American civilian information apparatus in Saigon, remarked in his book *Vietnam 10 Years Later*, 'One of our basic faults in Vietnam was that the communication of the war did not correspond to the reality of the war, and the further you got away from Vietnam the worse that gap became'. Quoted in Derrik Mercer, Geoff Mungham and Kevin Williams, *The Fog of War, the Media on the Battlefield*, London: Heinemann: 1987, p. 259.

37 Keen, op. cit., p. 87.

38 Robert Fisk, 'Clichés are a "real danger" to truthful news reporting', in *Action* (World Association for Christian Communication Newsletter), Vol. 123 (March 1988), p. 8.

39 Robert Fisk, 'Pejorative Words and Truth', an address given at the Arts Club, Dover Street, London, 14.12.87, on the occasion of Fisk being awarded the 1987 'Valiant for Truth Media Award'. This address is reprinted in the award booklet published by the Order of Christian Unity.

40 Crispin Aubrey (ed.), *Nukespeak, The Media and the Bomb*, London: Comedia, 1982.

41 Ibid., p. 95f.

42 Richard Keeble, in Crispin Aubrey op. cit., p. 123f.

43 Edward Said, *Covering Islam, How the Media and the Experts Determine How we See the Rest of the World*, London: RKP: 1981.

44 See, for example, the chapters in this volume by Peg Slinger, Jeanne Cover and Dorothee Sölle.

45 Henry David Thoreau, *Walden*, London: Everyman edition: 1912, p. 78.

46 Daniel J. Boorstin, *The Image, or What Happened to the American Dream*, London: Weidenfeld & Nicholson: 1961, p. 3.

47 Ibid., p. 9.

48 Ibid., p. 37.

49 Jerry Mander, *Four Arguments for the Elimination of Television*, Brighton: Harvester Press: 1980, p. 24.

50 Ibid., p. 351.

51 R. T. Brooks, *Communicating Conviction*, London: Epworth Press: 1983, p. 44.

52 Ibid., p. 113.

53 Gerhard Ebeling, *Introduction to a Theological Theory of Language*, London: Collins: 1973, p. 177. As quoted in Brooks, op. cit., p. 31.

54 Crispin Aubrey (ed.) op. cit., p. 123f.

55 International Commission for the Study of Communication Problems
    (the MacBride Commission), *Many Voices, One World: Communication
    and Society Today and Tomorrow, Towards a New, More Just and
    More Efficient World Information and Communication Order*, London:
    UNESCO: 1980.

56 Keen, op. cit., p. 96.

57 Peter Meggs in B. F. Jackson (ed.), *Television, Radio, Film for Churchmen*,
    New York: Abingdon Press: 1969, p. 71 and p. 105.

58 William, F. Fore, *Television and Religion, The Shaping of Faith, Values
    and Culture*, Minneapolis: Augsburg: 1987, p. 167.

59 Marshall McLuhan, *Understanding Media*, London: Ark Edition: 1987,
    p. 305.

60 Alvin Toffler, *The Third Wave*, London: Collins: 1980, p. 369.

61 Wolfgang Bartholomaus, 'Communication in the Church: Aspects of a
    Theological Theme', in Gregory Baum and Andrew Greely (eds.), *Concilium*
    1978 (issue theme: 'Communication in the Church').

62 John Bluck, op. cit., pp. 41–2.

63 Idries Shah, *Thinkers of the East, Studies in Experientialism*, London:
    Cape: 1971, p. 122.

64 Ibid., p. 41.

15 Television commercials: mirror and symbol of societal values

PEG SLINGER

> Human beings whose primal impressions come from a machine –
> it's the first time in history this has occurred . . . a cloud settles
> over the country from coast to coast, a cloud of visual and aural
> symbols creating the new kind of thought-environment in which
> Americans now live.[1]

> The ubiquitous box influences what we squirt, squeeze, smear.
> It has become the predominant inculcator of values. It has
> changed the long-standing institutions of government, religion,
> and family.[2]

Ruth Goldsen and Gail West have captured in words the essence of
television today. Viewing the 'programmed light-bulb' has become
a way of life for most of society, exemplifying and embodying
what is current in the culture. Television has changed the daily
rhythms of millions of people as it introduces and projects its
own views of the world, its own images and symbolic forms,
its own manner of interpreting reality. It serves as an amnesic
device, telling us that everything is fine and the whole world
consists of me and the other. It is a culturally revolutionary
presence among us which we may not ignore for it serves
as a most important source of images available to humankind
today. Of course, those who consider themselves 'TV snobs'
may easily turn off their sets, but they may not so easily turn
off the TV environment in which we live and breathe and have
our being.

What is the driving force of this powerful giant among us?
The ever-present commercial, the advertising of the 'thirty second
dream'. Those 'expensive, skillfully made playlets and works of
art made to shape our behavior and using every device available
to this end . . .'[3] are brief (twenty, thirty, or sixty second bursts),
fill twenty-two per cent of all broadcast time and in a typical

two hours of TV viewing, forty or fifty of these little messages will have flashed across the tube and implanted their imagery in the minds and hearts of millions. 'Shakable hair with that unshakable hold . . . Fibre you can trust . . . Everything you always wanted in a beer and less . . . Stronger than dirt . . . Tasting is believing . . . Fight back with Pepsodent . . . 24-hour protection . . . Trust Woolite . . . Timex, where everything is possible.' They play on every chord of the culture, linking products with patriotic values, religious themes, family caring, friendship, famous people and events. They introduce, interrupt, separate, amuse, offend, irritate. They disengage and abort our emotional reactions to news items, dramas, and documentaries as they make of the airwaves, 'an invisible midway.'[4] Our own heritage of capitalism with its system of profit, competition, and private ownership of the means of production, is the rich soil in which the consumer culture fostered by TV commercials grows. In a culture where the quest for a more comfortable existence and self-interest is the main pursuit, and where wasteful consumption is explicitly and systematically promoted, how can the TV commercial fail?[5] We owe it to ourselves to buy, own, and consume. For some, a slight embarassment may be felt over Jesus's message that our life does not really consist in an abundance of possessions, but then he didn't live in the twentieth century and even if he did, would he have been able to preach freedom and choice over consumption?

Analysing commercials is one way to get at the values and beliefs of the society in which they are broadcast. In this analysis and reflection, I intend to examine commercials on three levels: first, the basic facts – the aims, roles, techniques and dangers of TV commercials; secondly, commercials as the most distinctive 'icons' in our culture, including the manner in which symbols are packaged and 'transcendency' becomes commercialized; finally, I will explore the relationship between commercials, the Christian message and the model of radical change proposed by Holland and Henriot in their booklet, *Linking Faith and Justice*.[6]

What is the '30 Second Dream' actually about? What does it do to our thinking, our emotions, our whole being? Barnouw puts it concisely: advertising aims to sell us the unnecessary, creating emotionally charged values to make the unneeded seem necessary.[7] This creation of desires which constantly calls for new products and makes old ones obsolete is a very lucrative business. Jerry Mander in his book, *Four Arguments for the Elimination of Television*, describes the goal of advertising as that of discontent, an internal scarcity of contentment, even with what has just been purchased. The ideal world of the advertiser is one in which a product is used only once and then discarded.[8] High technology and much 'hype' is needed to convey this message to the public because generally we do not watch the commercial interruption with an 'absorbed reverence'. Catchy language, music, dancing, colour, action, special lighting, the use of familiar faces (Robert Young alias Dr Kildare for Sanka and Victoria Principle for hair spray) are just a few of the ways the ad-people attempt to capture our attention and our pockets. Commercials use language to angle our vision their way, thereby changing the way we actually experience reality. Concepts such as 'convenience packaging' and 'readily disposable' serve to cloud our vision of the mounds and mounds of waste material piling up in our world each day.[9] Music too has great selling power, calling up moods and mental pictures, opening us to the message of the ads. Goldsen relates the example of a Schaefer beer commercial which appeals to the listener's religious sense through music. A new truck driver amid his older confrères sings the commercial's praises for them in a pure, clear voice with bell-like tones. It is evident from the look of contentment and the tears in the eyes of the older men that memories of home, childhood, and church are conjured up within them.[10] And this clever musical symbol can sell a lot of beer to all of us who take it in or are taken in by it.

Another very powerful technique in TV commercials is to connect 'right' forms of social and personal behaviour with products. The need to pamper oneself is fulfilled at McDonalds ... 'You deserve a break today and we do it all for you!' The sexy woman caressing her body in the shower with soaps, oils, and perfumes exclaims, 'It's expensive, but I'm worth it!' The 'Pepsi generation' image links its customers to marriage, homecomings, and family reunions. A very consistent value statement emerges: happiness lies not in doing, serving or being, but in buying. A number of emotions are successfully used in commercials to continue the consumer frenzy; fear, loneliness and self-doubt. In examining these, some very interesting reflections may be found. The ads tell us (1) to fear nature ... buy chemicals to keep bugs away, sunglasses to keep eyes safe, sunscreen lotions to protect bodies, (2) to fear the constant judgement of others . . . bad breath, ring-around-the-collar, stringy dull hair, sneaker-smell, underarm odour, (3) to fear loneliness . . . buy products which will ensure love, relationships, happiness, success, making one irresistible and younger-looking, (4) to fear pain and our coping ability . . . take Aspirin, Pepto-Bismol, Anacin, Sominex, Alka-Seltzer *et al.*, (5) to fear un-cleanliness . . . go for whiteness, brightness, sterility and sudsiness. Fear reigns in the consumer's world as he or she suspect the worst of themselves and reach out desperately for the undeliverable promise of the '30 Second Dream'. Eric Sevareid pinpoints the issue well: 'The biggest business in America is not steel or automobiles, or television. It's the manufacture, refinement and distribution of anxiety . . .'[11] Barnouw comes to a brilliant conclusion – creation is definitely a disaster! All that was done in our making and our environment was a dreadful mistake and so products had to be invented to correct the error. Hair grows where it shouldn't, is too curly or too straight, the wrong colour, too oily or dry; skin is too pale, too dry, too dull; odours abound in our breath, our feet, our armpits; food is too coarse or too fine.[12] What a mess we find ourselves in! And so the primary danger in advertising is that the average person exposed to hundreds of these messages daily, begins actually to believe that insecurity, unpopularity, lack of success can be corrected with V-O 5 hair spray, Metamucil, Sealy mattresses, Miller Lite Beer, Toronados, and Kentucky Fried Chicken. The cries of the poor, the hungry, and the oppressed of the world are remote indeed when compared to the joy of finding the right shampoo or hair colouring.[13] Dedication to justice and service seem unnecessary when true happiness can be obtained with a Volkswagen, Reynolds Wrap, or Nestlés Quik: 'Advertising tries to conceal the emptiness and make life feel good. It is as if the forces of advertising had decreed that the individual man or woman must not be allowed to develop his or her own potentialities.'[14]

Having examined one level of the TV commercial, we now move to a second aspect of its influence; the power of the electronic image as 'icon' and 'symbol'. Images, which communicate as words cannot, with their great power to evoke feeling, cause something to happen to us though we may not be consciously aware of it. Advertising creates a world of mirrors in which we get new images of ourselves that fit well the purpose of the system.[15] Gregor Goethals in her book, *The TV Ritual, Worship at the Video Altar*, suggests that the TV commercial is a kind of electronic 'icon' for our time, appealing to hope and fear, promising miracles and calling forth fidelity, not to a king or a saviour, but to a product. Traditional icons of old represented hope to the believer and confirmed faith as they were contemplated with sustained love and devotion. The TV commercial weaves words such as faith, trust, loyalty, confidence, assurance, and happiness in and out of its thirty second message, becoming a visual, musical catechism affecting how persons see themselves and their world.[16]

> By buying a product everybody has a chance to become members incorporate in the mystical body of those who have been redeemed from obesity, ring-around-the-collar, bad breath, or simple human loneliness.[17]

A further attraction in commercials is the very human habit of raising questions, posing problems, and finding resolutions.

> Concern about body odour and the weekly wash could camouflage a need to ask more profound questions about mysterious and complex human experiences. The endless, mindless questions and answers encountered in commercials are a fractured, sometimes pathetic witness to the persistent human compulsion to raise questions and cope with life's problems. They also reflect the profound metamorphosis from Questions to questions, from the mysteries and miracles of traditional sacred truths to the mysteries and miracles of modern detergents. This transformation is accompanied by a metamorphosis of both images and faith; from gods to goods, from salvation to soaps.[18]

Symbols which call forth positive feelings are readily packaged into dramas, slogans, stories, and songs by clever advertisers. The strong emotional charge of patriotic symbols finds apt expression for Coca-Cola ... 'Look up America!' and for Pepsi ... 'Feelin' free!' Marches, bands, ball games, picnics, and hayrides readily accompany the phrases and songs. But the most ancient and revered symbols are those of a religious and spiritual nature. These too are boldly marketed in commercials in order to evoke positive charges in unsuspecting viewers. We see and hear that 'Datsun *saves* ... Zerox is a *miracle* ... Laura Secord candy is simply *divine* ... Natchos are the *ultimate*'. Coke and Pepsi bottles are wreathed in halos as the faces of those savouring Kentucky Fried Chicken are transformed through this sublime taste experience. As these products are linked with religious themes, the symbols of faith, hope, and love are turned back in on us. We are called to an unconditional belief in 'Tide', to trust fully in 'Ford Motor', to have sincere hope in 'S-O-S cleaning pads', to love deeply 'Mrs. Smith's Frozen Apple Pie' . . . 'Taste, prepare to meet your maker!' Transcendence has been defined as 'that particular quality by which the source and terminus of the religious relation surpasses absolutely the mind and all other reality.[19] This element, naming the relationship between God and all that is but is not God, has gained much popular interest today through mind-expanding drugs, altered states of consciousness, and mystical Eastern prayer techniques. It is no little wonder that TV commercial writers would also pick up and commercialize the concept for greater profits. A good illustration of this may be found in a recent commercial called 'The Stranger from the House of Levi'. In the mini-drama a mysterious figure enters a colourless town bringing Levis to improve everyone's life-style and then moves on in search of new towns to energize. The whole thing has a mystical quality with its sense of mission and divine bringer of the 'good news' of Levis. In this stranger, two themes, of the lonesome cowboy and the Christ figure, are cleverly combined to magically transform the townspeople. Even the title, 'The House of Levi' holds definite connections with the Tribe of Levi of the Old Testament where the priests were concerned with salvation. Hence, the merchandise becomes 'God-like' and who wouldn't buy into that theme?[20] The electronic 'icon' promotes not only products but a way of life, a philosophy, a transcendency which is difficult to resist.

What then does all of this have to do with the Christian message, the call of the Gospel to radical change and conversion? The Canadian Conference of Catholic Bishops urges Christians to build a humane world where no one fears another and where the resources of Creation are developed to supply what all people need to maintain a decent life-style.[21] Yet we have just seen that the ideology of the TV commercial contradicts this call. Based on fear and continuing to develop fear, it urges a minority of the world's population to devour a huge amount of its resources while millions of others drown in a sea of poverty. The Christian idea of transcendency offers the possibility of new life, not simply new looks, or new taste treats. Christ's call is to live beyond the normal boundaries of human nature. 'We live transcendently, exceeding the normal expectations of human persons, to the degree that we live the faith, hope, and love preached by Jesus Christ.'[22]

TV commercials fit well into the traditional model of change where the few direct the many, where those in control decide how things will function and how the common good is best served. Maintaining the status quo with order and harmony is at the heart of much advertising technique. Toyota – 'They all lived happily ever after' . . . Minute Maid Orange Juice – 'Goodness at its best' . . . Pepto Bismol – 'coats, soothes, relieves.' On the other hand the radical model of change with its critical view of economic, political, and cultural structures and social systems would threaten modern advertising considerably.[23] The encouragement of creative conflict along with community participation in what travels along the airwaves could change the whole concept of commercials as we presently know them.

> According to this radical interpretation of change, all parts of society are related to all other parts. Consequently a decision concerning any one part has implications for the whole. The rise of the price of oil affects the price of food. The amount of gasoline used by US motorists affects and is affected by our foreign policy. The fashions of New York determine employment patterns in South Korea.[24]

The implications of this principle for TV commercializing are tremendous. No longer could the consumer craze continue if such a world-view of humankind was internalized.

TV commercials are clever, expensive, persuasive, and anxiety-producing, holding out to us the carrot of a better life, a better body and better relationships through the consumer ethic. They have reversed the basic and traditional tenets of our society. Instead of reverencing nature, we process it; forgetting thrift, we see our duty as buying; work is not as important to us as consumption; modesty gives way to the super-sexual image; ego-restraint bends under the force of self-love as a consecrated ritual.[25] How can one survive in a world of such distortion? What choices are ours in such a seductive culture? Critical analysis, recognition of the devices of the persuaders, and constant reflection on what is being put forth in the world of advertising is absolutely essential if we are to remain sane and balanced. Dealing with the complexities of modern communication is a demanding and draining task. We can choose not to be persuaded but we must know what is going on for, without serious reflection, untold violence is done to our person. The social analysis models of change can assist us in this task.

> First, analysis helps us to understand the responses taken by those in positions of influence and authority to a given social situation. When action on behalf of justice confronts opposition, it is important to examine the model of change employed by those who support the status quo. We can then sort out the various tactics and strategies necessary to move toward further change . . . Second, the models of change help us know our own strengths and weaknesses. If we examine our own experiences honestly – personal experiences as well as institutional experiences – we probably are aware that we operate according to all models of change. At different times, in differing situations, we tend to support actions that are 'system preserving' or 'system-reforming', or 'system transforming' . . . But which time is it in the history of our social system? This question is one of discernment.[26]

Finally, we must continue to question the '30 Second Dream' philosophy:
- What claims are really being made?
- What or who is being linked with the product?
  (Love, family, patriotism, religion, stardom.)
- How am I portrayed as a person?
- What kind of person does this commercial call me to become?
- What is being left out?
  (Concern for others, world issues, global views.)
- What view of the world does this commercial give me?

The presence of the TV world of reality will continue to invade our homes and the privacy of our minds and hearts. Our response to this presence must be more and more conscious, reflective, and critical lest we become totally absorbed in the 'cloud of visual and aural symbols' penetrating our environment. Advertising, the turning of our attention toward something, could give us new images of ourselves as a people aware of others and of our life in the 'global village'. The question of whether or not it will remains unanswered.

NOTES

1 Ruth Goldsen, *The Show and Tell Machine*, New York: Delta Pub. Co.: 1975, pp. ix, 1.
2 Gail West, 'The Effects of TV: A Bibliography.' The Living Light, Vol. 17 (Fall 1980), p. 220.
3 Arthur Berger, *The TV Guided American*, New York: Walker and Co.: 1976, p. 57.
4 Goldsen op. cit., pp. 6–10.
5 Canadian Conference of Catholic Bishops, 'A Society To Be Transformed', *Witness to Justice*, Ottawa: 1977, p. 13.
6 J. Holland and p. Henriot, *Social Analysis: Linking Faith and Justice*, Washington DC: Centre of Concern: 1980.
7 Erik Barnouw, *The Sponsor, Notes on a Modern Potentate*, New York: Oxford University Press: 1978, pp. 82–3.
8 Jerry Mander, *Four Arguments for the Elimination of Television*, New York: Morrow Quill Paperbacks: 1978, pp. 128–9.
9 Goldsen, op. cit., p. 112.
10 Ibid., pp. 139–41 & 380.
11 Quoted in Erik Barnouw, *Tube of Plenty: The Evolution of American Television*, New York: Oxford University Press: 1975, p. 355.
12 Barnouw, *The Sponsor*, pp. 96–7.
13 'Preaching in the Marketplace', *America*, Vol. 136 (21 May 1977), p. 457.
14 Stuart Ewen, *Captains of Consciousness*, New York: McGraw-Hill: 1976, p. 87.
15 J. Mander, op. cit., p. 131.
16 Gregor Goethals, *The T.V. Ritual: Worship at the Video Altar*, Boston: Beacon Press: 1981, pp. 136–9.
17 Ibid., p. 137.
18 Ibid., p. 138.
19 Louis Dupré, 'Transcendence and Immanence as Theological Categories', *CTSA Proceedings*, Vol. 31 (1976), p. 1.
20 Berger, op. cit., pp. 57–61.
21 Canadian Conference of Catholic Bishops, op. cit., p. 2.
22 Kevin Culligan, 'Christian Transcendency and the American Dream,' *Spiritual Life* Vol. 22, (Spring 1976), p. 38.
23 J. Holland and p. Henriot, op. cit., pp. 16–17.
24 Ibid., p. 16.
25 Barnouw, *The Sponsor*, p. 98.
26 Holland and Henriot, op. cit., pp. 18–19.

16   Theological reflections: social effects of television

JEANNE COVER

> But he looked for justice but behold bloodshed; for righteousness, but behold a cry! (Isa. 5:7) . . . my people go into exile for want of knowledge (Isa. 5:13).

We, human beings, called to a covenantal relationship with God and humanity, and made in God's image and likeness, are being reduced to mere tools of the corporations of technology and the commercial world. In a world of broken relationships and individual isolation we have come to seek our solace in the panaceas and dreams provided by the consumer society, where 'freedom' is equated with 'choice' of material goods. Called to follow Jesus in radical discipleship, and to personal and collective conversion, we need a theology of kenosis, of emptying ourselves of our obsessions for material satisfaction, success, domination, and affluence. A radical transformation of society is called for, and a renewal of our covenantal priorities, whereby community-participation will replace privatization and passive receptivity; a search for justice will replace injustice, and love-in-service will replace the drive towards power. It is to be hoped that our survival will not be in jeopardy before this new redemption can take place.

As I commenced this theological reflection, which has really become a journey of discovery for me, it was not the power of the visual image and ritual employed by the medium of television, or even our addiction to it, which caused me surprise. For many years I have examined with history students Hitler's successful control of communications and propaganda in consolidating his regime. Films of the Nuremberg rallies give evidence of the power of symbols, strong rhythms, and processions to stir not only the Germans of his time, but even today's viewers. Religious liturgies, tribal celebrations, indeed sacred events in all ages have been accompanied by ritual and symbol. Two aspects in my study of mass media, religious awareness and values, have made a deep impression on me, and it is on these that I will attempt to reflect in this chapter in the light of the Word of God and of my own experience:

1. The ideologies of power and of consumerism which both govern and are reflected in our current rituals and symbols, especially through television.
2. The subservience of this ideology and of the media itself to the power structures of technology and large global corporations, and the consequences of this.

Theology is about what concerns us ultimately, and knowledge of God cannot be divorced from knowledge of humanity. Social analysis and pastoral ministry are not only consequences flowing from theological reflection; they also generate theology. It is vital, therefore, for one involved in any pastoral ministry (education in my case), to be aware of one's own role in reinforcing the cultural hegemony, and to be conscious of the controlling forces.

Lonergan[1] sees human consciousness as an ongoing process with five levels: experience which seeks the data and begs for understanding of 'how' and 'why', judgement of values, decision demanding action based on these value judgements, and the dynamism of love in commitment. Being a real person in today's world requires a genuine awakening of our consciousness for 'our responsible choices and actions constitute not only our world mediated by meaning, but our very selves.'[2] Prayerful meditative reflection on experience is basic. Indeed Baum calls critical theology a 'reflection on praxis',[3] and Holland and Henriot, influenced by the conferences at Medellin and Puebla, put experience with social analysis and theological reflection as essential components of their praxis of social action.[4] God wills that the gospel should transform not only our personal and private lives, but all social and public behaviour, and the attitudes and structures of our world.[5] For Jesus to know reality was to transform it, and in his alliance with the poor and the outcasts and his struggle against the structures of oppression, he encountered reality itself. Praxis is concrete action in discipleship with Jesus.

In this chapter I wish to put forward six propositions:

1. The ideology inherent in the advertising and majority of programmes offered by television channels reveals the social sin and collective blindness condemned by Jesus

and the Hebrew prophets, and is largely due to false consciousness;

2. This ideology has as its priorities affluence, power, efficiency and competition and undermines the basic stability of family life and community;

3. Not only has the secular replaced the religious, but sacred symbols have been removed from their religious contexts to give a spurious feeling of transcendence and sacredness to a 'theology' of consumerism;

4. The dignity of the human person made for self-transcendence and mystery[6] is threatened by the passive receptivity induced by the television medium, and the creativity and imagination required for theological reflection and social transformation are being stifled by the artificial moods, emotions, feelings and docility engendered and controlled by technology;

5. Global corporations exert their power to control the media, and create the psychological and physical needs that satisfy the requirements of their own growth. Not only the comparatively affluent countries, but the poorest peoples of the world, are being used as pawns in the hands of the powerful capitalist technology.

6. We need a new theology arising from a praxis which is modelled on that of Jesus, who revealed a God-in-humanity hanging powerless on a cross, and sought to establish the reign of God not by power but by service to the poor and the oppressed.

Their land is filled with idols; They bow down to the work of their hands, to what their own fingers have made (Isa. 2:8).

I invite you to worship with me at the Video Altar! Let us sit silent before the altar in a church set 'apart from the world' upon the limitless ocean with a background of wondrous coastlands, and harbours. The opening hymn promises 'something for everyone' and in just one hour we will be shown how travel on the *Love Boat* reconciles lovers, offers a first love, and brings new love to those who thought they would never love again. As the Captain performs marriage ceremonies for three happy couples his sermon assures us that 'love is more important than money'. However, in case we believe love can exist without money, the life on board ship reminds the congregation of rapt TV viewers that success, affluence, eternal youth, physical beauty and love are inseparable, and the twenty commercials interspersed throughout leave us in no doubt as to how to achieve these goals. *Love Boat* is easy to watch; no 'uncomfortable' social issues are introduced; our consciences are set at rest by the alleged concern of the ship's 'family', while the breathtaking scenes of nature's beauty raise us above our petty monotonous routine. Our belief in 'the good life' is reinforced by the constant assertions that our ideals can be realized by material acquisitions, and that relationships will endure because of them.

We are now well prepared for *Fantasy Island* where if we can afford the price, material and spiritual, we can have our fantasies realized. These fantasies fulfil personal ambitions and we achieve them alone.

Two hours of *McMillan and Wife* show us the success of an affluent, intelligent, happily-married couple. Any suspicions we may have that their life is unrealistic are soon removed as they argue over mundane domestic affairs with which we are familiar. We are allowed to identify with them and see ourselves as 'intelligent and superior'. Thirty-seven commercials reinforce our opinion. Each product is 'superior'. Wendy's hamburgers have 'class' and are for 'connoisseurs' (like us); we are invited by McDonald's to join the executive class for breakfast; Ontario Hydro assures us of their care – we are in safe hands – they 'do more than make electricity'. What this 'more' consists of is not clear. United Technologies are not to be feared – they are human beings like ourselves concerned only for our individual progress. We are presented with bath salts for our personal hygiene, and detergents for our luxurious kitchens and bathrooms. Labatt's beer will give us entry into this happy class, or alternatively we may join the successful group of Budweiser drinkers who in their superiority 'salute' those at sea, and those on the land. Blessed are the children, the parents, the dogs and the cats who have such riches offered to them! Surely we must accept these assurances of concern. We need take no positive social action, but leave it all to them for they will 'do it all for us'. Nor is there any place for guilt about our desires for affluence and success, for these are allegedly essential for family unity, personal dignity, meaning and fulfilment. There is little opportunity for consideration of alternative definitions of meaning and self-transcendence. Any suspicions we may have that there is more to life succumb eventually under our saturation by this constant barrage of consumerism and the values it puts forward.[7]

The afternoon soaps give further opportunity for 'escape' into the world of television heroes and heroines, with their intrigues and intricate 'relationships'. So realistic can these fictional characters become that in Australia recently the actor playing the role of the villain in *The Restless Years* had his life threatened! A fund-raising association successfully used the presence of the TV 'family' 'The Sullivans' as a drawing card for one of their functions. Farrah Fawcett (lately Majors) gave her hair-style to thousands of teen-agers (though Princess Diana's style is now in ascendence). *Class of '74* showed to young teenagers a group of students of their own age involved in drug-taking, sex, and abortion. In the same show teachers could be distinguished from students only by their illicit relationships, heterosexual and/or homosexual, with both students and other teachers. I found that older, more respon-sible, students were greatly concerned about the attraction these and similar shows had for their younger brothers and sisters. The theme song of *The Restless Years* explains away all aberrations and promiscuity. There is no responsibility or sin involved – all can be attributed to 'our restless years' – a restlessness which is common to all human beings. These partial truths and the seductive nature of the media itself make it difficult for many, especially the young, to recognize reality.

Crime shows further endorse the values of this cultural hegemony. Violence is acceptable if associated with efficiency and success. Starsky and Hutch show us successful aggression, or we can follow *Charlie's Angels* as they carry out the orders of the invisible *deus ex machina* – Charlie. There is nothing so blatant as presenting chorus lines of semi-naked girls for our entertainment. No! This would be exploitation. Instead we see the successful investigators capture those who engage in such exploitation and this incidentally necessitates some 10 – 15 minutes viewing of the chorus line. (For those who missed this spectacle, Pepsi offers a tempting minute of similar viewing in its com-mercials.) In American and Australian television most successful investigators are young and white. Recently in Australia a popular series on the non-commercial channel featured 'Boney' – the part-Aboriginal detective of Arthur Upfield's novels. It was a sad indictment of our society's degradation of the Aborigines that a New Zealand Maori actor had to be chosen for this part.

Many more instances of the impact of television in desensitizing our vision and imagination and forming our priorities could be given. Ruth Goldsen[8] portrays very clearly the television conceptions of sexuality, family life and human nature. Husbands, wives and lovers are as disposable as the 'elasticized diapers' and 'plastic containers' which the commercials recommend to us. Though commitment is trivialized, advertisers ironically feel the need to portray the family in their commercials. However, it is used as a symbol rather than as a reality. Television redefines 'family' as the 'crew' of a ship, the 'Odd Couple', Archie Bunker's oddly assorted members, and parentless groups. Only in historical dramas does the family appear intact.

Much of this may reflect the breakdown of family life and commitment in relationships which is present in today's world. However, television programmes legitimize and to some extent 'canonize' this situation. Moreover, the commercial world identifies spiritual ideals with the acquisition of consumer goods. The cultural emphases endorsed reflect a basically unjust society, with racist overtones, where women are still regarded as made for the use of men, where children are denigrated, where individualism and competition replace relationships and community, and where victims are treated as scapegoats or blamed for their inefficiency.

It is not new in the history of humanity that human beings seek the illusions and panaceas provided by literature, live theatre, and now television. What is new and far more insidious is the impact of the commercial world which has increasingly provided us with 'an idiom within which desires for social change and fantasies of liberation might be articulated and contained.'[9] We have now come to accept the priorities and attitudes of the powerful that permeate our televized lives – success, affluence, private property, efficiency and competition, consumerism, and the 'advantages' of technology. These market-place precepts have come to be given a universal validity.

These 'technicolour fantasies' and 'vicarious treats' cost television viewers over \$3 billion a year for the price of 40,000 commercials.[10] However, the consequences are more widespread than financial cost. We, like the poor tin god we set before us, are the tools of the global corporations who through their control of television control also the marketing and dissemination of ideas and create an ideology of 'salvation through profits and growth.'[11]

Yet 'no ideology can be legitimate unless the interests it defends are legitimate'.[12]

Go, therefore and make disciples of all nations (Matt. 28:19).

A Unesco study in 1974[13] showed the pervasive influence and widespread export of US television programmes. Canada and Australia import at least 50 per cent of their programmes, Guatemala 84 per cent, and Malaysia 71 per cent. Doctor Kekkonen, President of Finland, expressed his concern for democracy if 'only the dominant patterns of behaviour and pressure of public opinion offer content to people's views of the world;[14] but Herbert Schuller of the University of California sees 'social forces' as responsible for television in most countries and doubts whether locally produced programmes would indeed vary very much.[15] In 1970 the two largest US advertising firms had 56 per cent of the total billings in Latin America. The Columbia Broadcasting System distributes programmes to over 100 countries. In Peru Channel 5, which earned 63 per cent of all TV advertising revenues in 1969, derived more than 11 per cent from Procter and Gamble and Colgate-Palmolive. Seventy per cent of all newspaper news is supplied by two major wire services, Associated Press and United Press International.[16]

Thus we are offering not merely entertainment but attitudes, philosophies of life, and consumerism. By our complicity, even if unwitting, with these values and priorities, we are contributing further to social injustice both in our own countries and in those parts of the world where poverty predominates. We act in league with the global corporations whose technology is 'for enhancing private consumption, not for solving social problems'.[17] We join Coca Cola and Pepsi whose influence in Mexico has resulted in 'commerciogenic malnutrition' and we support the company campaigns which have succeeded in increasing the consumption of white bread, confections and soft drinks among the poorest peoples of the world.[18] In those less affluent countries we have been so successful in spreading our images of success, efficiency, leisure and pleasure that 'the mobile minority, encouraged by advertising to adopt the eating, wearing and travelling habits of the American upper middle class, live imported lives.'[19] Individual consumption, private cars, refrigerators, and expensive medical technology have received more emphasis than safe drinking water. It is appalling to realize that human beings outside our own countries have become of less importance to us than the 'cat-pianist' who demands 'Meow' Cat Food, or the dog whose welfare the commercials tell us is contingent upon 'Chunky Dog Food'.

These are instances of the false consciousness to which Baum refers, one 'created by these institutions and ideologies through which people involve themselves collectively in destructive action as if they were doing the right thing'.[20] In 1974 the Canadian bishops in their pastoral letter 'Sharing Daily Bread' criticized the 'free market system' which is legitimized by cultural and religious symbols.[21] This system, says Baum, 'has created a consciousness in us which makes us co-operate with it, . . . and apply its principle to even wider aspects of life'.[22] The corporate decisions can become the locus of free collective sins and increased injustices. The media, press, television and radio, so dependent on the commercial world for financial support, reinforce and legitimize our corporate sin.

This social sin is being compounded by the entry of 'religion' into the world of technology and television. Televangelical preachers reinforce a traditional conservative view of society which supports the status quo and the values which accompany it. Such preachers as Jerry Falwell, Pat Robertson, Rex Humbard and Don Stewart urge us to personal conversion to Jesus, but the lack of the need for any real change and their stress on accommodation with the present power structures of society, present a far cry from the repentance and conversion preached by Jesus who aligned himself with the poor and offered his disciples values which were the reverse of those of the world in which we live. Hadden and Swann, who themselves present a liberal evolutionary model of social analysis,[23] show the political and social power of these preachers, but I wonder how great their success would be if they preached 'transformation of' rather than 'accommodation with' the status quo, if they preached metanoia and community participation rather than individual salvation evidenced in material rewards. These TV preachers who do not challenge but reinforce what entertainment and commercials teach are the most successful.[24] Social concern has no part in their programmes.

Television can present Eucharistic sacrifices and religious events in a most moving fashion, as Goethals shows.[25] Yet television uses the same techniques and images, though not the same content, to give us a sense of participation, involvement, sacredness and awe, in its presentation of such events as the 'Superbowl', the 'Return of the Constitution to Canada' and the inauguration of presidents. We, creatures made for the 'unseen', with powers of creativity and imagination, with a capacity for I–Thou–We relationships imagining the Trinity of Community in God, have lost our sense of the supernatural and seek meaning in electronic 'ritual' images.

> What does the Lord require of you but to do justice, and to love kindness, and to walk humbly with your God? (Micah 6:8)

The whole prophetic message of Scripture teaches us that only in response to the neighbour can the claims of God be met and known. Theological statements are an analysis of the depths of personal relationships, or rather, an analysis of the depths of all experience 'interpreted by love'.[26] In the foregoing pages I have tried to reflect on my experience of television, seeking understanding and attempting judgement. This led me to the global corporations which control and condition our culture. Now I have reached the difficult task of responding to the call to move out of my own liberal/semi-traditionalist model of viewing change, into the unknown radical world presented by Jesus.

Once we begin to think in terms of transformation our 'creative imagination is freed, and this opening up of imagination, while not of itself bringing change, may be a key step towards it.'[27] Television need not condemn us to passive receptivity. Such programmes as *Fifth Estate*, *60 Minutes*, *Man Alive*, and certain Australian Catholic Communications programmes show the potential of television for involving us in evaluation and community participation. These are hopeful signs.

The Church cannot be exempt from this call to a conversion of consciousness and structure. It spans nations and like the global corporations has imposed cultural ideals and expectations. The Church must be seen to have aligned itself not with the powerful but with the poor and oppressed, and it is *we*, the people of God, who are the Church. To Jesus, the kingdom was present and future. It was a kingdom where the master was the servant, and the first guests to the banquet were from 'the highways and by-ways'. At the Last Supper, Jesus not only gave us his body, soon to be broken for us, and his blood, soon to be shed, but he became the servant of his disciples. The challenge today for me as I am engaged in education is to educate for transformation, not necessarily to turn my back on the well-to-do who seek education in our schools, but also not to stand alongside the forces that reinforce the 'sacredness' of power, affluence, competition and efficiency. In the school in which I was principal for the last eleven years, a high school of 600 students from the ages of eleven to eighteen, I saw what the young can offer to the work of transformation. It was easy to build community, reward personal and corporate effort rather than competition, and to serve the poor, elderly, and lonely in the nearby area. Yet we did not move beyond the liberal model which seeks to alleviate poverty, balance tensions, and accommodate change, without actually fundamentally altering the structures of society which produce and maintain these. A new type of evangelization is needed where discipleship of Jesus is a radical alliance with the powerless, and a new vision that sees the 'signs of the times'. The sinners to be converted so that they may enter the kingdom are those who help to maintain power and oppression and are unconscious of their personal contribution to this social sin, and here I cannot exclude myself.

To Jesus, power was service and the cross was love in the face of sin, the solidarity of God with the oppressed and suffering. Suffering is a by-product not a goal, and praxis is more than internal personal conversion. It is action involving a redefining of what it means to be a Christian. From the praxis of Jesus we can see what sin is – a saying 'No' to the cry of the poor and oppressed. Holland and Henriot advocate a move from 'Christ the King' to 'Christ the Servant', yet kingdom and service are not in opposition when one understands what Jesus means by kingdom. He redefined power as love in service.

Jesus's new covenant fulfilled the old; yet the old covenant was always seen in terms of relationships. Social injustice, a neglect of the poor, always resulted in a breaking of covenant. We must be aware of the violence that is produced by institutionalized injustice and ideologies that use force to win power. The very existence of global multinational corporations is a 'sign' of the need for communion and participation among nations. The base communities of Latin America 'work together to challenge the egotistical and consumeristic roots of society, and make explicit their vocation to communion with God and with their fellow human beings'.[28] Such a theology will be meaningful and will speak to today' secularized world. Indeed 'until institutionalized religion can ... evoke the fullness of human passion, television will nurture our illusions of heroism and self-transcendence'[29] rather than commitment in service and love.

There are hopeful signs in the growing questioning of the power and ideologies of technology and the global shopping centre with its resultant unemployment, inflation, crime, pollution, racial violence, terrorism, lack of meaningful work, and the psychological miseries of affluence – alienation, rootlessness and boredom.[30] Deeds of political power may be necessary to bring about the radical transformation that is called for, but the truly Christian praxis will have a new theology of liberation whereby power is seen as love in service to and identification with the poor and oppressed. In this way we will be called to complete in our own lives the redemptive work of Jesus.

Hope must be a primary tenet of our theology for Jesus has gone before us:

> In the world you have tribulation; but be of good cheer, I have overcome the world. (John 16:33)

In this chapter I have confined my analysis of the media to television. Space does not permit a similar coverage of the press, but it could be argued that it also is an agent in reinforcing the unjust power structures and cultural hegemony of our society and is bound to the global corporations of commerce and technology for the financial support it needs to exist.

In this reflection I have attempted to look at the effects of television on society, both through television programming and through its subservience to the powerful corporations controlling it. A radical transformation of society is required, one which involves personal and collective conversion from social sin to discipleship and service-in-love. Reflection on experience is the first step in the arousal of human consciousness, which I have viewed as a process with five levels – experience, understanding, judgement, decision and love. This love must be shown in action, in aligning ourselves with the powerless and with those who are exploited by the forces promoting the false values of our cultural hegemony.[31]

NOTES

1   Bernard Lonergan, *Insight: A Study of Human Understanding*, rev. ed. New York: Philosophical Library: 1958, passim.
2   Peter Beer, 'Meaning in Relation to the Trinity' in T. Dunne and J. M. Laporte (eds.), *Trinification of the World*, Toronto: Regis College Press: 1978.
3   Gregory Baum, *Religion and Alienation*, New York: Paulist Press: 1975, Ch. IX 'Critical Theology', p. 195.
4   J. Holland and p. Henriot, *Social Analysis: Linking Faith and Justice*, Centre of Concern: Washington-Union Labor: 1980, p. 3.
5   'A Society to be Transformed', a Pastoral Message by The Catholic Bishops of Canada, 1 December 1977 in *Witness to Justice*, Canadian Catholic Organization for Development and Peace: Toronto, p. 29.
6   Karl Rahner, 'The Concept of Mystery in Catholic Theology', *Theological Investigations*, Vol. 4, pp. 36–73.
7   A selection of prime-time television programmes shown on 8 May 1982 is given here.
8   Ruth Goldsen, *The Show and Tell Machine*, New York: Delta Paperback: 1977.
9   Stuart Ewen, *Captains of Consciousness*, New York: McGraw Hill Book Co.: 1977, p. 219.
10   Richard J. Barnet and Ronald E. Muller, *Global Reach: The Power of the Multinational Corporations*, New York: Simon and Schuster: 1974, p. 232.
11   Ibid., p. 253.
12   *Puebla and Beyond:* documentation and commentary, Maryknoll, N.Y.: Orbis Books: 1979, p. 323.
13   Kaarle Nordensberg and Tapio Varis, *Television Traffic – A One-Way Street?* Reports and Papers on Mass Communication No. 70, Unesco: Paris: 1974, pp. 13–15; *Canadian Radio-television and Telecommunications Commission 1977*, 'T.V. in Canada: What Canadians Choose to Watch', pp. 1–13. These reports give the following information: CBC Canada imports 34% of its programmes, 80% from US; RC Canada imports 46%, ⅓ from France, 50% from US; in the ten years up to 1977 the number of US stations viewed in Canada increased from 28 to 52; commercial channels in Australia import 75% of their programmes from UK and US (1974); US imports only 1% of its programmes (1974); in 1976 Canadians watched a daily average of 3.8 hours television per person between 6 p.m. and 12 a.m. For Anglo-Canadians 71% of this time was spent watching US programmes.
14   Kaarle Nordensberg and Tapio Varis, op. cit, p. 45.
15   Ibid., p. 49.
16   Barnet and Muller, pp. 143, 144 and 232.
17   Ibid., p. 165.

18 Ibid., p. 184.
19 Ibid., p. 174.
20 Baum, op. cit, p. 201.
21 Ibid., p. 202.
22 Ibid., p. 203.
23 J. K. Hadden and C. E. Swann, *Prime Time Preachers*, Addison-Wesley Co: Mass: 1982.
24 Ibid., p. 101.
25 G. T. Goethals. *The T.V. Ritual*, Boston: Beacon Press: 1981, Chapter 1.
26 Robinson, John A., *Honest to God*, London: SCM: 1963, Chapter 3, passim.
27 Holland and Henriot, op. cit, p. 27.
28 *Puebla and Beyond*, p. 317.
29 Goethals, op. cit, pp. 143–4.
30 Barnet and Muller, op. cit, p. 68.
31 The more active participation in Australia of family, community, and Church groups in actually campaigning with the Television Controls Board for different programmes and for more independence in choice of programmes has already given some signs of hope.

17 'Thou shalt have no other jeans before me'

DOROTHEE SÖLLE

Upon rereading Jaspers[1] I asked myself what might be implied by the category of 'existential unconditionedness' (*Unbedingtheit*), what he may have meant by it, whether if even today there might be a need for such unconditionedness and whether we have a language capable of articulating it, how it might be possible to clarify the theological background of this question, what assistance could be provided by the language of religious tradition to permit a better understanding of the spiritual and political situation of the 1970s.

In order to champion the notion of a 'more human life-world', Jaspers criticizes the 'universal apparatus of existence' that oppresses us:

> But should the time come when nothing in the individual's real and immediate surroundings is made, moulded, or handed down by that individual for his own purposes; when everything serves as nothing but the stuff for the instant gratification of needs, to be consumed and discarded; when living itself becomes mechanized and when the surroundings become despiritualized, when work counts only as a day's labour and ceases to play a role in shaping an individual's life – then the individual would be, as it were, without a world.[2]

These words, written long before the second industrial revolution, have lost even more of their subjunctive character. The number of people who through their work make, mould, and hand down something has undergone even further decline; a 'spiritual quality of one's own surroundings' can now be conceived only in caricature, having become fully privatized in summer homes on the Mediterranean; the 'continuity' of the individual self was already ridiculed by Gottfried Benn, who likened it to 'those garments which, cut from quality cloth, are guaranteed for ten years'.

If one asked what could save people from the apparatus, what would make their world human again or could preserve its human character, one would find in Jaspers's discussion such hackneyed phrases as 'the attainment of being', to 'turn to human existence', and, most important, the 'existential unconditionedness' that keeps alive the claim of existence. Today all these terms strike us as peculiarly impotent. Although once filled with meaning, they have now degenerated into elements of a cultural criticism that takes aim at Marxism and psychoanalysis, throwing them into the same pot as racism, the pot of 'ideology'. Apart from this unjustified and élitist critique of mass existence, it must still be asked whether there is something more concealed within Jaspers's formulations and his tumid prose ('will to destiny', 'authentic human existence') than the fear of loss in prestige that mass culture had instilled in the German bourgeoisie of the 1930s. For in the term 'existential unconditionedness' an attempt was made to secure something that, while already suspected of representing a form of 'irrationalism', seemed nonetheless to be more than a mere negation of critical rationality.

What is meant by unconditionedness? At the very least it signifies an interest in an existence that is not exhausted by the performing of functions defined by others, that does not consist in the means for externally imposed ends. Existence denotes what is irreducible, non-derivable, and incapable of being fashioned in terms of function. Existence is the basic category of a philosophy of liberation that struggles against precisely this functionalization of human life within the massive apparatus. 'I exist' means that I am not an object for others. I am more than what they know of me, more than what they can use. Even when I experience myself as conditioned in every respect, the meaning of life continues to consist in being an end and not simply a means, in existing and not simply in functioning.

As conservative and even reactionary as Jaspers's conclusion may seem to be, the task remains, even within a philosophy of existence, to distinguish between features that are emancipatory-humanistic and those that are repressive-élitist. The claim to exist, to be an end and not a means, to fulfill existence and not merely a function, is one of the most profound of all human needs, and it cannot be dismissed as merely irrational. Unconditionedness and absoluteness may indeed be misleading expressions, since, after all, unconditionedness can itself be achieved only under conditions that lend themselves to research and derivation, just as absoluteness can be understood only in ascertaining its relativity. Nonetheless the essence of unconditionedness, of the non-derivative meaningfulness of human life, cannot be disposed of in this fashion.

This essence found historical expression in the language of religion. Jaspers's entire analysis is imbued with a sense of grief regarding lost religions. It is a philosophy after the death of God, which aims to supersede and translate into existential terms that which was once designated by the word 'God'. Religion was a specific historical form of this longing for absoluteness; in a post-religious age we must find another language to express the nature of unconditionedness, one that gives human life a sense of meaning. Jaspers made this attempt. The experience of and adherence to an existential unconditionedness led him to a 'philosophical faith'. Yet did not Jaspers, even with this notion of a faith that has been rendered autonomous and severed from the tradition and institution of the church, remain more under the spell of religion than he himself knew? Is not the exaggerated demand for meaning, however philosophically it might be cast, itself still a part of religion? Might it not lie in the deepest interest of an existential unconditionedness to actualize religious traditions? Is it not possible that we cannot afford to dispense with those congealed experiences of meaning present in scripture and tradition, when the presentation and conveyance of existential immediacy is at issue?

Jaspers lived at the end of the age of bread. Plastics had not yet become the primary means of sustenance. Religion was in a process of decay, but the need for meaning had still in no way been rendered superfluous. By contrast, the situation in which we find ourselves today can be described as one in which there no longer exists a language to express the notions of meaning, existential unconditionedness, and faith. The age of bread (*Brot*) is over, and so too is the age of philosophical nourishment (*Brötschen*). We have been exposed to a manipulation of needs that has also transformed the need for uniqueness, novelty, and meaning into an obsession with possessions. Domination, the manipulation of consciousness, schooling in the destruction of one's own interests, are no longer performed by religion and the Church but by production and advertisement. The new religion is consumerism.

At the beginning of the 1970s an advertising jingle appeared recommending 'Jesus Jeans'. The Italian author and film-maker Pier Paolo Pasolini applied to this jingle a form of linguistic analysis in which he makes a comment on the spiritual situation of the age.[3] Pasolini sees a 'revolution from the right', which by the beginning of the 1970s had reached Italy as well. This revolution is profound, fundamental, and absolutely new, invested with sufficient power to destroy all existing institutions: family, culture, language, and Church. He calls this new state of affairs 'hedonistic fascism' or *consumismo* (consumerism). With regard to the theme advanced by Jaspers, this *consumismo* represents the perfect and inexorable repression of every form of existential unconditionedness. 'There is indeed no longer anything religious in the idealized image of the young husband and wife propagated and ordained by television. They are just two people whose lives gain reality through consumer goods.'

What is implied by the expression, 'no longer religious'? Did the ideal of a young couple at one time have a different significance? Was the subject matter different? Was there a promise of happiness filled by something more than consuming with each other? 'It is futile to want to preserve an unconditioned truth without God' (Horkheimer). The mythical basis for a life incapable of being made or being given as a thing was designated by the word 'God'. 'Without God' was therefore illusory, since – incidentally, as much to the Frankfurt School as to Jaspers – the danger was apparent that mundane, partial, conditioned, and particular ends might expand into universal, unconditioned, and divine ones. To live meaningfully and yet without God would appear unintelligible, as it is only *with* God that false gods and obtruding idols could successfully be repudiated. In fairness it must be conceded that in Horkheimer's philosophy as well God is in danger of being reduced to a mere function, a purifying and iconoclastic function oriented to the critique of ideology. Here, too, it is not possible to make positive statements about what God wants, where God stands – illuminating myths capable of instilling hope. Unconditioned meaning could be attained only in a leap from the conditioned. It was not the exodus from Egypt but the prohibition of idols that was incorporated into Horkheimer's philosophical position. Hence this approach is equally incapable of solving the difficulty that beset Jaspers's position – preserving

an unconditioned truth without God. Without a 'leap', without
a decision for life over death, unconditionedness is impossible.
To cite one example of existential unconditionedness becoming
a practical-political, there is no 'rational reason' not to kill mentally retarded children.

In a 1975 article entitled 'Herz' (Heart), Pasolini commented
on the practice of abortion in Italy. He had been criticized for
pursuing an irrationalist course and for seeing 'something holy
in life without reason'. In his analysis of the situation of the
age, Pasolini responds by posing a legitimate question: In whose
interest does free choice for abortion really lie? His answer: 'the
new consumerist and permissive forces', a new type of domination,
which, having no interest in the couple producing offspring (the
proletarian model), requires a pair that consumes (the *petit bourgeois* model). Its sanctuary consists in the 'ritual of consumerism
and in the fetishism of commodities'. In Pasolini's view, the issue
of existential unconditionedness is presented under the catchwords
'heart' and 'sanctuary'. 'To say that life is not holy and that feelings
are dumb amounts to doing the producers an enormous favor.'
Today the ruling powers are no longer clerical-fascist but secular-
consumerist. They assert themselves no longer in repressive but
permissive fashion. The decision that must be faced and in fact
is faced by the silent majority is that 'between the sanctity of life
and feeling, and capital and private property'.

In this context, I would like to make a personal comment on
the question of abortion. I participated in the campaign calling
for the abolition of Section 218 of the German Criminal Code
(the law regarding abortion), yet I was neither willing nor able to
support one of the essential features of this struggle: I could not
sign the women's declaration, 'I had an abortion'. Instead I could
only criticize the slogan, 'My womb belongs to me', since it merely
acknowledges, without surpassing, the moral level of capitalism,
which is always aware of 'what belongs to me'.

With the Italian feminists, I would like to criticize Pasolini
because he never once addressed the plight of those affected, the
women; he *de facto* instrumentalizes them. Just as before! Nonetheless I am in agreement with his stance, which involves a certain
tension between the bourgeois-liberal and the Christian positions. I
support the legalization of abortion and women's freedom of choice;
my commitment to life takes effect only after this liberalization. We

are living not in a Christian but in a secular state where the ever-diminishing minority of Christians has no right to impose ideas on those who think differently. The truly constraint-free dialogue about life, which indeed 'without reason' I take to be 'holy', can commence only at this point. I no more wish my daughter to visit an abortion clinic than my son an army boot camp. All training in killing destroys those who engage in it. Yet my existential unconditionedness with regard to life cannot assume the form of a legal norm; it can only be a call to life, an invitation.

'Set your hearts first on God's kingdom and righteousness, all these other things [meaning: food, drink, clothing] will be given to you as well.' (Matt. 6:33) This language of existential unconditionedness presumes the possible unity of our life. There are times when we see ourselves as undivided and free from dispersion, endowed with all capacities and dimensions (such as past and future). The oil in the lamp of the virgin awaiting her bridegroom is a symbol of this unity. Should she lack this oil, she lacks everything: she is 'foolish', unprepared, dispersed into a thousand parts. If her lamp is filled with oil, she has nothing to fear; she is, to speak in jargon, 'fully there'.

Existential unconditionedness is drawn from that indivisible totality to which I commit myself. 'Choose life' presupposes that there is 'life' in this emphatic, unconditioned sense and that it can be chosen and accepted or rejected and abused. 'I call heaven and earth to witness against you today: I set before you life and death, blessing or curse. Choose life, then, so that you and your descendants may live . . .' (Deut. 30:19)

To choose life over death implies participation in the great affirmation of life. In the biblical context this means to remain alive and to multiply, life and procreation being things endangered in Egypt; it means to live in a country, to be blessed, to live in peace.

We tend to affirm life in specific circumstances, under given conditions, as when it is expressed in youth, beauty, strength. But the affirmation in the emphatic, biblical context is an unconditioned affirmation, valid in sickness and in death and above all for those lacking in self-esteem, who, after perceiving themselves negatively for so long, have become resigned to this state of affairs. To choose life involves precisely the ability not to resign oneself to the blatant destruction of life around us and to its accompanying cynicism.

In the Christian tradition this commitment to life is known as 'belief' – belief in the existential sense of trust and not in the rational sense of holding something to be true. 'Choose life, then, so that you and your descendants may live, in the love of Yahweh, your God, obeying his voice, clinging to him; for in this life consists; on this depends your long stay in the land which Yahweh swore to your fathers Abraham, Isaac and Jacob he would give them.' (Deut. 30:19–20) Within this tradition a language developed that recalls, represents, and thus makes possible the emphasis on life, its imperilment and salvation.

The integrative moment ('totality') and the voluntarist moment ('decision') constitute what Jaspers termed 'existential unconditionedness'. But even if we trace this language back to its theological origin, a certain uneasiness persists.

It is precisely in its comparison with biblical language that the formalized and depleted character of the philosophy of existence becomes fully apparent. Terms such as blessing and curse, home and exile, as well as the kingdom of God, lamps, and marriage contain more than what can be conceptualized in the notion of existential unconditionedness. In a certain sense this philosophical language is as impotent as that of those young people whose most important approbative terms are 'real' and 'tough'. The philosophy of existence heightens the need for a non-functionalist foundation of life but cannot do much beyond that. The prevailing state of affairs is typified by the fact that we lack a language able to convey in comprehensible fashion something about life's assumed meaningfulness, about the human capacity for truth, about the unconditionedness and totality of existence. *Survivre n'est pas vivre* – thus it was written by students on the walls of Paris in 1968. But what is meant by *vivre*? Is it definable only in terms of its opposite, *survivre*? Are we only able to articulate what we do not want and what life does not mean? Pasolini grounds his critique of the reigning consumerism by referring to, among other things, the destruction of language, specifically the destruction of expressive language. Although we are still understood, we no longer say anything. People's expressive linguistic practices, especially apparent for Pasolini in dialect, are being extirpated along with the dialects themselves. The dominant language is the language of television, which suppresses and makes uniform regional, social, and group dialects. In this process Pasolini sees a loss of expressivity in language. No longer able to convey anything about oneself, one is no longer able to communicate with others. It is without detour, shall we say, that we make ourselves understood. The language of science has made expression taboo, and it is for this reason that women, in their role as bearers of expressivity, have difficulty making themselves understood in it. One always feels that one is saying nothing at all when uttering normal male sentences. The uniform character of ordinary language, disseminated by television commercials, promotes the language of science.

Linked with the loss of expressivity is the isolation from all forms of transcendence. The young consumer couple, owing to the ruling mode of television programming, has no need for a language capable of expressing personal anguish or desire. Life itself is not at stake; it has value, in fact, only in as much and as long as it can be purchased. 'The empty store windows, that drabness. What is life there good for anyhow?' – thus an American tourist commenting on his visit to the Eastern bloc. Pasolini characterizes this consumerism as a new fascism; it destroys all humanistic values without physical force, with its new tools of information and communication. If the age of bread is over, why still share bread and wine with one another? 'It is clear that superfluous goods render life itself superfluous.'

Religious traditions have articulated the consciousness that life itself is at stake, that it can cease to have meaning. It is here that people's anxiety in the face of a loss of meaning and identity has been given voice – and of course also rendered manipulable. 'Save us from hell' is a prayer centuries old. It enunciates something that today, simply in being felt, will guarantee entrance to the psychiatric clinic: the fear of a wasted life, of destroyed unity, of loss of self. Well-heated rooms are cold. 'Things are dead' is the standard reply of young people asked how things are going here and there.

It is possible to waste one's whole life, to throw it away, to treat it as a disposable object. One can win or lose it; in any case one does not 'have' it. Yet we lack a language sufficiently expressive and transcending to allow us to communicate with one another about it. Without this existential *Angst* about life, however, the more profound love of life also cannot exist; what remains is only a quick and ever-frustrated aggressiveness that at any moment can be turned into diffuse melancholia. One can only love something that is threatened and endangered – something potentially changeable or potentially non-existent, something that could die.

Existential unconditionedness goes hand in hand with existential *Angst* – the emphatic understanding of life as growth, being touched, touching, as the development of new qualities and experiences. This qualitative understanding of life contains an emphatic-traumatic relation to death. We are capable of dying. To know this is more important than repeatedly to acknowledge our mortality. Perhaps no one knows this better than someone suffering from mental illness. Life can be lost on the way to birth and before death. Were this not the case, it could not even be found.

Yet precisely this insight is expunged in the forgetful innocuousness of the blasphemy, 'Thou shalt have no other jeans before me.' This slogan 'contains the spirit of the second industrial revolution and the concomitant mutation of values.' The cycle of production and consumption functions most efficiently when people are severed from the experience of nature and history, that is, when they live in a purely technical and secular world, free of all religion.

When people are fully severed from the experience of nature, they cease to be aware that life requires renewal; that after work we need rest; after day, night; after befoulment, purification; after commotion, peace. Instead everything continues on an even keel. Rhythm is no longer a part of our lives. Independent of body and soul, the bleeding ordained by the monthly pill symbolizes this destruction of rhythm.

Just as people are severed from the experience of nature, so they are also severed from a transcending experience of history. Consumerism has generated an entirely new culture of communication, dominated by such pressing questions as how to save taxes or where to get a good deal; class differences are reduced to a question of the geography of good values. It is as if all historical experience, especially that viewed through the eyes of the forlorn, has been forgotten, has vanished. Its reference point, God's kingdom and its new justice, is now inconceivable. The cyclical understanding of history has overpowered the eschatological-teleological one. Loss of continuity and planned amnesia are prerequisites for the hedonistic culture, since memory requires behaviour inimical to consumerism. And since the loss of history is likewise the absence of a future, a sense of dramatic hopelessness sets in. Beckett's *Happy Days* is now being performed. One is buried in the sand, sitting motionlessly in one's hole and, in a perfect absence of all effect, awaiting sunrise and sunset.

What is blasphemous is not the use of the first commandment for an advertising slogan, but advertisement as such. Every attempt to direct my attention to hair spray, cat food, and trips to Ibiza is an attack on the one in whose image I was created.

Consumerism means eyes that are continually insulted, ears that are clogged, and hands robbed of their creativity. My relations with other people are subject to laws unimaginable to earlier generations. (I have the birthday party of an eight-year-old daughter in mind.) If everything is expressed and measured in terms of possession, then there remains no time, no energy, and no language for being with one another.

To believe means to struggle against the ruling cynicism. Yet the language of struggle is not adequate to conceptualize the courage and beauty of belief. We must learn to express more precisely the nature of the promises of happiness being made here, the nature of the experiences of happiness being discussed. To speak more precisely is to learn to speak in a more existential, more concerned, and therefore more coherent manner.

If life in the Judeo-Christian tradition has been concerned with what is at stake, with a thoroughly premortal hell and heaven-sent infusions of light, then we must assign the word 'happiness' a definition different from that prescribed by consumerism. The latter's advertising agencies are trying to dismantle the traditional values of frugality, family life, and altruism with the slogan, 'If it feels good, do it!' Yet the addressee of this ad is less and less the anal collector and the quiet enjoyer. The genital conqueror has now become the primary model. Happiness lies not in accumulation and consumption but in the seizure and taking possession of something previously seized and possessed by someone else. It is no longer the acquired item but the experience of acquisition itself that is the focus of advertisement; it is to be engaged in lustily. What thereby becomes even more incomprehensible is that essential element with whose aid religious traditions had attempted to define happiness: the experience of grace.

The young man and woman on television, no longer burdened by religion, are without grace. They do not need it, they do not expect it, and when we see them it does not occur to us to say, 'May God give you grace.' Yet it was just this promise, this hope, that in our culture once accompanied the idea of the young couple. Young people were once enveloped in an aura of frail happiness; it made them 'touching', a word that at the time was still part of our vocabulary. Today we cannot even wish *mazel tov* to our television models. Why should we? Whatever they hope for they can buy. Thus wishes freeze on lips, and the icy chill of relations devoid of all longing seeps from the television into every room.

Grace illuminates the depth of our possible happiness. When I choose life with existential unconditionedness, as Jaspers would say, when integration and decision fuse, when I take part in the great affirmation of life and am trained in the struggle against cynicism, then I shall experience the moment that is the basis of all true happiness, at least to the extent that it can be articulated within the context of the culture handed down to me. I realize that it is not owing to my own efforts that I have been brought into the particular circumstance that first establishes the objects of my own desires. I have no control over my affirmation. I am not in charge and forget that I may have wanted to be. 'Uncontrollability' (*Unverfügbarkeit*) is the other category employed by the philosophy of existence that cannot be ignored without deleterious consequences. Each true affirmation is an answer, a response, and this responsive nature is our very experience of happiness. Happiness means corresponding (*ent-sprechen*) with, not merely speaking (*sprechen*) to, someone or some situation. It is an integration into the process of give and take – not just taking, gaining, and appropriating and not just doing, making, giving. It is grace, and the more grace we experience in happiness, the greater its depth.

A young person untouched by religious tradition may ask how I know this. I would answer: the limits of my language are the limits of my world. The tradition in which I stand bequeathed to me a language that interprets, clarifies, makes transparent, and enriches my own experience. One of its words, 'grace', contains a conception of happiness that seemed more enticing than anything otherwise offered me. In it I found respect for my capacity for desire, a way of addressing my fears, and a total acceptance of my need for meaning. My capacity for happiness grew with my capacity for meaning (and, for that matter, with my capacity for pain, although in my tradition this belongs to the category of repentance). Therefore I regard consumerism as an attack on my dignity and do not by any means consider the word 'genocide' employed by Pasolini an exaggerated description of what occurs on a daily basis with consumerism. But the use of such terms presupposes the aforementioned emphatic understanding of life, which relies on the framework of heaven and hell.

What reason could exist to exchange this life between heaven and hell for a secular-trivial one? Why give up a tradition that regards bread and wine, fear and guilt, coitus and birth, death and the justice of the Kingdom of God as the unmarketable components of life? A tradition that continually surpasses the limits set by the language of the social sciences in favour of a promise of life for all; a tradition in which one person could reclaim for others the unseen light: 'He shall let his countenance shine upon you.'

NOTES

1   Sölle's chapter is taken from a book edited by Jurgen Habermas (*Observations on 'The Spiritual Situation of the Age'*) which, following the earlier lead of the philosopher Karl Jaspers (1883 – 1969) in *Die geistige Situation der Zeit*, attempted to give some contemporary assessments of 'the spiritual situation of the age'. Sölle's point of departure is Jaspers's concept of 'existential unconditionedness'. Whilst Jaspers's philosophy is not likely to be of immediate concern to readers of this book, Sölle's essay goes on to provide such a powerful critique of our modern media-society that it was thought important to include it (editor).

2   This is a modified version of the translation found in the English edition of Jaspers's *Die geistige Situation der Zeit: Man in the Modern Age*, Eden and Cedar Paul, translators, New York: Anchor Books: 1957, p. 42.

3   In P. P. Pasolini, *Freibeuterschriften: Die Zerstörung der Kultur des Einzelnen durch die Konsumgesellschaft*, Berlin: 1978.

18 Hymns and arias

D. P. DAVIES

Some years ago the popular entertainer, Max Boyce, achieved instant immortality as the impromptu choirs of the National Stadium gave voice to one of his ditties in among the traditional 'hymns and arias', to quote the catchphrase of his song, which caricatures the Welsh as a 'musical nation', given to praising the Lord in song on the slightest pretext. Not only is this a caricature, it is, as Max Boyce so mischieviously forces us to recognize, a self-caricature. The Welsh actually do believe themselves to be a musical nation, given to singing hymns, if not arias, at all times and in all places. They are even proud of it. Hallelujah! Praise the Lord!

This addiction to hymn-singing is symptomatic of a deep-seated, and as yet unresolved, national schizophrenia. The outside observer must find it mildly absurd that up and down the valleys of south Wales revivalist hymns are more often sung in rugby club houses by sweat-shirted choirs of prop forwards (or more likely prop forwards emeriti) to the accompaniment of enthusiastic beer-swilling than in the chapels founded on the zeal of the original revivalists. Yes, indeed, we are a musical nation! Wales seems to have turned on its head the old adage about the devil having all the best tunes. In the land of song God's tunes are commonly heard in the halls of the demon drink.

Admittedly, this is a notorious caricature, but like all caricatures it contains more than a modicum of truth. More seriously, it points to the indisputable fact that hymns, and particularly, and perhaps ironically today, hymns in the Welsh language, are deeply embedded in the folk memory, and indeed represent the folk religion of Wales, even among those who have long since lost contact with the culture and language of their ancestors (and this means the majority of the two million non-Welsh-speakers in Wales, i.e. 80 per cent of the population) and whose way of life seems in all outward appearances totally assimilated to that of their English neighbours. The words of Welsh hymns, imperfectly understood, continue to evoke resonances, maybe of a religious kind, but maybe not, in a manner that is difficult to explain. To sing the Lord's songs while supping the devil's brew could as easily spring from a dark, subconscious sense of guilt as from a primitive urge to rebel against the puritanical represssion of the Celtic spirit. There is in all Welshmen (and women) a constant inner conflict of identity between the *joie de vivre* of the playboy and the world-denying discipline of the puritan.

This folk religion and its close identification with Welsh language and culture is illustrated by the huge popularity on Welsh television of *Dechrau Canu, Dechrau Canmol*, a programme of hymn-singing. In terms of ratings it achieves viewing figures of soap-opera proportions, with around 100,000 viewers each week out of a total Welsh-language audience of little more than 500,000. To what extent such popularity indicates that, whatever may be the future of Welsh as an everyday channel of communication, it will continue to be a medium of Christian worship for years, if not centuries, to come is impossible to say. The conservatism of liturgical language is well attested by such examples as the centuries-long persistence of Latin in the Roman Catholic Church or the vestigial Hebrew phrases like Hallelujah and Amen that adorn Christian worship even today. On the same principle the abiding popularity of Welsh hymn-singing, even among non-Welsh-speakers in Wales, suggests perhaps that hymns are for many the liturgical vestiges of a far-off culture, which is still part of their subconscious, even though they have lost all other points of contact with the indigenous language of their native land.

That the liturgical, didactic and evangelistic needs of the Christian faith are responsible above all else for the survival of the Welsh language is widely accepted. For most Welsh-speakers, Welsh culture and the Christian religion are indissolubly linked. Many of those most deeply committed to the struggle to achieve equality of status with English for the Welsh language are motivated as much by missionary zeal for the gospel as an enthusiasm for things Welsh. And since the campaign to secure a separate television channel for Welsh-language broadcasting was throughout the sixties and seventies a primary aim of the language movement, it is not without significance that many of those who played a prominent part in the campaign were committed Christians.

With the British government at the start of the eighties still stubbornly refusing to yield to the almost unanimous will of the Welsh-speaking population, the turning point came with the well-publicized fast 'to the death' of Gwynfor Evans, president of Plaid Cymru, but also a sincere and active member of Undeb yr Annibynwyr Cymraeg (The Union of Welsh Independents). This led to a deputation of three 'wise men' visiting William Whitelaw, the Home Secretary, to plead with him to give way. The choice of the three was again significant since it provides another example of the deeply ingrained conviction of the Welsh establishment that religion and culture are indivisible; the three were the Archbishop of Wales (G. O. Williams), the Labour leader in the House of Lords (Lord Cledwyn), who was also a prominent Presbyterian layman, and a former Vice-Chancellor of the University of Wales (Sir Goronwy Daniel), who, like Gwynfor Evans, was one of the leading lights of Undeb yr Annibynwyr Cymraeg. The result was the establishment in 1982 of Sianel Pedwar Cymru (S4C), the Welsh fourth channel, probably the most significant milestone in the entire history of broadcasting in Wales. And for the success of the campaign to establish S4C much of the credit goes not only to individual Christians but to the churches in Wales, whose synods and assemblies had repeatedly called for the channel. It is therefore appropriate, ten years on, to review the ways in which S4C has sought to meet the needs of the Christian Churches in Wales, and the extent to which it has attempted to broaden the religious horizons of viewers in Wales by bringing before them the multi-faith dimension of the British, European and world community, of which Wales is part.

It would be difficult to exaggerate the political and cultural significance of S4C, let alone its potency as a national symbol, not only in the context of Wales, but also in the wider context of television broadcasting generally. Again it is no exaggeration to say that S4C was from the outset and continues to be the envy of cultural, linguistic and maybe even religious minorities all over Europe. With a brief to provide more than twenty hours of Welsh-language programmes a week and freedom to schedule these at peak times, as well as financial resources that by comparison with the provision for other minority groups in the UK and Europe generally were certainly generous, S4C had to succeed. Failure could not be contemplated, even if several influential commentators expressed serious misgivings about the capacity of half a million Welsh-speakers to sustain even the modest target of twenty to twenty-five hours viewing a week without a reduction in standards or the loss of audiences to a point where the venture would no longer be deemed viable. Ten years on, we can say that, while the service is far from perfect, the experiment has been an unqualified success; S4C has retained the loyalty of the Welsh-speaking audience at a level well beyond that initially predicted. Not even its strongest critics would now dare propose the abolition of S4C.

The channel was also fortunate to secure the service of able and dedicated broadcasters, people of vision and experience, from the outset. A further basic and vital feature of the channel's formative years was that its prevailing ethos was governed by the spirit of public-service broadcasting. The channel has genuinely sought to inform and to educate its viewers as well as to entertain them, and over the first decade of its existence has resisted the temptation to sacrifice these less popular responsibilities in a quest for ratings. It remains to be seen if the channel can maintain this ethos in the new market-forces environment. One further feature of the channel worthy of note is its funding. S4C was set up by the government as an independent authority but funded, like the fourth channel in the rest of the UK, from a levy imposed on the ITV companies. In addition, the BBC was required to provide the channel with some eight to ten hours of Welsh-language programmes a week free of charge. The result was a mixed economy, with the channel's provision coming in part from the BBC, in part from HTV, the local ITV company, and in part from independent production companies. As a consequence, Wales in the 1980s saw the growth of a flourishing independent sector, which has grown in direct proportion to the reduction of staff at the BBC and HTV.

This mixed provision was at once a blessing and a curse for the channel. By and large, the channel is obliged to take what comes from the BBC, and in its early years was in a not dissimilar position in relation to HTV. Whilst this arrangement guaranteed a certain basic standard of output, it considerably reduced flexibility and discouraged the kind of creative experimentation that became the hallmark of C4 elsewhere in the UK. Finally, it must be acknowledged that S4C was given the well-nigh impossible task of having to cater for all interests in the Welsh-speaking community in a service restricted to three or four hours a day.

How then have religious programmes fared? In terms of hours, religion has done well, that is, if the hours are seen in proportion to the total provision of the channel and compared with the provision made for religious programmes elsewhere in the UK system. In inviting bids for the franchise for Channel 3 the ITC, in accordance with the Broadcasting Act, imposed a requirement for religious programmes, suggesting a minimum of two hours a week. This corresponds to the existing provision on ITV. BBC1's provision is something similar, while both BBC2 and C4 devote less time to specifically religious programmes over the course of a week. ITV now broadcasts round the clock, so two hours a week represents a tiny fraction of its total output. By comparison, S4C broadcasts at least half an hour of religious programmes a week, and sometimes as much as an hour. This represents a significant proportion of its total output of around twenty-five hours. In that respect the religious constituency in Wales has no cause for complaint. They are as well catered for as other special interest groups, and such generosity of provision on S4C almost certainly reflects a recognition that the religious constituency forms a significant part of S4C's audience. The viewing figures for *Dechrau Canu, Dechrau Canmol* provide the evidence for this judgement.

So much for quantity, but what of the nature of the provision and its quality? Here commissioning editors have had to strike a balance between the apparently conservative tastes of the viewers and the innovative instincts of programme-makers. The same dilemma confronts the BBC and ITV. Do schedulers pander to the evident popular appeal of *Songs of Praise* or *Highway*, or do they divert resources to more exciting and challenging series such as *Everyman* or *Encounter*? In Wales, the dilemma is to some extent resolved for S4C since *Dechrau Canu, Dechrau Canmol* comes free of charge from the BBC. The programme is relatively cheap to produce and cheaper still now that two programmes are recorded together at the same venue, whereas in earlier more prosperous years the programme changed its venue each week. *Dechrau Canu* is now modelled on *Songs of Praise*, with interviews as well as hymns, though BBC Wales is unable to match the resources available to its English counterpart. Consequently, the viewer has not infrequently to endure the embarrassment of predictable and poorly-researched interviews, interspersed with a relatively restricted range of well-worn hymns. Nevertheless, the programme still attracts one of the channel's highest weekly audiences.

In terms of the public-service broadcasting requirement to inform, educate and entertain, *Dechrau Canu* must surely be in the category 'entertainment'; it is rarely informative and even less educational. Nor can it really be classified as worship, which forms an essential ingredient of the menu of religious programmes on BBC1 and ITV. Ironically, in serving a population where church/chapel attendance is proportionately higher than it is in English-speaking circles, S4C offers little or nothing by way of 'broadcast worship'. This deficiency has been the subject of adverse comment from individuals, Churches and advisory panels; it is therefore encouraging to learn that the channel has plans to rectify it in the future. A basic requirement, however, must be a willingness to invest adequate financial resources in the experiment. The channel needs also seriously to address the basic theological and practical questions relating to the broadcasting of worship on television. This is a real challenge, but one fears that inadequate financial resources and lack of theological reflection may lead to programmes that are little more than radio programmes with pictures.

On the information and education front, recent experience has been more encouraging and reflects the growing self-confidence of a new breed of specialist religious programme-makers. HTV, for example, has supported a religious broadcasting unit that produces a regular magazine programme on the religious scene in Wales (*Ffiniau*). The series is well made, with individual programmes almost invariably both interesting and informative. Moreover, the series has resisted the temptation to confine its attention exclusively to the mainstream Christian denominations, by including occasional items on communities and individuals representing faiths other than Christianity. HTV is to be commended on maintaining support for this specialist unit, alongside its equally successful English-medium religious broadcasting unit. Like the BBC in Wales, HTV has to serve the needs of an English-speaking audience as well as preparing Welsh programmes for S4C and this inevitably gives rise from time to time to competition for resources within the organization.

There are signs, then, that Welsh-language religious programmes are not all exclusivist and introverted, something which is vitally important for a minority channel where the temptation to do no more than let the minority speak to itself and see itself must be very great, particularly when the big wide world is already on offer to the vast majority of viewers on other channels. S4C must continue to resist this temptation. A culture turned in on itself, exclusively preoccupied with its own state of health and with the problems of survival, deserves to perish. Not for nothing is incest prohibited by law and custom. If S4C is concerned with *broad*casting and genuinely determined to avoid the trap of *narrow*casting, the channel must, first, present the world outside to the Welsh-speaking community and, second, present the Welsh-speaking community to the world outside. In other words, it must facilitate a dialogue between Wales and the world. Furthermore, in the specific context of religious broadcasting, this dialogue must extend to promoting mutual understanding between religion, on the one hand, and society at large, on the other.

In this connection it may be helpful to remind ourselves of the CRAC[1] guidelines on religious broadcasting offered to the BBC and ITV in the context of the UK as a whole. Religious broadcasting should seek to (1) 'reflect the worship, thought and action of the principal religious traditions in the UK', recognizing that they are mainly Christian; (2) 'present . . . those beliefs, ideas, issues and experiences . . . which are evidently related to a religious interpretation or dimension of life'; (3) 'meet the religious . . . needs of those on the fringe of or outside . . . the major religious groupings.' Applied to a Welsh-speaking context, these guidelines suggest, first, a need for programmes which reflect the worship and life of the Welsh-speaking Christian community. As we have noted, this requirement is largely met or about to be met. Secondly, Welsh-speaking viewers need to be challenged by beliefs, ideas, issues and experiences that point to a religious dimension of life. Such ideas and experiences come not only from the Welsh-speaking community itself, but from an endless variety of sources the world over. S4C is not unaware of the need to provide programmes of such a kind. As for the third guideline, there is little evidence that S4C in its provision for *religious* programmes makes any attempt to cater for the *religious* needs of fringe groups outside the main Christian denominations. If challenged, the channel would doubtless respond that resources do not permit it to meet the needs of what must be a minority within a minority.

But to return to the kinds of programmes that challenge the viewer to reflect on the religious dimension of life by bringing to the attention of the Welsh-speaking community the experiences, ideas and beliefs of others around the world. Recent experience has shown that S4C is willing to respond to this challenge by commissioning independent companies to produce series that bring the religious world outside to the screens of Welsh-speaking homes. For example, the Cardiff-based Cwmni Elidir has produced more than one series of *Troeon*, comprising individual documentary pro- grammes on a variety of religious themes, ranging from the Muslim community in Wales to the contribution of the Churches to the downfall of Communism in Eastern Europe. The programmes have usually been made from the perspective of the Welsh-speaking com- munity looking at a religious phenomenon foreign to it. This helps the home audience, even if it lessens the potential general appeal of the series. Nonetheless, we have here a commendable attempt to inform and to educate the Welsh religious (i.e. Christian) com- munity about the religious world outside Wales, particularly on the continent of Europe.

More ambitious, more experimental, and consequently more of a gamble, is the series on *Credo* in Europe, produced by the Lampeter- based Cwmni'r Gannwyll in partnership with Cambrensis, to be screened early in 1993. The series will look at each of the major reli- gious traditions of Europe (Catholic, Orthodox, Protestant, Jewish and Muslim) through the eyes of the tradition itself as seen from within a pair of countries, one in Western Europe and the other from the former Communist bloc. To facilitate this approach the series involves co-production partners in countries such as Sweden, the Netherlands, Poland, Hungary and Greece, and will appear on the networks of these and other European countries, appropriately subtitled. This is an ambitious attempt to enable a range of dif- ferent religious traditions to tell others, including a Welsh-speaking audience, about themselves. In that sense the series is primarily edu- cational, which reflects the academic base of Cwmni'r Gannwyll in the Department of Theology and Religious Studies at Lampeter. In previous years Cwmni'r Gannwyll has experimented with several series of five-minute meditations (*Y Duw Byw*), aimed at raising questions rather than giving answers. The quality of the individual meditations varied, as did the audience reaction, but the experiment proved its worth (as consultant and script editor of these series the author declares an interest!) in that it provided a number of useful pointers to the kinds of experimental programmes that might be tried in the future.

What then of the future? After ten years, where do we go next? Where should we consolidate? What should we scrap? Where should we be more innovative? On the positive side, S4C has undermined the caricature by demonstrating to its Welsh-language viewers, and through them to the rest of Wales, that religion involves a great deal more than 'hymns and arias'. Magazine programmes like *Ffiniau* and its predecessors and documentary series like *Troeon* and *Credo* should continue. In such series, however, the programme-maker is seeking to communicate with the viewer in what is essentially a one-way traffic system. Two-way traffic, i.e. interaction with the viewer, has yet to be seriously tried in the context of religious programmes. Admittedly, we have interviews with individual, and maybe typical, viewers in *Dechrau Canu*, but these are stereotyped set pieces; what we are looking for is genuine dialogue between the grassroots and the professionals. This should be easier in a relatively small viewing population like the Welsh-speaking community. S4C has successfully interacted with viewers in producing, for example, entertainment and some current affairs discussion programmes. An experiment of a similar kind would be worth conducting in relation to religious programmes. One possible forum could be the televising of worship. At present there is little or no worship broadcast on S4C. With the channel's declared intention of remedying this, it will be interesting to see if those commissioned to produce worship will be encouraged to experiment, particularly in facilitating genuine grassroots involvement. Furthermore, the visual potential of the medium in presenting worship needs to be fully exploited, which again calls for a readiness to experiment.

If, as was suggested above, the channel should be a means of allowing Wales to speak to the world and the world to speak to Wales on religious issues, then a greater willingness to set up co-production partnerships is required. To be fair, S4C has pursued a vigorous policy of facilitating co-production deals in recent years and become much more European in its orientation. One idea that might be worth pursuing would be to form a network of production companies across Europe with the aim of producing a weekly magazine/news programme to be broadcast all over Europe, concentrating on religious issues and interpreting the religious dimension of current affairs.

Certain gaps in the provision of S4C are all too apparent: first, there is little provision for the religious needs of children and young people, even though young children are relatively well catered for otherwise. This problem area needs to be addressed in the context of Wales, just as in the rest of the UK. The pitfalls and difficulties involved in meeting this challenge have deterred most broadcasters; however, children and young people now form so significant a part of the viewing population that they have a right to appropriate 'religious' programmes. Similarly, S4C has failed to make provision for those on the fringe of or outside institutional religious groups (in Wales, the Churches), but who are nonetheless deeply interested in religion and in many cases very religious.

To achieve all this will, of course, require substantial investment. The current state of retrenchment in the industry, in Wales as elsewhere, combined with future uncertainties of funding consequent upon the new financial arrangements covering C4 and S4C, lead one to be less than optimistic. It is well known that in the television industry you get what you pay for. Poorly-resourced programmes are frequently poor programmes. Ten years of achievement are now threatened by a potential cash crisis as S4C enters its second decade, and this is not good news for religious programmes.

What, finally, are the general conclusions that may be drawn from the experience of S4C? First and foremost, the Welsh experiment shows that a relatively small minority (linguistic or otherwise) can, with dedication and commitment, sustain a credible television service. The talent emerges, provided that the general climate is favourable and supportive. To this extent, S4C has been a trend-setter, indicating to minority cultures and communities elsewhere in the UK and the rest of Europe that a 'local' television service is possible and worthwhile. As we move towards an environment of community television and specialist (satellite) channels, the experience of S4C can only be encouraging to those prepared to venture. Furthermore, S4C has shown that providing for the needs of a relatively small linguistic and cultural minority need not lead to *narrow*casting. S4C's first task was to win the loyalty of its own community; having achieved that objective, in recent years it has made a commendable effort to become an integral part of the European broadcasting system, and in so doing it has brought Wales and Europe much closer together. What has been demonstrated in Wales over the past ten years is that a minority-interest channel cannot evade its responsibilities to *broad*cast. Certainly it has to provide for its audience the kinds of programmes that reflect their internal interests and needs, but at the same time it must be the means of extending the horizons of the minority community to take in other societies and cultures in the environment of the global village, which the mass media of communication have helped to create.

NOTES

1   The Central Religious Advisory Committee (CRAC) advises both the BBC and the ITC (formerly the IBA). Its membership represents the mainstream of religious opinion in the UK and its remit is to offer advice on policy regarding religious programming output. The CRAC Guidelines on Religious Broadcasting are available from the Religious Broadcasting Department of the BBC or the Religious Broadcasting Officer at the ITC.

19 Religious broadcasting on independent television

RACHEL VINEY

Religious programmes are an integral part of television output in the United Kingdom. Between them, the BBC, ITV and Channel 4 broadcast several hundred hours of religion each year at a cost of many millions of pounds. So accepted a part of our broadcasting landscape has such programming become that few people stop to ask themselves why it is there or to wonder why it takes the form it does. In this chapter I hope to explain, with particular reference to the system within which I work – independent television – the way in which religious broadcasting in this country has developed, to look at how it may change in the future and, finally, to consider some of the likely implications of such change.

First, because the development of religious broadcasting in the United Kingdom can only be understood within the context of overall broadcasting provision, there will be discussion of some of the general principles which inform public-service broadcasting (PSB) and of how these have been applied to independent television. Secondly, the position of religious broadcasting within the PSB framework will be examined, with particular reference to the development of religious broadcasting policy. The third section of the chapter will highlight some of the changes which face broadcasters as a result of the changes introduced in the Broadcasting Act of 1990. Finally, I shall briefly assess the possible implications of these changes for religious broadcasting as we currently know it in this country.

If necessity is the mother of invention, scarcity could be said to be the mother of public-service broadcasting – and John Reith, the first director-general of the British Broadcasting Corporation to be the father: for it was the limited availability of spectrum allied to the view that, as a scarce resource, broadcasting should be organized in the public interest that gave birth to the broadcasting ethos which we know as public service. It was Reith who first articulated the principles according to which the BBC was run, and who laid the foundations of an approach to broadcasting which continues to inform not only the BBC, but also commercial television in the UK. The definition of PSB has, in the seventy years since the establishment of the BBC, evolved into something more complex – and less paternalistic – than the responsibility 'to carry into the greatest possible number of homes everything that is best in every department of human knowledge, endeavour and achievement'.[1] Nonetheless, at the heart of the PSB ethos remains a belief that, in the words of a latter-day exponent and former director-general of the IBA, Sir Brian Young, 'broadcasting belongs in some way to all the people and all their needs and is not just something to be bought and sold.'[2]

For the first twenty years or so of the BBC's life, the notion that scarcity and monopoly should go hand in hand went largely unquestioned. It was not until after the Second World War that the inevitability of this relationship, and of monopoly as a pre-condition of PSB, was subjected to close scrutiny. By this time substantial changes were also afoot within the BBC itself, which was not only reorganizing radio into three new services – Home, Light and Third – thereby providing its audience with the opportunity of more segmented listening, it was also developing further the television transmissions which it had begun at Alexandra Palace shortly before the war. Reith's vision of a single service offering the best of everything to everybody was already being reinterpreted in the light of the possibilities offered by developing technology and of a new awareness of popular taste. This fragmentation of the BBC's own services was followed in 1955 by the breaking of its monopoly in the form of a competitor to its television service – ITV.

Prior to the establishment of ITV under the Television Act of 1954, the idea of a new service underwent several years of debate, within and outside Parliament. The eventual arrival of ITV was achieved in the face of vigorous opposition from a number of quarters. One of the most outspoken opponents was John Reith, now Lord Reith, who by this time had left the BBC. Speaking in a House of Lords debate in May 1952 he went so far as to compare the introduction of what he described as 'sponsored broadcasting' with that of 'smallpox, bubonic plague and Black Death'![3]

Even though with the benefit of hindsight that comparison has proved to be more than a little extreme, it reflected a frequently expressed concern about the new service and, in particular, about the implications for the high standards of broadcasting which the British public had come to expect of a television service financed by private enterprise. In the event, many of the concerns about standards and the accountability of the new service were met by the establishment of a public controlling body to oversee the setting up and running of the new system – a body which began life in 1954 as the Independent Television Authority (ITA). The ITA not only had extensive powers and responsibilities in respect of programme content and the control of advertising, but it was also – whilst not a maker of programmes – the broadcaster of the programmes transmitted on the new channel. This meant that the ITA owned and operated the transmitters which it then leased to private companies based in different regions of the United Kingdom. In return for a rental payment to the ITA the companies would provide the programmes broadcast on the transmitters and sell the advertising space which paid for the programmes.

Although the new system was fully commercial in the sense that it was financed by the sale of advertising and supplied by privately-funded companies, it was subject to a range of public obligations which continued to be developed by the ITA and its successor the Independent Broadcasting Authority (IBA). A crucial principle had been established from the outset, however: that a commercial service financed by advertising did not have to mean that the *programmes* broadcast on that service were supplied or 'sponsored' by advertisers. A clear distinction was made between advertisements and programmes, with the programmes companies appointed by the ITA editorially responsible for the programmes they transmitted, while appearances by advertisers were restricted to 'spots' in breaks in between or during programmes. The new service continued a number of important principles which had first been seen at work within the BBC. They included, with the establishment of the ITA, independence from direct government control and freedom from editorial pressure from commercial sources or particular interest groups. Access to programme airtime was not to be dependent on the ability or willingness of individual groups to pay for it.

The principle of vesting editorial control in the broadcasters was an important pillar of the structure of ITV. Commercial, and indeed ideological, *laissez-faire* was not envisaged. Indeed, it had even been proposed in early discussions about a possible commercial competitor to the BBC to ban religious and political broadcasting altogether. This rather draconian suggestion was subsequently lifted for programmes – although religious and political *advertising* were prohibited in subsequent legislation – and safeguards introduced to prevent abuse.

The Television Act of 1954 and subsequent Acts, up to and including the Broadcasting Act of 1981, have all included the following cautionary formula: 'Except with the previous approval of the Authority, there shall not be included in any programme broadcast by the Authority any religious service or any propaganda relating to matters of a religious nature.' The legislation did not contain any requirement for religion to be included in the output of the new service – a fact which comes as a surprise to those who imagine that religious broadcasting owes its existence to a legislative guarantee rather than to the discretion exercised by the ITA and in later years by its successor bodies, the Independent Broadcasting Authority (IBA) and latterly the Independent Television Commission (ITC) to require its programmes contractors to include certain types of programmes as part of a diverse programme output.

Not surprisingly, there are Reithian precedents for the tenor of the legislative requirements. The 1954 Act, for example, required the ITA to arrange to take advice from a committee representative of the main streams of religious thought in Britain. From the earliest days the BBC had had a religious advisory committee, at first known as the Sunday Committee and later as the Central Religious Advisory Committee (CRAC). The ITA consulted CRAC, and also appointed its own panel of religious advisers to advise it on day-to-day programme matters. Reithian ideals can also be seen at work in the emphasis which the ITA laid on the professionalism and the breadth of purpose and appeal of religious programmes.

As a recent BBC head of religious broadcasting, Colin Morris, has put it: 'Though the mainstream churches were encouraged to use the airwaves, it was made clear that they had no absolute rights of access; they broadcast by invitation.'[4] And as Morris goes on to point out, Reith insisted that religion should be judged according to general professional standards, not indulged or treated as a special category. Religious broadcasting, no less than any other kind of output, should fulfil the tripartite public-service mandate to inform, educate and entertain.

The principle that religious broadcasting should function as an integral part of public-service broadcast output can be seen too in the range and type of programmes available on Independent Television – which since 1982 has included a second service, Channel 4. On ITV, for example, religious programmes mainly fall into the broad categories of: 'worship', 'information' and 'inspiration' which between them aim to address as wide an audience as possible. Programmes of worship currently take the form of a 'live' outside broadcast from a different church each week and aim to reflect, as far as possible, the range of Christian denominations found throughout the United Kingdom. The logistics of this are far from straightforward: the denominational breakdown in England, for example, is different from that of Scotland, Wales and Northern Ireland. Added to this is the difficulty of calculating on anything approximating a pro rata basis how many services each grouping – broadly Anglican, Roman Catholic and Free Church (including the Church of Scotland) – should have each year, when individual denominations have their own different ways of calculating membership. Given both that any formula for allocating services on the basis of denominational allegiances can only be approximate and that the viewers, who tend to come from a church background, are committed to so many different things, the week-by-week transmission of church services meets with a high degree of approval: half a million or so viewers tune in on an average week, many of them sick or housebound, the majority elderly; the audience appreciation index – which measures viewers' enjoyment of and interest in programmes, as opposed to the numbers of people watching – frequently numbers *Morning Worship* among the top ten most-appreciated programmes; the postbag for *Morning Worship*, and for the *Meditations* which occasionally replace it, is the highest of any religious programme.

In contrast to *Morning Worship*, the informational religious programme which follows it does not assume a religious commitment on the part of its viewers. The format may be that of a documentary, a current-affairs programme or an interview. Such programmes may look at faith at work in the life of an individual or a community, or may explore issues relating to belief in the modern world. The religious connection may be explicit or implicit, looking, for example, at the response of the human spirit to adversity or danger. Where the subject is explicitly religious, the faith explored is often Christian, but not necessarily so. Whatever the faith, an attempt is made to explain it in a way which does not assume that the audience shares those beliefs. The quality of much of this output is such that it would fit quite easily into many documentary strands. It is an unfortunate result of the need to categorize particular slots as 'religious' that many excellent programmes do not find their way into the mainstream of programming. They would surely find an appreciative audience if they did.

The last of the three strands which currently form ITV's religious output is a popular, usually music-based, programme shown at 6.40 on Sunday evenings. Religious programmes shown in peak time on ITV have an unenviable path to tread between appealing to as broad an audience as possible and retaining their religious distinctiveness. For the past nine years Sir Harry Secombe's *Highway* has performed this difficult task with considerable success, regularly attracting audiences of eight million viewers or more and showing faith at work in the lives of the famous and not-so-famous. The future for *Highway* or other programmes of its kind is uncertain, however, as is that of the designated slot for religious programmes early on a Sunday evening. The 'God slot', or more properly the 'closed period' between 6.40 and 7.15 p.m. on BBC1 and ITV, is what remains of the otherwise defunct tradition of broadcasting no television programmes at all between 6 and 7 p.m. on weekdays and 6.15 and 7.30 p.m. on Sundays. ITV turned matters on their head in 1956 by securing agreement to broadcast the UK's first weekly religious television programme in the Sunday 'closed period' – which had originally been instituted in order to prevent competition with Evensong! The closed period subsequently evolved as a time in which both the BBC and ITV broadcast religious programmes. After a number of years the duration of the 'closed period' was reduced to thirty-five minutes, the agreement between the BBC and the IBA to broadcast religious programmes back-to-back continuing to this day.

This arrangement has not always found favour with some of the ITV companies who have increasingly criticized it as an anachronism and a handicap to maximizing audiences on Sunday evenings. Those who support the continuation of the 'closed period' see it as a signal that commercial values should not always prevail, particularly on the day still viewed by many people in Britain as a day of rest. One of the consequences of the Broadcasting Act of 1990 – which will be discussed in greater detail below – will be to pass responsibility for adhering to the closed period from the ITC to the ITV companies themselves.

No discussion of religious broadcasting on Independent Television would be complete without mention of Channel 4 which, in fulfilling its statutory remit to appeal to tastes and interests not generally catered for by ITV and to encourage innovation and experimentation in programmes, explores religious issues using a wider variety of approaches and formats than is possible on its sister channel. These include not only documentaries and current affairs but film, drama, dance, music and animation. The subjects covered may be as diverse as Rastafarianism, Gnosticism, Zoroastrianism or the significance of the Mass in the lives of everyday Catholics. The approach too can be unexpected – a Jewish rabbi in search of English spirituality, for example, or the monastic life seen from the perspective of the production of the alcoholic beverages made by many religious orders.

The range of religious programmes broadcast by ITV and Channel 4 has in no small measure been enabled by the presence of a regulatory body committed to the principle that religious programmes have a proper place in a balanced television output and the belief that religious programme-makers should be supported and encouraged in the enterprise of producing religious programmes of quality and integrity. That the IBA/ITC has also been the broadcaster of the programmes it regulates has enabled it to be pro-active in making programming policy, in consultation with its religious advisers, and in communicating that policy to programme-makers. The latter has been achieved through regular discussion with the companies about their programme plans and, from time to time, through consultations bringing together programme-makers, regulators, advisors to the IBA and the ITV companies, and theologians to take stock of the current position and to look to the future. Such consultations have been underpinned by extensive audience research into who is and who is not watching religious programmes and why.

If the pattern described above sounds comfortable and rather traditional, it is worth emphasizing that policy for religious broadcasting has always been active rather than static, evolving to take account of new developments within broadcasting and – as the reference in the previous paragraph to audience research indicates – to changes within society itself. Until recently, such policy developments have occurred within a public-service broadcast context. However, the emergence during the 1980s of cable and satellite broadcasting systems, with their ability to deliver tens of channels into viewers' homes, has moved the debate about broadcasting into a completely new area. From broad acceptance of a system based on a limited number of channels paid for by everybody and offering a wide range of programmes to as wide an audience as possible, recent discussion of broadcasting issues has included descriptions of the arrangements for terrestrial broadcasting as a 'cosy duopoly'; of the licence fee as an imposition; of ITV as the 'last bastion of restrictive practices',[5] with the emphasis on the right of the consumer to make his or her own choices about what to watch from an à la carte television menu, rather than the set meals hitherto on offer. Whether one chooses to see the new mood as technology or ideology led, or a combination of the two, it has been clear since the mid-1980s that change was on the way.

The principal agent of this change was the Broadcasting Act of 1990 which signalled a radical shift in the organization of non-BBC broadcasting in the United Kingdom. (At the time of writing many of the provisions of the Broadcasting Act have been or are about to be implemented with public attention shifting to the future of the BBC, whose Charter is due for renewal in 1996.) Under the legislation, which established the Independent Television Commission as the new regulatory body for all non-BBC television services, the IBA's status as broadcaster – and with it the legal responsibility for the content of programmes – passes from the regulator to the Channel 3 (ITV) companies and Channel 4. The ITC's new responsibilities include the licensing and regulation of satellite and cable channels originating in the United Kingdom. From having day-to-day involvement with the programme companies and powers to approve programme schedules in advance, the ITC's powers will become retrospective. They will include ensuring that its licencees observe the provisions of the Broadcasting Act and the provisions of the various codes which it is required to draw up under the legislation.

Although the government White Paper which heralded the 1990 Act was lukewarm about imposing on ITV the kind of programming requirements which had come to be associated with its public service role – intending that these should devolve to Channel 4 – after lengthy debate many of its proposals were amended and the ITC empowered to ensure that, in addition to a number of specific programme categories required under the Act, taken as a whole the service offered by a regional Channel 3 licensee should be calculated to appeal to a wide variety of tastes and interests. This has been translated into the Channel 3 licences as minimum amounts of programmes in a range of categories which, when taken together, amount to what is, effectively, a public service.

The place of religion within this scheme has been strengthened by a statutory guarantee of its presence on Channel 3 and Channel 5 – a new terrestrial channel provided for under the legislation. It is perhaps paradoxical that a piece of legislation widely regarded as deregulatory should be the first ever to make the broadcasting of religion a legal requirement. Its inclusion points to fears that religion would be one of the types of programmes associated with public service provision which would be vulnerable in a more commercialized ITV system. It is fair to say, however, that even had there been no mandatory requirement, the ITC would have required its licencees to offer religious programmes. Either way, it is a condition of a Channel 3 licence that its holder broadcast a minimum of two hours a week of religious programmes, including acts of worship and a range of other programme types. The ITC has no power, however, to require these programmes to be scheduled at specific times, although the structure of the ITV network makes it likely that they will be broadcast on Sundays.

The requirement on Channels 3 and 5 to broadcast religion is only one of several 'firsts' in the Broadcasting Act of 1990. Others include: clauses about the content of religious programmes on all services; the repealing of the prohibition on religious advertising on terrestrial channels; and ownership by religious groups of certain types of cable and satellite (though not terrestrial) channels. Religious programmes are, for the first time, the subject of rules contained in a legally enforceable programme code. The Code is designed to enable the ITC to ensure that in addition to its powers and duties applying generally to licensed services, in every licensed service 'due responsibility' is exercised with respect to the content of any religious programme, as required by Section 6(1)(d) of the Act. In particular such programmes may not involve 'any improper exploitation of any susceptibilities of those watching the programmes, or any abusive treatment of the religious views and beliefs of those belonging to a particular religion or religious denomination'.

Devising rules which can be applied fairly to all religious groups has not been easy. There are those who fear that the Code's provisions are unduly restrictive of their right to proclaim a particular creed whilst others, fearful of the spectre of American 'televangelism' or cults whose activities they regard as harmful, feel that they do not go far enough. At this early stage it remains to be seen whose view is correct. A couple of points are worth making here, however. First, the Code is designed to give maximum flexibility, within the terms of the legislation, to licencees and their programme-makers whilst safeguarding the interests of the viewer, whatever his or her religious belief. Second, the Code reflects the differences between various types of service and the effect that such differences are likely to have on the expectations of their audiences. This is particularly true of specialist channels owned by religious groups, which the ITC is given discretion to licence under the Act. Such channels may operate an editorial policy which, by contrast with general-audience channels, reflects a particular religious point of view. Given that audiences will be aware of this, the Programme Code offers scope for religious programmes broadcast on these channels to be designed for the purpose of recruiting viewers to a particular religious faith, provided that other requirements of the Code, such as clear identification of the religious body involved and not preying on people's fears, are met.

However effective the Code, it is a mechanism designed to prevent abuse, not a guarantor of quality religious programmes. On satellite and cable channels, which under the Act are not subject to any positive programme requirements, quality and diversity within an individual programme service will be the responsibility of the licensee. In contrast, statutory requirements relating to the maintenance of high standards *do* exist in relation to the output of Channels 3, 4 and 5; it will be one of the ITC's responsibilities to define and monitor quality on these services.

Broadcasting in the United Kingdom has come a long way since the days when it consisted of a single radio service presided over by Sir John Reith. As I have attempted to show, although monopoly is now a faint historical memory, many of the ideals which accompanied it persist to this day, having been developed and redefined as new broadcast services have come on air. We have seen, for example, how the principles articulated in the early days of the BBC informed the setting up and development of a new commercial television service.

Until as recently as 1982, when Channel 4 came on air, it continued to be assumed that new broadcast services would fit in to the public-service mould. That assumption changed with the introduction of cable and satellite services which were not free at the point of use and to which viewers could pay to 'opt in' if they so chose. In other words, the ecology of broadcasting has changed and with it expectations of what broadcasting is about. The Peacock Committee, for example, appointed by the government in 1985 to look at the future financing of the BBC, offered an 'operational definition' of PSB as 'any major modification of purely commercial provision resulting from public policy' and saw the main role of PSB in a 'full broadcasting market' as 'the collective provision . . . of programmes which viewers and listeners are willing to support in their capacity as taxpayers and voters, but not directly as consumers'.[6]

There is no doubt that, in a plural society, increasing demands are made of a system of broadcasting paid for by everybody and available to everybody. Policy changes in religious broadcasting clearly demonstrate this. For example, between 1960 and 1977 one of the objectives for religious broadcasting, as recommended by the Central Religious Advisory Committee, underwent a major change from reflecting 'the worship thought and action of those Churches that represent the mainstream of Christian belief in Britain' to reflecting 'the worship thought and actions of the principal religious traditions represented in Britain, recognizing that these are mainly though not exclusively Christian'.

If addressing the plurality of religious faiths now present in the United Kingdom were not challenge enough – and it is arguable whether religious broadcasting has yet seriously grasped that particular nettle – even those who continue to regard themselves as part of the Christian tradition cannot be assumed to hold the same values in common. The IBA's research monograph *Godwatching: Viewers, Religion and Television*, published in 1988, showed that, although religious feeling *as a whole* had declined since a previous survey in 1968, the proportion of people describing themselves as 'very religious' had risen from 6 to 9 per cent, while a recent poll by MORI into moral values was accompanied by the comment that 'British people may still like to call themselves Christian though . . . their beliefs are shaky and their enthusiasm for worship slight. But when it comes to morals they have removed themselves even further from conventional Christianity than we have yet suggested. The British today, we have to report, are scarcely in touch with anything recognizable as a traditional Christian moral agenda.'[7]

The question surely arises as to whether in these days of increasing opportunities, when – in broadcasting terms at least – each religious group has the possibility of sitting under its own fig tree, PSB and its approach to religion should not take their place as one option among many, or even disappear altogether. At this point the discussion about religious broadcasting becomes relevant not just to questions about the future of broadcasting, but to the wider debate about the kind of society we want to inhabit. Chief Rabbi Jonathan Sacks has argued the case for PSB more persuasively than most in his 1990 Reith lectures on Radio 4:

> Anyone who has ever delivered a religious broadcast knows how difficult it is to speak to an unknown and open audience. To our fellow believers, we can address words of fire; to a wider public, only the vaguest of generalities. Broadcasting as opposed to narrowcasting is low in authenticity. But if we are to have a public culture, and one with a religious dimension, it is a discipline we have to undergo. We have to learn to speak to those we do not hope to convert, but with whom we have to live. Narrowcasting frees us from that burden. But it moves us nearer a situation in which opinion is ghettoized into segmented audiences. And where the increase of choice means that we only have to listen to voices with which we agree.[8]

Diversity of choice in broadcasting is here to stay – and I for one welcome it. But having worked for several years now within public-service broadcasting, I am convinced both that it has a future, and that this future is full of potential to explore more deeply what it means to do religious broadcasting which is truly relevant to a plural society.

NOTES

1   John Reith, *Broadcast over Britain*, p. 34 (Hodder and Stoughton: 1924) – quoted in *Public Service Broadcasting: A Reader* by James McDonnell, Routledge: 1991.

2   Sir Brian Young, from his 1983 Watt Club Lecture entitled 'The Paternal Tradition in British Broadcasting 1928–83', quoted in *Public Service Broadcasting: A Reader*, op. cit.

3   *Hansard, House of Lords Official Report*, vol. 176, cols 1293–1302, 22 May 1952.

4   Colin Morris, *God in a Box*, Hodder and Stoughton: 1984, p. 97.

5   Margaret Thatcher, to a seminar of broadcasting industry leaders held at 10 Downing Street on 21 September 1987. Quoted in, *inter alia*, the *Independent*, 22 September 1987.

6   *Report of the Committee on Financing the BBC* (Chairman: Professor Allan Peacock), HMSO: London: 1986, para 580, p. 130.

7   Eric Jacobs and Robert Worcester, *We British: Britain under the MORIscope*: Weidenfeld and Nicholson: 1990, p. 85.

8   Jonathan Sacks, from 'Paradoxes of Pluralism', the fourth of his 1990 Reith lectures on 'The Persistence of Faith', published in *The Listener*, 6 December 1990.

20 Privatism, authority and autonomy in American newspaper coverage of religion: the readers speak

STEWART M. HOOVER

Newspapers plan their coverage from a broad perspective. They cannot have the close identification with their stories that the individuals and institutions they cover have. Instead, they take a stance which is broadly interpretive and attempts to serve the discursive interests of the mainstream of society, which they understand to be their 'readers'. There is, of course, debate about the extent to which this discourse is a 'popular' or an 'élitist' one, but American journalism's *self-perception* is one of being the guardian of a great 'common ground' of interests.

Traditionally there has been a gap in this coverage. Even though the mass of the American public is now, and always has been, remarkably 'religious' (at least in contrast with the other major Western democracies) the press has generally not given religion much space or attention. The typical coverage pattern in the past was for religion to appear on a Saturday 'church page' which carried both church advertisements and church 'announcements'. As such an approach did not even necessitate a religion reporter, copy could be produced literally by *anyone*. Where there *was* a religion reporter, that person rarely saw his or her output placed anywhere beyond this church page.

Beginning at some time in the recent past, coverage of religion has become less marginal in some American media. While the exact extent of it is hard to document, a number of trends and events seem to have brought about this change. The politicization of conservative religious movements, collectively called the 'new right', the election of a 'born-again Christian' to be President of the United States, and the Islamic Revolution in Iran combined to push religion from the 'church page' to the 'front page.'

But these and other trends meant that religion was also changing. It was becoming non-institutional. Observers speak of 'privatization' and 'restructuring' to describe the new face of American religiosity which finds expression in diffuse and atomized locations and practices.[1] This new form of religiosity is not, at the same time, exlusively *personal*, however. Religious social and political activism are also important parts of the recent religion story. As a result, the newly prominent religion beat is now becoming more complex, and many newspapers have responded by expanding it.[2] This expanded scrutiny by the press has not been universally welcomed by the world of religion, however. The power of the press to make private behaviours public, places institutions such as churches in a curious position. On the one hand, they desire to maintain control over their own stories. On the other hand many of them desire the validation and credibility conferred by publicity in the public sphere.

This public validation has its own dangers, however. If religious interests withhold themselves entirely, they get no publicity at all (unless something goes seriously wrong). If they do submit to scrutiny (for instance, by co-operating fully with press coverage) but yet attempt to control the interpretation too much, then they run the risk of losing the sought-after credibility. To go into public fully, and with credibility, churches have to surrender control over their stories, something that they are reluctant to do.

First and foremost among journalistic perceptions is that religion is still seen as a *local* beat at many papers. Allied with the perception of localism is the fact that religion is also covered as a *parochial* issue, with the stress placed on the beliefs and behaviours of specific local groups.[3] We must ask whether, in an era of change, these and other journalistic practices fit the reality of religious interest and behaviour in the society at large. When covering religion as an institutional story only, definition is easy. Coverage of religion is simply coverage of the institutions of the religious 'establishment'. When covering religion in an era of diversity and privatism, definition becomes more difficult.

The research reported here assumes that there has been recent improvement in the status and quality of religion coverage by American newspapers. At the same time, it is clear that many of the traditional understandings of the news industry about the religion beat, and some of the new understandings, deserve empirical and critical investigation. In particular, there appears to be no normative definition of religious news underlying today's coverage, practices and traditions other than the assumptions of privatism and localism. The data reported here come from two national surveys, each a national probability sample of 1,100 adults, administered in 1988. The survey focused on religiosity and news-readership measures. This was a personal (not a telephone) interview, and allowed us to administer more complex items than would have been possible over the telephone.

The first survey was intended to address the relationship between various measures of religious behaviour and religious interest and newspaper readership. The second survey contained more refined measures of qualitative interest in religious coverage. While it should come as no surprise to us given the widely noted religiosity of the American public, it is still noteworthy that the vast majority of daily newspaper readers are religious people. One way to look at this is presented in Table 1 which compares the reported frequency (in Survey I) of newspaper reading among our sample with the 'importance of religion in their lives'.

Table 1
Newspaper readership by religiosity

	Importance of religion		
Reading Frequency:	Very %	Fairly %	Not very %
every day	71.6	69.4	73.6
a few times a week	23.3	23.7	19.2
once a week or less	4.6	6.5	7.3

As can be seen, there is little difference in reported frequency of reading newspapers between those for whom religion is 'very important', 'fairly important', or 'not very important'. Nearly the same percentage of each of these categories report reading a newspaper every day, and it is a large percentage. As with the overall figures for various classes of religiosity, vast majorities reported reading a paper every day. Members of evangelical churches reported less frequent reading than did others, Catholics slightly more frequent reading.

There is as much variation in belief *within* some American Protestant denominations as *between* them. This tendency, which

Martin Marty has called the 'two-party system of American Protestantism',[4] has been a major factor in the recent unrest in
Protestant churches[5] and the essential element of a contemporary
restructuring.[6] The rise of the evangelical movement over the past
fifteen years has found expression in ways quite distinct from
church membership, meaning that there are evangelicals within
non-evangelical churches, and vice versa. To measure this factor,
respondents were asked whether they were 'born again' or 'evangelical' (30% of respondents answered 'yes'). Table 2 shows while
there is some difference in newspaper readership between those who
consider themselves to be 'born again' and those who do not, the
difference is quite small.

Table 2
Newspaper readership by 'two-party' dimension

Reading Frequency	Born-again %	Non born-again %
every day	67.3	72.5
a few times a week	27.0	21.0
once a week or less	5.4	6.2

Those who consider themselves to be 'born again' are less likely
by five percentage points to report that they read newspapers every
day. We found, however, that they were much more likely than
others to be regular readers of *religious* periodicals. In general,
the data suggest that the general readership for daily newspapers
is both fairly religious (much more so than would be the case in
other Western industrial countries, for instance) and not generally
as exposed to the specifically 'religious' press as would be the case if
they were looking to that source for information about religion.

Where they do look is to the 'secular' press. Responses to the
question 'how important is it to you, personally, that the newspapers you read cover religion?' suggest that 65.5 per cent of all
respondents felt it was at least 'fairly important' that newspapers
cover religion. Among those who reported reading newspapers
every day, 66.1 per cent felt it was 'very important' that those
newspapers cover religion. It is clear from other research that
readers have a clear understanding of the structure of the typical

newspaper.[7] That is, they understand the difference between the 'front' and 'back' matter in the newspaper, and understand the difference between the 'hard news' sections of the paper and the sections devoted to features and softer news. While it can be argued that coverage of religion as only a feature or 'soft' beat is a limited vision of its place in the paper, it is nonetheless the case that a major way it is defined in the context of the typical daily paper is as a stand-alone identifiable department or feature. Thus, how religion stacks up against 'sports', or 'food', or 'entertainment' is one way newspapers and their readers evaluate the priority it gets.

With that in mind, the second national survey presented repondents with a list of nine 'special-interest' topics. Respondents were asked to rate, on a scale of one to seven, how important it was to them, personally, that the newspapers they read cover each of these topics. Table 3 presents the overall score of each item, ranked highest to lowest.

Table 3
Importance of nine 'special interest' topics

	Scores (scale of 1 – 7)
Education	5.69
Health	5.60
Business	4.85
Food	4.54
Religion	4.50
Entertainment	4.40
Sports	3.46
The Arts	3.78
Personal Advice	3.72

Religion was not the highest or lowest ranked in interest. Surprisingly, it did come out ahead of sports in overall interest. We next looked at rankings within demographic sub-groups, asking whether religiosity or demographic differences lead to differences in perception of the importance of these topics. Education and income differences seemed not to make much difference in rankings.

Neither did gender, with the exception that men ranked business and sports higher than did women.

There was a difference in ranking for those who call themselves 'born again', who ranked religious coverage much higher than those who do not call themselves 'born again'. There were also interesting differences by size of community of residence. Table 4 presents these scores for people who live in 'small' (under 50,000 in population), 'medium' (between 50,000 and one million), and 'large' (over one million) communities. The order of categories presented in Table 4 is the same as in Table 3.

Table 4
Size-of-place differences in importance of religion as a 'special interest' topic

	Small	Medium	Large
		(scale of 1–7)	
Education	5.85	5.90	5.49
Health	5.75	5.49	5.63
Business	5.15	5.17	4.82
Religion	5.23**	4.56**	4.03**
Food	4.66	4.23	4.48
Entertainment	4.25	4.45	4.53
Sports	3.88	4.34	3.94
The Arts	3.87	3.67	4.08
Personal Advice	3.70	3.52	3.57

It is not too surprising that the score given to religion was highest among those who live in the smallest communities, and the lowest for those who live in large cities. As respondents in the larger cities scored all categories lower than did others, it was necessary to look at rankings alone, where religion ranked fourth for both the smaller and medium-city dwellers, and slipped to sixth for those who live in large cities. This suggests that there are real differences in interest between city dwellers and others.

There were also regional differences in perception of the importance of religion coverage. Residents of the South and South-east ranked religion as higher in importance than did residents of the

New England states or the Far West.

Table 5 reports responses to the question of which of these nine topics respondents were 'most likely to read'. This was a *forced* choice. Respondents could only choose one 'most important' (seven on the scale) one 'next most important', and so on.

Table 5
Likelihood of reading 'special interest' topics

(scale of 1 – 7)

Education	6.65
Business	5.82
Health	5.60
Entertainment	5.04
Food	4.81
Religion	4.56
Sports	4.22
The Arts	3.99
Personal Advice	3.88

The most striking thing about this list is that the order came out nearly the same as with the earlier item where respondents scored topics by their inferred importance rather than their likelihood of reading them. Readers seemed to be reporting behaving in ways consistent with their beliefs about what it is important for newspapers to cover. The male – female differences in ranking on this item were not large. Women ranked religion slightly higher than did men. Those who call themselves 'born again', however, ranked religion much higher than did others. Size-of-place and regional rankings were similar to those on the earlier 'importance' item.

As a final measure of readership interest and response to religious coverage, respondents were asked to rank the paper they 'most often read' for the *quality* of its coverage of the nine 'special interest' topics. Table 6 reports results for this item.

Again, the score represents relative position on a seven-point scale, where seven is the highest score and one the lowest. What

Table 6
**Respondents' satisfaction with coverage by newspaper
'most often read'**

(scale of 1 – 7)

Sports	5.74
Business	5.29
Entertainment	5.18
Education	5.00
Food	4.99
Health	4.76
The Arts	4.67
Personal Advice	4.39
Religion	4.32

is remarkable here is the sharp reversal of position of both sports and religion. While religion generally ranked a bit higher than sports in the various ratings of importance of religious coverage, when readers are here asked to rate actual coverage, the roles are reversed. The message is pretty clear, readers do not feel that the newspapers they read give religion the kind of coverage they want and expect.

Table 7 compares this item with circulation size of the newspaper 'most often read'. Small papers are those with a circulation under 50,000, medium papers those with a circulation between 50,000 and 200,000, and large papers those with circulations over 200,000. While the satisfaction scores overall are higher for the large papers, the ranking of items (their order) came out *nearly* the same as for the smaller papers. For the large papers, religion remained at the bottom of the list in satisfaction. For the medium papers, it ranked eighth out of nine. It ranked highest for the smaller papers, but still only seventh out of nine.

Respondents were next asked *directly* how frequently they read *religious news* when it does appear in the newspaper. Some interesting gender and 'two-party' differences were found. Table 8 presents the male – female results, and Table 9 the differences for those who say they are 'born-again evangelicals' and others.

Table 7
Satisfaction with coverage by circulation size of newspaper 'most often read'

| | Circulation Size: | | |
	Small	Medium	Large
Sports	5.39	5.58	5.31
Business	4.98	5.13	5.11
Entertainment	5.02	4.98	5.28
Food	4.88	4.56	4.84
Education	5.02	4.33	4.67
Health	4.46	4.51	4.86
The Arts	4.13	4.03	4.59
Personal Advice	4.04	3.70	4.03
Religion	4.26**	3.90**	3.57**

Women and evangelicals seemed much less likely than men or non-evangelicals to read religious news when it does appear in the newspaper. This is not consistent with other aspects of religiosity and religious behaviours, where women and evangelicals generally express higher levels of religious interest than others. However, it *is* consistent with overall newspaper reading behaviour, where men are, for instance, much more likely than women to report regular newspaper reading. It seems that women are more likely

Table 8
Frequency of reading religious news (How frequently do you read religious news when it appears in the newspaper?)

	Women (%)	Men (%)
Whenever it appears	19.6	28.6
Frequently	12.3	18.6
Occasionally	22.9	21.5
Infrequently	18.4	17.3
Just about never	25.7	13.9
Don't know	1.0	0.2

Table 9
Frequency of reading religion by two-party dimension

	Born-again (%)	Non-born-again (%)
Whenever it appears	11.3	30.7
Frequently	8.3	19.0
Occasionally	20.1	23.3
Infrequently	25.5	13.9
Just about never	34.3	12.4
Don't know	0.4	0.7

to report preference for, or interest in, religious news, but men are more likely actually to read it. The same tendency held for 'born-again' versus 'non-born-again' respondents.

Definition of what constitutes religious news is one of the major challenges in this area. In order to test definitional ideas with this sample, a list of sixteen 'types' of religion coverage was developed. This battery was intended to test directly the commonplace hypothesis, discussed earlier, that religious news interest is primarily local and parochial. The list was presented so that local and parochial concerns were first, with the scope of coverage moving outward conceptually and physically from the respondents' home locations with subsequent categories. Table 10 presents the complete list of response 'types' in the order in which they were administered.

Respondents were asked again to score each of these sixteen types on a seven-point scale. Table 11 presents the overall results of this item, with the categories ranked from highest (most important) to lowest (least important) rated. This was perhaps the most surprising result of the entire survey. Far from being oriented only toward local and parochial interests or issues of faith experience, respondents overall seemed to have a trans-local and universal scope in their interest in religious news. Further, the findings that (1) high percentages of newspaper readers are interested in religion, (2) that they expect religious coverage, (3) that most of them do not turn to 'religious' sources for news which fits this interest, and (4) that they are generally not very satisfied with the coverage that religion gets from the daily press, paint a picture of religious news that is

Table 10
Sixteen categories of religious coverage

1. Stories of individual faith experiences.

2. Local church news and announcements.

3. Coverage of local religious issues besides church news and announcements.

4. Coverage of national religious groups and denominations.

5. Coverage of the ecumenical movement and co-operation between religious groups.

6. Coverage of the beliefs of various religions besides your own.

7. Coverage of major American religious movements (such as fundamentalism, evengelicalism, the charismatic movement, etc.).

8. Coverage of 'alternative' or 'new' religious movements (such as the 'new age' movement, cults, etc.).

9. Coverage of national religious issues and controversies (such as scandals, textbook controversies, etc.).

10. Coverage of the role of religion in American politics.

11. Coverage of the role of religion in foreign or international politics (such as the Middle East, Iran, Northern Ireland, etc.).

12. Coverage of ethical and social issues.

13. Coverage of social and ethical positions and pronouncements by major faith groups (such as on abortion, nuclear policy, the economy, etc.).

14. Presentation of opinion and commentary (such as columns or editorials by major religious leaders).

15. Presentation of humour or cartoons relating to religion.

16. Results of surveys or polls on religious topics.

far removed from the traditional or 'received' definitions of it.

To the extent that there was support in these data for the localism/parochialism hypothesis, it held more strongly for women than for men. Women ranked local church news and local religious issues higher than did men. However, interest in social and

Table 11
Mean scores of religious coverage 'types'

Positions and pronouncements	4.77
Ethical and social issues	4.63
Local church news and announcements	4.34
Local religious issues	4.29
Religion in American politics	4.26
Foreign or international politics	4.25
National issues and controversies	4.22
National groups and denominations	4.11
Other religions besides your own	4.01
Ecumenism and co-operation	3.96
Opinion and commentary	3.96
Faith experiences	3.83
Surveys or polls	3.66
American religious movements	3.61
'Alternative' or 'new' movements	3.49
Humour or cartoons	2.91

ethical issues, and the positions and pronouncements of faith groups on social issues, was higher for both men and women than we might have expected. This also turned out to be the case for the other demographic classes which are the more traditionally 'religious': 'born-again' evangelicals; older people; residents of smaller communities; residents of the South; and lower education and income respondents. All seemed to be more interested than others in the local issues. However, these groups generally reported *lower* levels of news readership than did others. Those cohorts who report *higher* levels of news readership (men, for instance) are the ones who are the least interested in local and parochial religious coverage.

These surveys call into question some of the common perceptions held by the press about religion and religious news. They showed that religious people are also newspaper readers. This should not have surprised anyone, but somehow it did. The idea that religion was not of interest to journalism seemed inferentially to indicate that it was not of interest to its *readers*. This turned out not to be true. We know from other surveys that the typical American reports a high degree of religious belief and behaviour. It was thought to be possible that regular newspaper readers might be atypical in this regard and less interested in religion than cohorts who read newspapers less frequently. However, regular newspaper readers did not significantly differ from the general population in this regard. Demographic controls did not seem to affect this pattern, either.

These findings, taken together, suggest that there are a great number (indeed, a majority) of readers who consider themselves to be religious people, yet who do not read religious publications. The secular media are increasingly where they turn to find significant information about the world of religion. When we asked readers to compare religion with other things newspapers cover, we found that it was neither the *most*, nor the *least* important to them. It consistently ranked in the middle in importance, below such things as education and business, but (surprisingly) above sports. There were clear *regional* differences in how important religious coverage is to readers. Respondents in the South-east expressed a higher degree of interest than those in the West and North-west. Other demographic characteristics, such as education and income, seemed to make less difference than did region.

When asked directly how frequently they read religion when it appears in the newspaper, some interesting gender and belief differences emerged. Men were more likely to report frequent reading than were women. 'Born-again' respondents reported much lower levels of religious reading than did others.

Finally, it is clear that readers want to see coverage that is far less local and parochial than is often thought. Respondents seemed to have a broad definition of religious coverage, one that entailed religion on a local, national, and international level, and that saw religion as an important dimension of much of the rest of the news. While the local items did rank fairly high in interest, respondents placed national and institutional items high as well. There seemed to be relatively little interest, for instance, in newspapers covering spiritual or inspirational matters.

These findings suggest that many common assumptions about reader interest in religion may be misperceptions. Readers understand the news process fairly well, and understand what kinds of things qualify as news. They see much that *could* fit in

the newspaper that does not. They are not expecting newspapers to cover their own local group so much as they
expect religion in general to find its way into the news in
general. They would like to see more evidence in the papers
they read that religion is an important part of daily life for
many Americans. They want to see religion *mainstreamed* in the
newspaper.

These data also have some important things to say about the
broader relationship between religion and the media in contemporary American life. The widely expected 'secularization' of
society is not as complete as many, particularly those in the
news business, have thought it to be. Religion is no longer a story
that can be covered by reporting on its institutions and establishments, however. Events in the Middle East, Northern Ireland, and
in Washington have also become 'religious news'. The media have
begun to respond, at least according to our interviews with journalists and editors.[8] The news audience seems to be asking that,
as they do so, they keep in mind a vision of religious news as *news*,
not as a localized and parochial 'beat' that can be defined entirely
in terms of formalized, institutional beliefs and practices.

NOTES

1   See, for example, Thomas Luckman, *The Invisible Religion*, New York:
    Macmillan: 1967; Robert Wuthnow, 'The Social Significance of Religious
    Television', *Review of Religious Research*, Vol. 29 no. 2 (1987); and
    Phillip Hammond, *Religion and Personal Autonomy: The Third Dises-
    tablishment in America*, Columbia, SC: University of South Carolina
    Press: 1992.

2   See Stewart M. Hoover, Barbara Hanley and Martin Radelfinger, 'The
    RNS-Lilly Study of Religion Reporting and Readership in the Daily Press',
    New York: The Religious News Service: 1989.

3   This is shown by Hoover *et. al.*, op. cit.

4   Martin E. Marty, *Righteous Empire*, New York: Dial Press: 1970.

5   See Dean Hoge, Everett Perry and Gerald Klever, 'Theology as a Source
    of Disagreement About Protestant Church Goals and Priorities', *Review
    of Religious Research* Vol. 19 no. 2 (1978), pp. 116–38.

6   See Robert Wuthnow, *The Restructuring of American Religion*, Princeton:
    Princeton University Press: 1988.

7   Hoover *et. al.*, op. cit.

8   For a complete discussion, see Hoover *et. al.*, op. cit.

ADDENDUM:
a profile of the World Association for Christian Communication

This book has been published with the support of the World Association for Christian Communication (WACC). WACC is an organization of corporate and personal members who wish to give high priority to Christian values in the world's communication and development needs. It is not a council or federation of churches. The majority of members are communication professionals from all walks of life or media critics and theorists pursuing academic studies.

WACC is organized in seven regions which determine the composition of its governing body, the Central Committee. The latter focuses on the regions' need for professional guidance and inspiration of members. It also funds communication activities which reflect regional interests, and encourages ecumenical unity among communicators.

As a matter of principle WACC is truly ecumenical in its membership and project activities, in its encouragement of grassroots co-operation between Protestant, Orthodox and Roman Catholic communicators, in its challenge to denominational communication activities to seek a broader base, and in its search for co-operation between people of other faiths and ideologies.

As a professional organization, WACC serves the wider ecumenical movement by offering guidance on communication policies, interpreting developments in communications worldwide, discussing the consequences which such developments have for churches and communities everywhere but especially in the Third World, and assisting the training of communicators.

WACC has a Third World bias because at this time in history it believes it to be the most valid interpretation of Christ's teaching. Five of the seven regional associations of WACC are in the developing world.

For further information contact: World Association for Christian Communication, 357 Kennington Lane, London SE11 5QY, United Kingdom. Tel: (0)71 582–9139. Fax: (0)71 735–0340.

The following documents state the principles on which WACC's philosophy of communication is based.

I   CHRISTIAN PRINCIPLES OF COMMUNICATION

Information and communication are drastically changing the world we live in. Instead of establishing commonness and solidarity, public communication now tends to reinforce divisions, widen the gap between rich and poor, consolidate oppression, and distort reality in order to maintain systems of domination and subject the silenced masses to media manipulation. Yet communication remains God's great gift to humanity, without which we cannot be truly human, reflecting 'God's image'. Nor could we enjoy living together in groups, communities and societies steeped in different cultures and different ways of life.

It is both the potential for solidarity and the threat to humanity which modern communications contain, that has prompted the members of the World Association for Christian Communication to examine their communication practices and policies on the basis of the Good News of the Kingdom. The guidelines which follow are an expression of our common witness to Jesus Christ and to the hope He has given us through the transforming power of His own communication.

1. Communication from a Christian perspective

Jesus announced the coming of God's Kingdom and commissioned us to proclaim the Good News to all people until the end of time. Hearing the Good News, living by it and witnessing to it, is the basic calling of all Christians.

To enable them to carry out this task, they have been promised the power of the Holy Spirit. It is this Spirit that can change the Babel of confusion into the Pentecost of genuine understanding. But the Spirit 'blows where it pleases' (John 2:8), and no one, neither church nor religious group, can claim to control it.

The Good News addresses itself to the whole person and to all people. We pray for the coming of the Kingdom as well as for our daily food, for God's reign in the world-to-come and the here-and-now. For Christian communicators, the material and the spiritual are part of each other.

Christ's own communication was an act of self-giving. He 'emptied himself, taking the form of a servant' (Phil. 2:7). He ministered to all, but took up the cause of the materially poor, the mentally ill, the outcasts of society, the powerless and oppressed. In the same way, Christian communication should be an act of love which liberates all who take part in it.

The Gospel, being the Good News for the poor, needs to be constantly reinterpreted from the perspectives of the poor and oppressed. This challenges church hierarchies to disassociate themselves from the power structures which keep the poor in a position of subservience. In this sense, the Good News for the poor embodies genuine reconciliation by means of which the dignity of all people can be reaffirmed.

By accepting Christ's sovereignty, the Christian communicator proclaims God's Kingdom rather than our divided churches. The churches do not exist for their own sakes, but for the sake of the Kingdom. For this reason, the Christian communicator gives preference to ecumenical communication so that Christians of different denominations can speak with one voice, thus bearing witness to the one body of Christ.

Christian communicators, as witnesses to the Kingdom, should awaken and reflect the corporate witness of the church. The lives of Christians, as well as the work of communicators, need to be set free from the individualism which characterizes some cultures and traditions. We need to rediscover the early Christian community's understanding of a witnessing and communicating church.

The church as a community of believers is God's chosen instrument for promoting the Kingdom. This is because the Church is meant to embody and testify to the central values of the Kingdom, among which are oneness, reconciliation, equality, justice, freedom, harmony, peace and love ('shalom').

Furthermore, Christian communicators are conscious of and show respect for God's mysteries. God's ways can never be grasped, let alone be explained. Likewise, the crown of God's creation, people, cannot be fully understood. Christian communicators, therefore, are always aware of their inadequacies when speaking of God, and conscious of 'mystery' when telling the story of God's people.

The communication of Christians is ultimately meant to glorify God. In that sense, all Christian communication is an act of worship, a praise of God through the shared word and action of a community living in the consciousness of God's presence. Christian communication is challenged to witness to God's transforming power in all areas of human life. Paul calls himself and all servants of the Word, 'servants of your glory' (Eph. 1:12) and thus 'servants of your joy' (2 Cor. 1:24). The glory of God and the joy of the people should be the hallmark of all Christian communication.

These general principles of Christian communication will now be elaborated in the context of today's communication problems.

2. Communication creates community

Many people today fear or deplore the loss of community and community spirit. Rather than bringing people together, the mass media often isolate or divide them. Yet communication, including the use of alternative media, can revitalize communities and rekindle community spirit, because the model for genuine communication, like that for communities of all kinds, is open and inclusive, rather than unidirectional and exclusive.

But a community must not be seen as the local community alone. A community of peoples and nations, as well as a community of different churches and religions, has to emerge if humankind is to survive. Therefore, one aim of our work is the breaking down of all kinds of barriers which prevent the development of communities with rights and justice for all – particularly such barriers as race, sex, class, nation, power and wealth. Genuine communication cannot take place in a climate of division, alienation, isolation and barriers which disturb, prevent or distort social interaction.

True communication is facilitated when people join together regardless of race, colour or religious conviction, and where there is acceptance of and commitment to one another.

3. Communication is participatory

The mass media have been organized along one-way lines: they flow from top to bottom, from the centre to the periphery, from the few to the many, from the 'information rich' to the 'information poor'. This has conditioned the minds of many people – not only in terms of the media's content but also by creating a 'mass media mentality'. Many think that this is the way the media have to work. Even those who advocate horizontal flow are often only concerned with an increase in the number of channels, the diversification of content and localization of media. They still adhere to the basic top-down principle.

On the other hand, there is now a growing awareness that there are information and communication needs, felt by individuals and groups, which the mass media cannot meet. Modern communication technologies could allow a much higher degree of participation than those who control the media systems are willing to grant or to develop.

Communication is, by definition, participatory. It is a two-way process. It is interactive because it shares meaning and establishes and maintains social relationships. The more widespread and powerful the media become, the greater the need for people to engage in their own local or inter-group communication activities. In this way, they will also rediscover and develop traditional forms of communication.

Only if people become subjects rather than objects of communication can they develop their full potential as individuals and groups. Communication is now considered an individual and social necessity of such fundamental importance that it is seen as a universal human right. Communication as a human right encompasses the traditional freedoms: of expression, of the right to seek, receive and impart information. But it adds to these freedoms, both for individuals and society, a new concept, namely that of access, participation and two-way flow.

Participatory communication may challenge the authoritarian structures in society, in the churches and in the media, while democratizing new areas of life. It may also challenge some of the 'professional rules' of the media, whereby the powerful, rich and glamorous occupy centre stage to the exclusion of ordinary men, women and children. Participatory communication, finally, can give people a new sense of human dignity, a new experience of community, and the enjoyment of a fuller life.

4. Communication liberates

The mass media are a form of power and often part of a system of power. They are usually structured in such a way as to reinforce the status quo in favour of the economically and politically powerful. Mass-media power thus has a dominating effect which is contrary to genuine communication.

We cannot communicate with people whom we regard as 'inferior', whose basic worth as humans we do not respect. We can simply impart information to them or sell 'media products' to them. Genuine communication presupposes the recognition that all human beings are of equal worth. The more explicit equality becomes in human interaction, the more easily communication occurs.

There are crude and subtle ways of silencing people. The dictates of modern nationalism and the demands of ruling ideologies are examples of how freedom has been curtailed and contrary views suppressed. When media boast of or clamour for freedom of the press or of broadcasting, they should be asked: Whose freedom and whose liberty? Freedom of communication is bound up with the quest for community and the fulfilment of the individual and social needs of all, rather than of just a few.

Communication which liberates, enables people to articulate their own needs and helps them to act together to meet those needs. It enhances their sense of dignity and underlines their right to full participation in the life of society. It aims to bring about structures in society which are more just, more egalitarian and more conducive to the fulfilment of human rights.

5. Communication supports and develops cultures

A people's basic culture and need for cultural identity are part of the dignity of the human person. Many countries and peoples are now rediscovering and redefining their basic cultural identities. This is particularly urgent where culture, language, religion, gender, age, ethnicity or race have been attacked or treated with contempt by members of other cultural groups.

Global communication structures are now being set up in such a way as to threaten the cultures and priorities of many nations. More seriously, the entertainment industries, particularly television and home video programmes, are creating a media environment which is alien and alienating.

The Western criteria of the mass media have already been adopted by the national élites in countries of the South. They set the 'standards' of what can rate as 'professional' in media productions, often preventing the emergence of alternative forms of communication.

Communicators now have an awesome responsibility to use and develop indigenous forms of communication. They have to cultivate a symbolic environment of mutually shared images and meanings which respect human dignity and the religious and cultural values which are at the heart of Third World cultures. One of the greatest assets of today's world is its many different cultures, revealing the richness of God's image in all its diversity.

6. Communication is prophetic

Many media workers are trying to interpret the signs of the times, because this is part of the public information work to which they are committed. For Christians, the events of the day are part of God's agenda for action. In it, God's plans are revealed through changing circumstances and new opportunities. In order to discern and interpret the situation correctly, Christian communicators must listen to God and be led by the Spirit. This is a condition of prophecy.

But words are only part of prophecy. They take on real meaning only when they are accompanied by action. Prophetic communication expresses itself in words *and* deeds. Such prophetic action must be willing to challenge the principalities and powers, and may carry a high price.

Prophetic communication serves truth and challenges falsehood. Lies and half-truths are a great threat to communication. Prophetic communication stimulates critical awareness of the reality constructed by the media and helps people to distinguish truth from falsehood, to discern the subjectivity of the journalist and to disassociate that which is ephemeral and trivial from that which is lasting and valuable. Often it is necessary to develop alternative communication so that prophetic words and deeds can be realized.

Conclusion

These principles should guide the work and mission of Christians in communication. They also set out the corporate agenda of the World Association for Christian Communication – for project support, studies and dissemination of policies. Communication must be seen as central to the churches, as the process in which God's love is received and shared, thus establishing communion and community.

II COMMUNICATION AND COMMUNITY:
THE MANILA DECLARATION

More than 450 people from over eighty countries responded to the call of the World Association for Christian Communication (WACC) to participate in its first international Congress in Manila. For five days (15–19 October 1989) they discussed the theme 'Communication for Community', dealing with the issues of participation, people's culture, liberation, and the task of prophecy.

Many fields of communication were represented at the Congress. There were media professionals, grass-roots activists, teachers and communication researchers. Their religious backgrounds were equally diverse. United by the ecumenical movement, participants shared the following concerns about the state of communication and people's rights and dignity in tomorrow's world.

Communication: God's gift to humankind

1. Communication is a crucial issue for the 1990s and for the future of humankind. It can lead to reconciliation or destruction. It can bring knowledge, truth and inspiration, or withhold knowledge and spread disinformation and lies. Communication is God's unique gift to humankind, through which individuals and societies can become more truly human. Genuine communication is as essential to the quality of life as food, shelter and healthcare. It is the process of interaction through communicative symbols which creates a cultural environment.

2. Communication, therefore, is part of every aspect of life. It has to serve society as a whole and, ultimately, humankind in its entirety.

As a social necessity communication is, therefore, the responsibility of everyone – governments, formal and informal organizations of people. It should not be manipulated by a few or misappropriated by a single centre of power.

A new vision for the 1990s

3. The search for new principles of communication for the 1990s is grounded in the historical experience of the last fifteen years. The imbalance in the state of public communication was analysed in detail by an international commission ten years ago. It produced the MacBride Report under the title 'Many Voices, One World: Towards a new more just and more efficient world information and communication order' (NWICO). Though the report was adopted unanimously, several governments soon opposed some of its main features. Other governments stood by, doing nothing to implement it.

4. The Congress participants, committed to a vision of democratic communication, are anxious to enter into a new phase of dialogue with related organizations and all people of goodwill to achieve a common understanding of communication in the service of free, just and peaceful communities at the local and international levels. The growth of technology, the increase in the monopolization of the media and the vulgarization of content, make this task all the more urgent. The principles of communication envisaged should be based on the power of the people, going beyond the formal processes of party politics and seeking new ways of participation which increase the freedom of all people to communicate.

5. The search for peace, both regionally and internationally, is likely to characterize the 1990s. The media must abandon their often militaristic language and the stereotyping of nations and cultures. The time has come for the media truly to work for peace and international understanding.

Media ecology

6. The total human environment is made up of two interlocking spheres: nature and the human-made environment of culture, energized by communication. Both these environments can only

be protected and cultivated by local, regional and international efforts. Issues such as militarism, racism, apartheid, sexism, the debt burden, the consumerism of the few and the misery of the many threaten both the natural and the cultural environments.

7. Underlying all of these problems is the urge to exploit which has poisoned both the cultural ethos and the natural environment. To change this, communication has a decisive role to play, not only in challenging the exploitation of the natural environment, but also in giving voice to the human victims of that same exploitation. A sound natural environment goes hand in hand with a communication environment which perceives humankind as one family, inhabiting one world. This calls for a revolution in social values and priorities.

8. A positive reponse to this exploitation of the natural and human environments is found in the ecumenical programme for Justice, Peace and Integrity of Creation. The Congress commits itself to this programme.

Communication and power

9. Mass media and the information industries are structures of power. They are intertwined with national centres of political, economic and military power and are increasingly linked at the global level. Ordinary people are victims of media power and are treated more and more as objects rather than subjects. This is particularly true for women, manual labourers, indigenous minorities, senior citizens and children.

10. Great efforts are required to reverse this trend. In the first place, churches should democratize their own media. They and other social institutions should give priority to media which the people can control and through which they can speak. There is a wide range of traditional media, rooted in local cultures, which need to be further developed, like the vigorous popular theatre movement in many parts of the South. Group media or group communication for social transformation are another form of grass-roots communication which needs to be cultivated. Some new communications technologies, such as video, desk-top publishing and computer networks, provide further opportunities for the empowerment of people.

11. In an age when families are enticed to spend a great deal of their leisure time as consumers of media, there has been a gradual deterioration of communication within the family. Initiatives need to be taken to restore the family's own capacity to communicate and extend it to the neighbourhood community. The more mediated our communication environment becomes, the more we need to develop our skills in interpersonal communication.

12. Media-awareness training demystifies mass communication. Media education should become part of the curriculum in schools at all levels, including church-related institutions and theological seminaries. This must be complemented by informal media education in the family, among youth, in men's and women's associations, and church groups. Media education should lead to a new and more constructive relationship between media workers and media consumers.

The responsibility of communication workers

13. Communication professionals and other cultural workers carry an awesome responsibility. Many have to work under appalling conditions. Some are silenced and lose their jobs. Others are persecuted or even killed for telling the truth. They are prophets of our times. This Congress expresses its deep respect for and full solidarity with them. This should not only be expressed in words, but also in actions.

14. Communication workers live with the responsibility to meet high professional standards. Such standards, however, need constant examination. Established professional rules for the mass media may serve to legitimize the maintenance of unjust power structures. This Congress regrets the preoccupation of many journalists with the politically and economically mighty while neglecting the efforts of people's movements for freedom and justice.

15. Much of public communication in the Third World takes place in languages which are not the mother-tongues of the majority of people. This tends to relegate the importance of indigenous languages and dialects, which are rooted in people's cultures. This situation has to be remedied in order to involve all people in the communication process and promote cultural integrity and renewal.

16. Regrettably, advocacy journalism is scorned by many professionals. Yet it has done well in serving the struggle for human rights, environmental protection and the exercise of people's power. Ultimately, Christian communicators have no other option but to throw in their lot with the poor, oppressed and marginalized who bear the hallmark of God's communication.

17. Participants in this Congress feel privileged to work towards a new communication environment which challenges unjust power structures. It calls for new alternatives in communication and a pledge to continue working for a better future for humankind.

18. In conclusion, Congress participants call upon WACC and its partner institutions to take the following course of action as a matter of priority and urgency.

Recommendations

19. WACC should build up and widen its network of Christian and secular groups and institutions, and of all people of goodwill, to accelerate the implementation of the right to communicate.

20. WACC should advance the process of working out a set of common principles of international communication which should guide the NWICO debate in the 1990s.

21. WACC should promote, and provide opportunities for interaction between, traditional communication and alternative media. At the same time, WACC should encourage study and documentation of the social problems and potentials of modern communication technologies.

22. WACC should strengthen its programmes in media education in and across different cultures and promote communication studies in theological education.

23. WACC should give priority to the empowerment of women through communication training and other activities. Likewise, it should promote the use of non-sexist, inclusive language.

24. WACC should strive to be in a position to increase its assistance and service to church-related institutions and other groups to develop communication policies and programmes that respond to the challenges of the 1990s.

Bibliography

This bibliography consists of a selection of items recommended by the editor and contributors. It is not intended as an exhaustive listing of material available in the area, simply as a means of facilitating further inquiry on the part of interested students.

Abelman, R. and S. Hoover, (eds.), *Religious Television: Contro-versies and Conclusions*, Norwood, N.J.: Ablex: 1990.

Arthur, Chris, 'Tigers: Some Reflections on Communication and Theological Education', *Religious Education*, vol. 84, no. 1 (1989), pp. 103–30.

—'Justice, Peace and the Integrity of Creation; a role for Communication', *New Blackfriars*, vol. 72, no. 846 (1991), pp. 66–76.

—'Media Ecology as a Moral Priority', *The Month*, vol. 24, no. 11 (1991), pp. 506–8.

Atkinson, John, *The Media, a Christian View*, London: Epworth Press: 1979.

Babin, Pierre (ed.), *The Audio-Visual Man, Media and Religious Education*, Dayton, Ohio: Pflaum: 1970.

—*The New Era in Religious Communication*, Minneapolis: Fortress Press: 1991.

Beeson, Trevor, *An Eye for an Ear*, London: SCM: 1972.

Bluck, John, *Beyond Neutrality, a Christian Critique of the Media*, Geneva: World Council of Churches: 1978.

—*Beyond Technology, Contexts for Christian Communication* (with contributions from the WCC's Sixth Assembly), Geneva: World Council of Churches: 1984.

Boorstin, Daniel J., *The Image, or What Happened to the American Dream*, London, Weidenfeld & Nicholson: 1961.

Brooks, R. T., *Communicating Conviction*, London: Epworth Press: 1983.

Bruce, Steve, *Pray TV, Televangelism in America*, London: Routledge: 1990.

Buddenbaum, Judith, 'Analysis of Religion News Coverage in Three Major Newspapers', *Journalism Quarterly*, vol. 63 (1986), pp. 600–6.

—'The Religion Beat at Daily Newspapers', *Newspaper Research Journal*, vol. 9 no. 4 (1988), pp. 57–69.

Centre for the Study of Communication and Culture, *Communication Research Trends* (a quarterly information bulletin).

Christians, Clifford G., Kim B. Rotzoll and Mark Fackler, *Media Ethics, Cases and Moral Reasoning*, New York: Longman: 1983.

Concilium, *Concilium (1978)* (Special issue on Communication in the Church, (ed.) Gregory Baum and Andrew Greeley), New York: Seabury Press: 1978.

Eisenstein, Elizabeth L., *The Printing Press as an Agent of Change: Communications and Cultural Transformations in Early-Modern Europe*, (2 vols), Cambridge: Cambridge University Press: 1979.

Eldridge, John, 'Through a Glass Darkly: Reflections on Television', *Churchman*, vol. 98, no. 2 (1984), pp. 117–25.

Ellul, Jacques, *The Humiliation of the Word*, Grand Rapids: Eerdmans: 1985.

Elvy, Peter, *Buying Time: The Foundations of the Electronic Church*, Great Wakering, Essex: McCrimmons: 1986.

—(ed.), *Opportunities and Limitations in Religious Broadcasting*, Edinburgh: Centre for Theology and Public Issues: 1991.

Falconer, Ronald, *Message, Media, Mission*, Edinburgh: The Saint Andrew Press: 1977.

Ferré, John, 'Denominational Biases in the American Press', *Review of Religious Research*, vol. 21 (1980), pp. 271–83.

—(ed.), *Channels of Belief*, Ames: Iowa State University Press: 1990.

Fore, William F., 'A Theology of Communication', *Religious Education*, vol. 82, no. 2 (1987), pp. 231–46.

—*Television and Religion: the Shaping of Faith, Values and Culture*, Minneapolis: Augsburg: 1987.

—*Mythmakers: Gospel, Culture and the Media*, New York: Friendship Press: 1990.

Gaddy, Gary D., 'The Power of the Religious Media: Religious Broadcast Use and the Role of Religious Organizations in Public Affairs', *Review of Religious Research*, vol. 25 (1984), pp. 289–302.

Gerbner, George *et.al.*, *Religion and Television* (a Research report by the Annenberg School of Communications, University of

Pennsylvania and The Gallup Organization), Annenberg School of Communication: 1984.

Gerbner, George and Kathleen Connolly, 'Television as New Religion', *New Catholic World*, April/May 1978, pp. 52–6.

Goethals, Gregor T., *The TV Ritual: Worship at the Video Altar*, Boston: Beacon Press: 1981.

—*The Electronic Golden Calf: Images, Religion, and the Making of Meaning*, Cambridge, MA: Cowley: 1990.

Goody, Jack (ed.), *Literacy in Traditional Societies*, Cambridge: CUP: 1968.

Goody, Jack, *The Logic of Writing and the Organization of Society*, Cambridge: CUP: 1986.

Gronbeck, Bruce, Thomas J. Farrell and Paul Soukup (eds.), *Media, Consciousness and Culture: Explorations of Walter Ong's Thought*, London: Sage: 1991.

Hadden, Jeffrey, K. and Charles E. Swan, *Prime Time Preachers: The Rising Power of Televangelism*, Reading MA: Addison-Wesley: 1982.

Hart, Roderick P., Kathleen J. Turner and Ralph E. Knupp, 'Religion and the Rhetoric of the Mass Media', *Review of Religious Research*, vol. 21, no. 3 (1980), pp. 256–75.

Hoover, Stewart, *Mass Media Religion: The Social Sources of the Electronic Church*, London: Sage: 1988.

Hoover, Stewart, Barbara Hanley and Martin Radelfinger, *The RNS-Lilly Study of Religion Reporting and Readership in the Daily Press*, New York: The Religious News Service: 1989.

Horsfield, Peter G., *Religious Television: The American Experience*, New York: Longman: 1984.

—'Religious Dimensions of Television's Uses and Content', *Colloquium*, vol. 17, no. 2 (1985), pp. 62–7.

—'Larger than Life: Religious Functions of Television', *Media Information Australia*, vol. 47 (1988), pp. 61–6.

Hubbard, Benjamin (ed.), *Reporting Religion: Facts and Faith*, Sonoma, CA: Polebridge Press: 1990.

Hynds, E. C., 'Large Daily Newspapers have Improved Coverage of Religion', *Journalism Quarterly*, vol. 64 (1987), pp. 444–8.

Jackson, B. F. (ed.), *Television–Radio–Film for Churchmen*, New York: Abingdon Press: 1969.

Katz, Elihu and Daniel Dayan, 'Media Events: On The Experience of Not Being There', *Religion*, vol. 15 (1985), pp. 305–14.

Keen, Sam, *Faces of the Enemy. Reflections of the Hostile Imagination: the Psychology of Enmity*, San Francisco: Harper & Row: 1986.

Knightley, Philip, *The First Casualty. From the Crimea to Vietnam: the War Correspondent as Hero, Propagandist and Myth Maker*, London: André Deutsch: 1975.

Knott, Kim, *Media Portrayals of Religion and Their Perception*, University of Leeds: 1984. (The final report of a project funded by the Christendom Trust.)

Kuhns, William, *The Electronic Gospel: Religion and Media*, New York: Herder & Herder: 1969.

Lester, Paul, 'Faking Images in Photojournalism', *Media Development*, vol. 35, no. 1 (1988), pp. 41–2.

Lichter, Robert, Daniel Amundson and Linda Lichter, *Media Coverage of the Catholic Church*, Washington, DC: Centre for Media and Public Affairs: 1991.

Lowe, Kathy, *Opening Eyes and Ears, New Connections for Christian Communication*, Geneva: WCC/WACC: 1983.

MacBride Commission/International Commission for the Study of Communication Problems, *Many Voices, One World. Communication and Society Today and Tomorrow: Towards a New More Just and More Efficient World Information and Communication Order*, London: UNESCO/Kogan Page: 1980.

McDonnell, James and Francis Trampiets (eds.), *Communicating Faith in a Technological Age*, Slough: St Paul Publications: 1989.

McDonnell, James (ed.) *Public Service Broadcasting: a Reader*, London: Routledge: 1991.

McLuhan, Marshall, *Understanding Media, The Extensions of Man*, London: Ark: 1987.

Mander, Jerry, *Four Arguments for the Elimination of Television*, Brighton: Harvester Press: 1980.

Marty, Martin E., *The Improper Opinion. Mass Media and the Christian Faith*, Philadelphia: The Westminster Press: 1961.

Mattingly, Terry, 'The Religion Beat: Out of the Ghetto, into the Mainstream', *The Quill*, January 1983, pp. 13–19.

Media Development (quarterly journal of the World Association for Christian Communication).

Montefiore, Hugh (ed.), *The Gospel and Contemporary Culture*, London: Mowbray: 1992.

Morris, Colin, *God in a Box: Christian Strategy in a Television Age*, London: Hodder & Stoughton: 1984.

—'Love at a Distance – the Spiritual Challenge of Religious Broadcasting', *Media Development*, vol. 33 (1986), pp. 40–1.

—*Wrestling with an Angel: Reflections on Christian Communication*, London: Collins: 1990.

Muggeridge, Malcolm, *Christ and the Media*, London: Hodder & Stoughton: 1977.

Myers, Kathy, *Understains. The Sense and Seduction of Advertising*, London: Comedia: 1986.

Ong, Walter J., 'Communications Media and the State of Theology', *Cross Currents*, vol. 19, no. 4 (1969), pp. 462–80.

—'Technology Outside us and Inside us', *Communio*, vol. 5 (1978), pp. 100–21.

—*Orality and Literacy: The Technologising of the Word*, London: Methuen: 1982.

Postman, Neil, *Amusing Ourselves to Death: Public Discourse in the Age of Show Business*, London: Methuen: 1987.

Religious Education, vol. 78, no. 1. (1983), (Special issue on 'The Formation of the Public Mass Media').

Religious Education, vol. 82, no. 2 (1987), (Special issue on 'The Electronic Media').

Robinson, Haddon W., 'The Impact of Religious Radio and Television Programmes on American Life', *Bibliotheca Sacra*, vol. 123, no. 490, pp. 124–35.

—'The Audience for Religious Broadcasts in the United States', *Bibliotheca Sacra*, vol. 123, no. 489 (1966), pp. 69–72.

Said, Edward W., *Covering Islam. How the Media and The Experts Determine How We see the Rest of the World*, London: RKP: 1981.

Schleifer, S. A., 'Conflict Coverage in the Middle East', in *Media Credibility and Social Responsibility*, Proceedings of the Seventh World Media Conference, Tokyo, 1984, pp. 337–55.

—'Islam and Information: Need, Feasibility and Limitations of an Independent Islamic News Agency', *American Journal of Islamic Social Sciences*, vol. 3, no. 1 (1986), pp. 106–24.

—'Mass Communication and the Technicalization of Muslim Society', *Muslim Education Quarterly*, vol. 4, no. 3 (1987), pp. 4–12.

Schlesinger, Philip, *Putting 'Reality' Together*, London: Constable: 1978.

Shulman, Milton, *The Ravenous Eye: the Impact of the Fifth Factor*, London: Cassell: 1973.

Soukup, Paul, *Christian Communication, a Bibliographical Survey*, New York: Greenwood: 1989.

Svennevig, M., I. Haldane, S. Spiers and B. Gunter, *Godwatching: Viewers, Religion and Television*, London: John Lilley/IBA: 1988.

Tillmans, W. G., 'Symbolism in the Mass Media: A Theological Approach', *Kerygma*, vol. 15, no. 36 (1981) pp. 72–9.

Traber, Michael (ed.), *The Myth of the Information Revolution: Social and Ethical Implications of Communication Technology*, London: Sage: 1986.

Turner, Victor, 'Liminality, Kabbalah and The Media', *Religion*, vol. 15 (1985), pp. 205–17.

Warnock, Mary, 'Broadcasting Ethics: Some Neglected Issues', *Journal of Moral Education*, vol. 13, no. 3. pp. 168–72.

Warren, Michael, 'Images and the Structuring of Experiences', *Religious Education*, vol. 82, no. 2 (1987), pp. 247–57.

Communications and Cultural Analysis, a Religious View, Westport, Connecticut: Bergin and Garvey: 1992.

The Way, Supplement no. 37 (1986) (on 'Communications, Media and Spirituality').

Name Index

Subject Index